DEVELOPMENTAL MANAGEMENT

Developmental
MANAGEMENT

Developmental Management

PRINCIPLES OF HOLISTIC BUSINESS

RONNIE LESSEM

Basil Blackwell

British Library Cataloguing in Publication Data
A CIP catalogue record for this book is available from
the British Library.

Library of Congress Cataloging in Publication Data
Lessem, Ronnie.
Developmental management: principles of holistic business / Ronnie Lessem.
p. cm. – (Developmental management)
Includes bibliographical references.
ISBN 0–631–16844–3.
1. Organizational change. 2. Comparative management.
I. Title. II. Series.
HD58.8.L47 1990
658.4'06–dc20   89–48321 CIP

Typeset in 11 on 13pt Ehrhardt
by Hope Services (Abingdon) Ltd.
Printed in Great Britain by
William Clowes, Beccles, Suffolk

Contents

Preface

The origins of *Developmental Management* lie in the early 1960s when, as the son of a self-made businessman, I became a student of economics in Zimbabwe. Having studied the principles of economics for three years I found myself, at the end of it all, little closer to finding an answer to the questions *Why do some individuals, enterprises and nations develop more fully than others?*, and *How can I myself help to bring such development about?*

Having found no obvious economically based answers, I turned to psychology and then to Eastern philosophy for new insights. However, at the time I was still too young to appreciate the significance of what I was investigating, and got (seemingly) diverted in succession to accountancy, industrial economics and business administration. At the same time I moved from Africa to Europe, then to the Middle East, to the United States, and finally back to Europe.

Of course, as I now realize with hindsight, the 'diversion' was not in vain. For when I came, four years ago, to write my book *Global Business*[1] I found myself travelling to all four quarters of the globe and across all the commercial functions to find the inspiration as well as the content for the book. In the event I discovered that the fully developed business – like the whole person – has body, mind, heart and soul. Moreover, such 'whole' development is contingent upon a cross-cultural approach to business, as to life.

Two years later, in setting out my *Global Management Principles*,[2] I conjectured that the body and mind of business are represented in what I have termed *primal* and *rational* management. Whereas Tom Peters has become the high priest of the former, instinctively based, strain of management,[3] Peter Drucker is the philosopher king presiding over the latter, intellectually based, variety.[4] That left the heart and soul of business still to be accounted for.

The soul, or spirit, of business – what I have termed *inspirational* or *metaphysical* management – is the most difficult of all to access. In fact I have left it to my American friend and colleague, Harrison Owen, to plumb the depths of such organizational transformation, through the recovery and release of spirit.[5] I have chosen to focus on the heart of the organization, as revealed through what I have now termed developmental management.

In my global management text, then, I first set out the basis for a developmental approach that underpins the evolution of individual people, business functions, managed organizations and even whole societies. I have revisited those basic elements in this book, paying due attention to the roots, the core and the branches of such a developmental approach. In fact, as you will see, the roots are *biological* and *ecological* rather than economic in nature. Similarly, the evolving organization at the core is ultimately *humanistic* rather than commercial or administrative in its fully developed form, though it assumes an economic and technical orientation along its evolutionary way. Finally, the developmental grounds, in which the business tree of life is rooted, stretch across the globe, from *transpersonal* psychology in the West to *Buddhist* psychology in the East, from *existential* philosophy in the North to *mythological* philosophy in the South.

The developmental approach branches out – interestingly – towards on the one hand *individuation*, rather than enterprise or individuality, and on the other *organizational synergy*, rather than community or teamwork. The fruits of such developmental activities are contained within the *learning organization*, which draws on the whole person – that is, his or her actions, thoughts and feelings. In this book I have discussed one such organization, Dexion, which was started in Britain by a remarkable Greek-Australian, Demetrius Comino.

The grounds not only for this book but for the whole series of which it is a part, therefore, cross the four quarters of the globe. While, for example, the Anglo-American Charles Hampden-Turner, in *Charting the Corporate Mind*, draws on existentialism, the Japanese Yoneji Masuda, in his *Managing in the Information Society*, draws on Buddhism. The ecological roots of developmental management are reflected in the work of the Englishman John Davis – *Managing Sustainable Development*. The developmental core is depicted not only in *Foundations of Business* by the Russian Ivan Alexander, but also in the Dutchman Bernard Lievegoed's *Managing the Developing Organization*.

The developmental branches will be represented by the African Albert Koopman's *Bridging the Cultural Gap*, as well as by *Unity in Variety* from the Anglo-Egyptian writer Pauline Graham. Finally, in depicting the developmental fruits the Englishman Gerry Rhodes focuses on *The Thinking Organization*, whereas the Frenchman Alain Minc deals with *Europe 1992 as a Learning Community*. It is my hope that these and the other titles that will appear in the series will resolve not only my own developmental questions but many of your own, as individual managers and as managers of organizations.

Ronnie Lessem
London, 1990

Notes

1 R. Lessem, *Global Business*. Prentice Hall, 1987.
2 R. Lessem, *Global Management Principles*. Prentice Hall, 1989.
3 T. Peters and R. Waterman, *In Search of Excellence*. Harper & Row, 1982.
4 P. Drucker, *Management: Tasks, Responsibilities and Practices*. Heinemann, 1979.
5 See Lessem, *Global Management Principles*, chapter 26.

Acknowledgements

It was a good twenty years before *Developmental Management* was first conceived, and it took a further twenty-five for it to advance from conception to birth. Before it was even conceived I had, firstly, my parents to thank for sowing seeds in fertile grounds. My father's Lithuanian heritage and my mother's Austrian descent seeded my developmental thinking – as may be implied by events in Eastern Europe today. Similarly, their combined entrepreneurial and artistic influence has provided fertile ground for much of the developmental content that has followed.

Secondly, in that formative period before the book's conception, I have to thank my African and, specifically, Zimbabwean heritage for positioning me within a developmental context. I would particularly like to thank the late Dr Michael Gelfand and Lovemore Mbigi – my mentors in Zimbabwe – and Professor Raymond, who taught me at Harvard Business School, for belatedly exposing me to that context in which I had lived, largely unknowingly, for a good twenty years.

For the conception of the developmental idea, I owe a debt of gratitude to my wife, Joey, who, as a counsellor and designer, opened my eyes not only to art and beauty, but also to my own emotions. The artistic influence has extended through my children Talya and Gabriel, both of whom are musicians, linguists and interpreters of life. Their emotional influence, combined with the intellectual nourishment provided especially by Mary Parker Follett and Abraham Maslow in the US, Bernard Lievegoed and Rudolf Steiner in continental Europe, Kevin Kingsland and Reg Revans in Britain, and Agha Hasan Abedi in the Indian subcontinent, has rounded out my soulful African orientation.

Finally, I have to thank particularly Richard Burton at Basil Blackwell, and subsequently Rosemary Roberts, for acting as midwives in the birth not only of this book but also of the Developmental Management series as a whole.

Ronnie Lessem

*   *   *

Publisher's Note

Chapters 3, 4 and 5 of this book and some parts of Chapter 2 are revised and reworked versions of sections drawn from *Global Management Principles* (Prentice Hall, 1989). We thank Cathy Peck at Prentice Hall for granting permission for the use of the original material.

TO BERNARD LIEVEGOED

*who gave me my first managerial insight into the
developmental way*

What is Developmental Management?

Management has entered its mid-life crisis. The rational approach that has dominated organizational life for the greater part of this century is now under siege. Where management goes from here is still open to question. Will it regress to its youthful, entrepreneurial and primal origins, or can it surmount its mid-life crisis to reach a more highly evolved state?

Developmental management is this new state. It comprehends, but is more advanced than, either enterprising or effective management. Whereas the youthful, enterprising manager is represented by economic man, and the more established, responsible manager by organizational man, the developmental manager in mid-life is represented by the whole, rounded person. In other words, for the manager in mid-life, for the first time, business becomes an extension of his or her whole being.

The Emergence of the Conventional Wisdom

From the 1950s to the early 1980s scientific wisdom dominated the management scene. A fertile combination of European thought and American practice resulted in a rational approach to management, championed by Peter Drucker, a central European who emigrated to the US.

Drucker argued, as a scientific thinker, that management is not just a matter of experience, hunch or native ability.[1] Its elements, he claimed, can be analysed, organized systematically, and learned by anyone with normal intelligence. At the same time, as the achievement-oriented American that he became, Drucker claimed that the ultimate test of management is not analysis but performance.

This amalgam of scientific analysis and goal-oriented performance became the hallmark of professional management in Europe and the US. Moreover, it was exported in this form all over the world. In Latin America, southern Africa, Hong Kong and Singapore business schools sprang up to disseminate this conventional wisdom. Production and marketing, finance and human resource management were all developed as offshoots of this rational core.

There emerged, particularly in the 1960s, a bitter dispute between the so-called behavioural scientists, who favoured a democratic and qualitative approach to organizational behaviour,[2] and the management scientists, who followed a more bureaucratic and quantitative line. But the softer approach failed to infiltrate the commercial end of business, which still held fast to social-scientific principles. Rational man was still very much in charge.

Cultural Re-orientation

A fundamental shift occurred, however, in the early 1980s. It was brought about by the loss of economic and managerial hegemony in Europe and the US. For the first time in business and managerial history the social engineering of the West and the North was called into question.

> Managerial reality is not an absolute; rather, it is socially and culturally determined. Across all cultures and in all societies, human beings coming together to perform certain collective acts encounter common problems having to do with establishing direction, coordination and motivation. Culture affects how these problems are perceived and how they are resolved. Societal learning also establishes horizons of perception.[3]

The Japanese economic miracle, particularly in the 1970s, made the rationalists think again, for it appeared that something had been stirring in Japan of a non-rational, if not irrational, nature. The two American investigators, Pascale and Athos, conveyed this at two levels.

At one level – which the management establishment was less ready to perceive – the non-rationality involved a subtle blend of forces, an 'approach to ambiguity, uncertainty, imperfection and to inter-dependence as the most approved form of relationship'.[4] At a second level – more accessible to conventional managers – it involved soft-edged, shared values.

Back to Basics

It was to this second level that Tom Peters led his fellow Americans, as well as many other admiring managers around the world. In the face of increasing business and environmental turbulence, managers as far apart as Latin America, southern Africa, northern Europe and the Indian subcontinent have retreated from advancing complexity. Spurred on by the resurgence of *enterprise cultures* worldwide, Tom Peters – following just one aspect of the Pascale–Athos theory – has overturned the rational establishment and regressed in his theory to a more primal state.

Shortcomings of Rational Management

- To be rational is often to be *negative.*
- The exclusively rational approach leads to *heartless* philosophy.
- The numerative component has in-built *conservative* bias.
- Today's version of rationality *devalues experimentation.*
- Anti-experimentation leads to *over-complexity.*[5]

In effect, spurning complexity and abstraction, Peters has returned to the homespun American virtues of personal enterprise and a strong sense of community. In so doing he has achieved three things. Firstly he has released management from the stranglehold of rationality as an all-pervasive organizational norm. Secondly he has introduced a balance between soft and hard business attributes. Thirdly he has interwoven commercial and organizational functions and behaviours, which were growing increasingly apart.

However, in going back to basics Peters has adopted a brand of parochialism that merely shelters us from the implications of the emerging global business. To take account of this new globalism we have to turn from primal and rational to developmental management.

Developmental Management Defined

Whereas primal management is economically based, and rational management is administratively oriented, developmental management is *humanistic* in essence. Whereas the primal manager values economic man and the rational manager values organizational man, the developmental manager values the *whole person.*

In other words primal management recognizes people for their independence, rational management acknowledges them for their dependability, and developmental management values them for their *interdependence*. Similarly the primal manager champions independent enterprise, the rational manager serves the public or private corporation, and the developmental manager orchestrates interdependent *joint ventures*. Finally, as has already been suggested, primal management is parochial, rational management is national, and developmental management is *transnational* in orientation.

Understanding Developmental Management

A useful metaphor for developmental management is one that I used in *The Roots of Excellence* – the *tree of life*.[6] In explaining this I shall first review the philosophical *grounds* of this style of management in humanistic psychology; secondly the disciplinary *roots* in biology and ecology; thirdly the organizational *core* in the developing organization; fourthly the managerial *branches* reflected in self-development and organizational and societal development; and fifthly the *fruits* – the learning organization.

In seeking to understand developmental management we shall focus throughout on its evolutionary nature (that is on its developmental stages) marked by crises and resolutions. In generalized terms this evolutionary force in the individual, the organization and the surrounding environment is first *formative* or action-oriented, second *normative* or rational, and third *integrative* or infused with feeling. This third, so-called *developmental* stage incorporates an appreciation of the whole (stages one to three). In other words in the integrative phase we combine an accommodation of individuality with an appreciation of interdependence.

The Developmental Ground

Whereas primal management is grounded in economics and rational management in technology, the grounds of developmental management are to be found in humanism.

A new psychology of *self-actualization* was first established by a political and organizational philosopher, Mary Parker Follett, and later enriched by her compatriot in the US, the psychologist Abraham

Maslow. A move towards *individual learning* and *organizational renewal* was initially made by the Austrian social philosopher Rudolf Steiner, and later pursued by a management educator in Britain, Reg Revans. An important influence was exercised by a group of management philosophers concerned with *Buddhist economics*. And the last contribution was made by the Pakistani founder and president of the Bank of Credit and Commerce, Agha Hasan Abedi.

The new psychology of self-actualization: the US

Mary Parker Follett was a political and management philosopher in the US during the 1920s. At the time she exerted significant influence over progressive captains of industry in both her own country and Britain. Parker Follett sought a new principle of political and economic association. 'Life is enriched', she said, 'by collaboration with all the powers of the universe.' Man lives on several planes at once and his development depends on uniting them. His life, therefore, is one of manifold relations. 'The power of our corporations depends upon this capability of men to interknit themselves into such genuine relations that a new personality is evolved.'[7] Abraham Maslow took off from this point by relating the several planes on which man lives to a hierarchy of needs. For Maslow the need for 'self-actualization' lay at the top of the hierarchy.[8]

Individual learning and organizational renewal: Europe

While Parker Follett was a lone philosophical force in the US in the 1920s, existentialism had a major philosophical influence across Europe in the 1950s and 1960s. Its major emphasis was on the *free assertion of individual identity* and *subjective experience as the foundation of knowledge*. Interestingly, whereas the British were noticeably unmoved by the continental existentialists, intellectually several management thinkers were significantly affected by them. For the Englishman Reg Revans, the manager who challenges reality must first ask 'What view of the here and now is appropriate in using any of my knowledge?'[9]

The philosophical perspective that has probably exercised the most powerful influence on developmental management is Rudolf Steiner's anthroposophy. Although much of his thought is inaccessible to the lay person his ideas on social renewal, coupled with the economic and organizational perspectives of his contemporary disciples, have formed probably the strongest pan-European stream of management

thought. What Steiner did, starting from his threefold view of man –
as a willing, thinking and feeling being – was to document the
evolution of individuals, organizations and whole societies.

> Everything that happens to man is an image, having its prototype amidst
> those great events of cosmic evolution with which his existence is bound
> up . . . the weal and woe of the individual is bound up with that of all the
> world. Man does harm to the world and to all other beings if he fails in the
> right development of his own powers.[10]

Buddhist economics: Japan

It was the Anglo-German management philosopher and author of
Small is Beautiful in the early 1970s, Fritz Schumacher, who coined
the term 'Buddhist work'. He described the purpose of such work in
the following terms:

> to give man a chance to utilise and develop his faculties; to enable him to
> overcome his egocentredness by joining with other people in a common
> task; and to bring forth the goods needed for a becoming existence.[11]

In fact the originator of capitalism in Japan was probably a Zen
Buddhist priest, Shoshan Suzuki, who advised merchants in the
1600s to travel around the country distributing goods as if they were
on a pilgrimage.[12]

'Real' or 'natural' management: the Indian subcontinent

Similarly the Bank of Credit and Commerce in Pakistan, following
the principles of 'real management' evolved by its president and
founder, Agha Hasan Abedi,[13] now concerns itself with the physical,
mental and spiritual well-being of its employees, clients and
communities across the globe. Drawing on the 'natural laws of
totality, integrity, latency and flow', Agha Hasan Abedi has drawn up
a developmental philosophy that the members of his senior management team have put into commercial practice.

The Developmental Roots

The philosophical grounds are wide-ranging, both geographically and
culturally. Whereas primal management draws heavily on political
and cultural economics, and rational management draws on the

administrative and behavioural sciences, developmental management is rooted in biology and ecology.

Developmental biology

The eminent American biologist and management consultant George Ainsworth Land wrote a book with the provocative title *To Grow or to Die*. In it he described the pattern of organization – for individuals, organizations and societies – as universal.

> A formative period of establishing the initial pattern, a normative period of extending and improving and repeating the pattern; and then a third phase of integrating and combining previously excluded material and sharing differentness.[14]

A second American biologist, Barry McWaters, who founded the Institute for the Study of Conscious Evolution, has added another evolutionary element, one that regulates the three that Land has cited. Evolution for McWaters is the development of any type of energy or organization that progresses towards a more conscious or meaningful role in the universe.[15]

Social ecology

By contrast with Land and McWaters – American biologists with an interest in humanistic psychology – Martin Large is an English anthropologist with an interest in what he terms *social ecology*. Large too has been heavily influenced by Rudolf Steiner. Social ecology, he says, like natural ecology, begins with the cultivation of a consciousness appropriate to the understanding of life and development processes.

> Whereas objective thinking gives rise to mechanistic thinking appropriate to understanding the inorganic world, life-consciousness gives rise to holistic thinking appropriate to the development of human and social forms over time.[16]

Large, then, drawing on his ecological insights, goes on to cite the characteristics of development that apply to individuals, organizations and societies. Development, he believes, involves the unfolding of structure over time, encompassing ever more complex levels of organization.

The Developmental Core

While the core of primal management is contained in Tom Peters's 'passion for excellence', and that of rational management in Peter Drucker's 'managing for results', the developmental core is contained within the *developing organization* conceived by Bernard Lievegoed, a leading Dutch psychiatrist and another student of Rudolf Steiner.[17]

Out of the developmental roots there emerges the core:

- action becomes formative,
- thought becomes normative,
- feeling becomes integrative.

Lievegoed describes these three stages of the developing organization as:

- pioneering,
- differentiated,
- integrated.

Developmental management at its core is concerned with the evolution of an individual, organization or society from a state of independence (formative) to dependence (normative) to inter-dependence (integrative). In this cumulative process each comes to realize its unique whole or 'transcendent' identity. Let us now approach each stage of development in a little more detail.

Formative enterprise: pioneering

Primal management, which goes back to basics, is highly appropriate for the small enterprise where a personal, parochial and independent frame of mind is necessary. Similarly, where there is a need to re-energize a moribund organization, such primal instincts have their place.

Normative organization: differentiated

If, however, such an enterprise is to negotiate its growth crisis successfully and become an established organization, the rules of its business game need to change. There is now a need for an impersonal, national, dependable outlook, in which rational strategies and structures are given due attention. Intelligence, or thought, becomes primary and instinct secondary. Personality and community should be replaced by professionalism and organization.

Integrative association: integrated

Increasingly both public and private organizations are evolving from independent to interdependent entities. We are witnessing a development from personalized enterprise to depersonalized bureaucracy to the individual learning organization; from parochial to national to transnational; from independence to dependence to interdependence.

At each stage of its development, moreover, the business requires a balance of hard and soft attributes if it is to succeed. A business veers one way or another to take on a different form, albeit within the context of a particular stage. So the primal business alternates between a *personal* and a *cooperative enterprise*. The established organization alternates between a *hierarchy* and a *network*. The truly developmental organization alternates between what might be called a *learning organization*, facilitating self-development and organizational development, and a *molecular organization*, fostering individual and organizational synergy.

The developmental manager is there to stimulate organizational evolution, taking due care of primal and rational business attributes in the process. In other words, he or she must be able to envisage and implement a passage from formation to integration, alternating along the way between soft and hard.

The Developmental Branches

The primal branches personalize enterprise. The rational branches depersonalize business, management and organization. The developmental branches, emerging out of root and core, give rise to individuality in people, organizations and societies.

Individuals, organizational functions and whole societies – like the organization itself – all evolve through stages, reflecting each of the root elements in turn. Primal or formative products and markets, for example, reflect active youth in individuals and organizations. Rational or normative approaches to functional management reflect thoughtful adulthood in societal development. Finally a developmental or integrative approach to organization or environment reflects the emotionally evolved nature of renewal in mid-life.

The individual: self-development

The developmental manager will be concerned, firstly, with the evolution of managers from youth to maturity and with their self-actualization. Like the business as a whole, the manager undergoes his or her phases of development. These evolutionary phases, characterized by structure-changing and structure-building episodes, need to be fostered by the developmental manager.

At an early stage of their managerial development, that is, in their youthful twenties, individuals engage in experimentation and exploration. These are the primal years. Subsequent attempts to consolidate, in later adulthood, require a degree of rationality and responsibility not previously needed. Mid-life, in the forties, is a time of renewal, when a conscious and purposeful attempt to develop the whole person – in intimate association with others – becomes imperative for growth. Finally, in maturity, the manager, if he has successfully negotiated his earlier transitions, is able to find the true centre of his being and becoming.

The enterprise: organization development

Enterprises are created by thrusting *entrepreneurs*, or enterprising managers, in association with what may be called loving *animators*, or people managers.

Rational organizations are developed by freedom-loving *agents of change*, or adaptable managers, in association with responsible *executives*, or analytical managers.

Associations of enterprises, while acknowledging the other roles, are headed by *enablers* or facilitative managers, who spearhead individual evolution, and by *adopters*, or attuned managers, who ensure that personal, organizational and societal evolution are in harmony.

At any one point in time, however, developing business organizations, specialized functions, managers and societies will all have constituent parts operating at different stages of evolution. A manager may be mature in his commercial dealings and immature in his personal and organizational ones. A business may have one youthful, enterprising division and another in the process of its mid-life renewal. A society may have a mix of parochial (rural) and transnational (technological) points of focus.

Society: global development

The truly developmental manager will be concerned with the evolution of societies from a parochial to a transnational state, and with his or her own process of self-realization. Like the individual manager and the business entity, whole societies evolve or decay. It is the developmental manager's role to ensure that his or her organization not only responds to but in some cases participates in the evolution of the surrounding environment. This could apply, on the one hand, to individual market places and, on the other, to whole cultures.

In fact the developmental manager will be concerned with the evolution of both corporate and national cultures. Primal business cultures have strong 'Western' features to them, which duly combine enterprise with community. Rational ones are more 'Northern' in character, combining individual and organizational learning with organizational structure and corporate strategy. Developmental cultures are an amalgam, combining Western and Northern approaches to personal and organizational individuality with Eastern forms of group, organizational and inter-organizational harmony.

Applying Developmental Management

Developmental Fruits

The fruits represent the culmination of the developmental activity, grounded in humanistic soils, rooted in biology and ecology, held in place by a solid developmental core, branching out towards individual, functional and societal development.

These fruits are borne of the threefold nature of humanity. Developmental management, then, through its roots, draws upon those three fundamental elements that recur constantly and recombine in philosophical and psychological thought. Steiner referred to them as will, thought and feeling. The Anglo-Indian psychologist Kevin Kingsland identifies cognitive, affective and behavioural aspects of our being. As we shall see later, the Spaniard Salvador de Madariaga regards these attributes as combining to form the spirit of Europe.[18]

In effect, as should by now be clear, these three elements mirror the three stages of evolution (Table 1.1). In effect, in applying developmental management we move away from an appreciation of evolutionary phases. Instead we become involved with the active manipulation of the three key elements. In other words, the three stages,

- formative,
- normative,
- integrative,

become three forces

- action (the behavioural force),
- thought (the cognitive force),
- feeling (the affective force).

The structural field, accommodating these three forces, is not the economic enterprise nor the bureaucratic institution but the learning organization. The dynamic field, in which these forces flow, is an alternating field of learning, both horizontal and vertical.

Table 1.1   The Fundamental Elements and Stages

Source	Perspective	Element		
		1	2	3
Steiner	Philosophical	Will	Thought	Feeling
Madariaga	Cultural	Action	Thought	Passion
Kingsland	Psychological	Behavioural	Cognitive	Affective

Source	Perspective	Stages		
		1	2	3
Land	Biological	Formative	Normative	Integrative
Lievegoed	Organizational	Pioneering	Scientific	Integrated
Lessem	Managerial	Primal	Rational	Developmental

The horizontal spectrum of learning

Different kinds of manager, as well as different aspects of an organization, arise across the horizontal spectrum. Each individual or institution is differentiated in varying degrees, behaviourally, cognitively and affectively. Seven combinations result from the different permutations of these three:

- action management and physical activity;
- people management and corporate culture;
- management of change and adaptive information systems;
- enterprising management and new business ventures;
- analytical management and formal strategy and structure;
- developmental management and the learning organization;
- innovative management and the creative nucleus of the corporation.

All these have complementary roles to play.

The vertical spectrum of learning

Learning proceeds vertically upwards and innovation downwards, again in sevenfold form. Learning proceeds upwards:

- from attention to action;
- from action to involvement;
- from involvement to experimentation;
- from experimentation to pattern formation;
- from pattern formation to formal conceptualization;
- from conceptualization to fundamental insight;
- from insight to origination.

Conversely, creativity or innovation, just like the process of setting up a business, proceeds downwards:

- envisioning the future is followed by
- recognition of technological, market or human potential;
- from the combination of these a concept is born;
- the concept must be energized by people and resources;
- continuing adaptation is needed to fulfil the creative act;
- social involvement is required if creativity is not to be foiled by the human factor;
- plans must be acted on and the consequences of action attended to.

The fruits of developmental management – a transformation of human will (or actions), thoughts and feelings – spread across and up and down. In the horizontal dimension they combine to form a spectrum of managerial, organizational and national individualities. In the vertical dimension they combine cumulatively, yielding, in an upwards direction, the individual or societal learning spectrum and, in a downwards direction, the spectrum of innovation.

The learning organization

The learning organization, then, facilitates participative (horizontal) and innovative (vertical) development within and between people and institutions, commercially, technologically and socially. It thereby transcends not only the business enterprise but also the hierarchical institution.

Conclusion

It is the aim of this book to explain developmental management from grounds to roots, core, branches and fruits. It therefore encompasses, from an evolutionary and interdependent perspective, not only the manager as an individual and the functions of the business being managed but also the manager's external environment. As such it is *interdisciplinary* and *cross-cultural* in its approach.

The book falls into two parts, 'Understanding Developmental Management' and 'Developmental Management in Action'. In the first part I outline the philosophical grounds of developmental management (Chapter 2), before going on to investigate the developmental roots, core and branches of management, drawing on biological and ecological concepts that are of particular relevance. There follows a review of the developing organization and the evolving business functions. In Chapters 6 and 7 I assess the development of the European Community in the context of the increasing globalization of business.

Part II examines the implications for individual, commercial, organizational and societal learning of the developmental approach to management, and relates these findings to the case of a company in which it has been applied successfully – the Dexion Group.

Notes

1 P. Drucker, *Management: Tasks, Responsibilities and Practices*. Heinemann, 1979.
2 W. Bennis, *Changing Organizations*. McGraw Hill, 1966.
3 R. Pascale and A. Athos, *The Art of Japanese Management*. Penguin, 1982, p. 22.

4 Pascale and Athos, *The Art of Japanese Management*, p. 204.
5 T. Peters and R. Waterman, *In Search of Excellence.* Harper & Row, 1982, p. 57.
6 R. Lessem, *The Roots of Excellence.* Fontana, 1986.
7 M. Parker Follett, *The New State.* Peter Smith, 1926, p. 8; 2nd edn, 1965.
8 A. Maslow, *Motivation and Personality.* Harper & Row, 1964.
9 R. Revans, *Developing Effective Managers.* Longman, 1971, p. 21.
10 R. Steiner, *Occult Science.* Pharos, 1979, p. 266.
11 E. F. Schumacher, *Small is Beautiful.* Abacus, 1973, p. 45.
12 B. De Mente, *Japanese Etiquette and Ethics in Business.* Passport Books, 5th edn, 1987, p. 6.
13 R. Lessem, *Global Business.* Prentice Hall, 1987.
14 G. A. Land, *To Grow or to Die.* Random House, 1973, p. 21; 2nd edn, John Wiley, 1985.
15 B. McWaters, *Conscious Evolution.* Turnstone, 1983, p. 68.
16 M. Large, *Social Ecology.* Published by the author, 1981, p. 10.
17 B. Lievegoed, *Organisaties in ontwikkeling.* Lemniscaat, 1969. Eng. trans. as *The Developing Organization.* Tavistock, 1973; new edn, Basil Blackwell, 1990.
18 S. de Madariaga, *Englishman, Frenchman, Spaniard.* Howell, 1922.

PART I

Understanding Developmental Management: the Grounds, Roots, Core and Branches

Introduction

For some fifty years the substance of general management has remained unaltered. While concepts and techniques of manufacturing and marketing, finance and personnel, have advanced apace, the generalities of management have endured. The basic activities of planning, coordination and control – allowing, of course, for innumerable variations on the common theme – have remained sacrosanct, in both theory and practice. This rational approach, vigorously championed by Peter Drucker, has prescribed, and indeed limited, our understanding of management.

During the 1980s a yearning to go 'back to basics' has resulted in an altered state of managerial consciousness. Essentially, according to Tom Peters and his colleagues, the generalities of management can now be reduced to three elements, less complex and abstract than the rational principles. For management is now a matter of caring for customers, innovating constantly and exercising leadership – especially by 'wandering about'. This new, primal approach has once again limited our managerial understanding, although it has shifted our field of awareness towards more tangible, visible, basic qualities.

A developmental understanding of management, in fact, precludes neither a rational nor a primal approach. On the contrary, the developmental perspective invites you, as a manager, to exploit the best of both those worlds, as and when appropriate. A small enterprise or a new business venture lends itself to a primal and localized style of youthful leadership. Conversely a more established public or private, national institution requires a more rational approach to its management. But the development outlook transcends the parochial and the national, the youthful and the consolidated, the small and the medium-sized organization.

Neither the rational nor the primal approach adequately caters for managers in mid-life, organizations in need of renewal, transnational businesses, or cultures outside of the Western sphere of influence. For the developing individual, the developing organization, the developing business and the developing society new concepts are required to replace the old style of management. Concepts of individuality, attunement and alignment supplant those of planning, coordination and control, and those of customer care, constant innovation and management by wandering about.

Understanding developmental management, then, is not only a matter of commercial instinct and managerial thought, but also one of individual feeling and intuition. Instinct is wrapped up with primal enterprise, thought with rational organization, and feeling and intuition with development in itself.

Section A

Developmental Philosophy

2

The Humanistic Grounds for Development

Introduction

Unlike rational management, whose origins lie mainly in Europe, and primal management, whose source is the US, the humanistic grounds for developmental management are spread across the entire globe – from the US and continental Europe, to Britain and Japan, as well as the Indian subcontinent. The individuals and movements that supplied these developmental grounds are, in the US, the political scientist Mary Parker Follett and the humanistic psychologist Abraham Maslow; in continental Europe the social philosopher Rudolf Steiner; in Britain the management educator Reg Revans; in Japan Buddhist economics, also espoused by the Anglo-German management philosopher Fritz Schumacher; and finally in Pakistan the founder and president of the Bank of Credit and Commerce, Agha Hasan Abedi. (Figure 2.1.)

The Western and Northern sources, in the US and Europe, are centred on the individual, albeit in the context of organizational and socio-economic evolution. The Eastern and Southern sources, in Japan and the Indian subcontinent, are socially and economically centred, albeit in the context of personal and human evolution. I shall begin this chapter in the West, with Maslow and Parker Follett, and then go North, to Revans in western Europe, and to Schumacher, before moving to Steiner in central Europe. Finally, I shall cross to the Far East, to unravel Shoshan Suzuki's Japanese adaptation of Buddhist economics, before turning South to Agha Hasan Abedi's 'real' or 'natural' management.

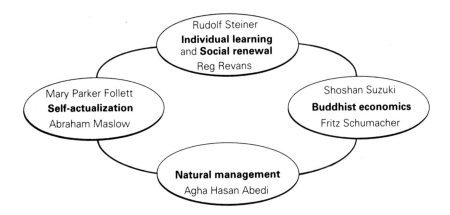

Figure 2.1 The Developmental Grounds

Self-actualization

The New Psychology

Mary Parker Follett, who rose to pre-eminence in America in the 1920s and 1930s, started out in life as a political scientist. As a democrat, in the truest sense, she wanted to introduce a 'new psychology of individuality in community' into public awareness. While starting from a social and political perspective, she ended by having a significant influence on prominent industrialists of the day, particularly such Quaker businessmen in the UK as the Cadbury and Rowntree families.

As a management analyst Parker Follett focused on the power of the group.

The New Psychology

By the 'new psychology' I mean partly that group psychology, which is receiving more attention and gaining more influence every day, and partly I mean simply that feeling out for a new conception of modes of association which we do see in law, economics, ethics, politics, and indeed in every department of thought. It is a short way of saying that we are now looking at things not as entities but in relation.[1]

Immediately we can see the broad sweep of Parker Follett's analysis and synthesis. She is combining psychological, social and political insight into one grand synthesis. She is playing the role of a 'gatherer', but from a conscious and analytical rather than from a subconscious and instinctive perspective. She also extends her reference point, with no great difficulty, from a social to a commercial context:

> The business world is never again to be directed by individual intelligences, but by intelligences interacting and ceaselessly influencing one another. Every mental act of the big businessman is entirely different from the mental acts of his predecessors, continuing to manage their own competitive businesses. There is of course competition between our large firms, but the cooperation between them is coming to occupy a larger and larger relative place.[2]

These might appear to be, especially in the 1920s, the words of a romantic idealist. However, what is noteworthy is the real influence Parker Follett had on practising businessmen and community leaders and management consultants in Great Britain, of whom Seebohm Rowntree, a captain of industry, and Lyndall Urwick, a leading business consultant, were the most prominent. Her analysis was certainly a compelling one, coming, as it did, in the trouble-torn years between the wars, and just before the Great Depression. As always, she combined economics and politics with psychology and sociology.

Group Life

> Our political life is stagnating, capital and labour are virtually at war, the nations of Europe are at each other's throats – because we have not yet learnt to live together. The twentieth century must find a new principle of association. Crowd philosophy, crowd patriotism, crowd government must go. The herd is no longer sufficient to enfold us. Group organization is to be the new method in politics, the basis of our future industrial system, the foundation of international order. Group organization will create the new world we are blindly feeling after, for creative force comes from the group, creative power is evolved through the activity of group life.[3]

The great American psychologist William James was a contemporary of Parker Follett. While he maintained that man is a complex of 'many selves in one', she saw society as a complex of groups, all of which together make up a social whole. Within the group process is contained the secret of collective life, the key to democracy, the master lesson for every individual to learn, and the chief hope for the political, social and international life of the future. What, more specifically then, is this extraordinary group process, in which Parker Follett had so much faith?

The group process

The key to unlock Parker Follett's group process is the human craving for totality, or for wholeness. Democracy, for her, is not a spreading out and an extension of suffrage. That is merely its external aspect. It is rather a drawing together. 'It is the imperative call for the lacking part of the self.' Democracy is the finding of the one will to which the will of every single man and woman must contribute. 'We have an instinct for democracy because we have an instinct for wholeness.'

The human being, then, craves totality. This craving is in fact the motor of social progress. The process of getting and growing is not one of adding more and more to ourselves, but one of offering more and more of ourselves. For Parker Follett, contribution, not appropriation, is the law of growth. What our special contribution is, as an individual, is for each of us to discover. The definition of individuality must therefore be, finding one's place in the whole. 'One's place' pertains to the individual; 'the whole' pertains to the society. The connecting agency is the small, adaptable group. If I fail to make my individual contribution to the group, the whole of society suffers.

In the 1920s Parker Follett wrote, 'the individual is being submerged, smothered, choked by the crowd fallacy, the herd theory. Free him from these, release his energies, and he will work out, together with all other free men and women, quick, flexible, constantly changing group forms, which shall respond sensitively to every need.'

Creativity in Unity

Imitation is for the shirkers, like-mindedness for the comfort lovers, unifying for the creators. . . . The unifying now demanded of us is that which is brought about by the enlargement of each by the inflowing of every other. Then I go forth a new creature.

But to where do I go forth? Always to a new group, to a new 'society'. There is no end to the process. A new being springs forth from every fresh contact. My nature opens up to a thousand influences. I feel continuous new births.[4]

Integration not compromise

What Parker Follett had to say had very direct implications, not only at a philosophical level, but also at a practical business level. In fact the whole of 'industrial relations', as conventionally practised, cut completely across her convictions, and her understanding of constructive human behaviour.

As far as Parker Follett is concerned, whoever advocates compromise – which is the stuff of everyday negotiations – abandons the individual. The individual has to give up part of himself in order that some action might take place. The integrity of the individual can only be preserved through integration. If you believe in compromise you see the individual as static. So what is integration? Integration is a qualitative adjustment, whereas compromise is a quantitative one. In the first case there is a change in the ideas and their action tendencies; in the second there is mere barter of opposed 'rights of way'. In a compromise situation the underlying conflict continues.

Compromise, then, is on the same plane as fighting. Integration, on the other hand, involves, first, the discovery of difference, and, second, the unifying of apparent opposites. Differences must be integrated rather than annihilated or absorbed. Every difference that is swept up into a bigger conception feeds and enriches society; every difference that is ignored feeds on society – or on a business – and eventually corrupts it. Heterogeneity, not homogeneity, makes for unity. The higher the degree of business or social organization, the more it is based on a wide variety among its members.

Friendship and Sympathy

The deep and lasting friendship is one capable of recognizing and dealing with all the fundamental differences that must exist between any two individuals, one capable therefore of such an enrichment of our personalities that together we shall mount to new heights of understanding and endeavor. Pleasant little glows of feeling can never be fanned into the fire which becomes the driving force of progress.

Sympathy is a whole feeling; it is a recognition of oneness. Suppose six manufacturers meet to discuss some form of union. What these men need most is not altruistic feelings, but a consciousness of themselves as a new unit, and a realization of the needs of that unit. True sympathy, therefore, is not a vague sentiment they bring with them. It springs from their very meeting, to become, in its turn, a vital factor in the meeting.[5]

The law of the situation

Among all this wealth of group analysis and integration, only a very small amount has been picked up and assimilated by management posterity. I find this extraordinary, especially given Parker Follett's powers of communication during her lifetime, which Lyndall Urwick considered to be exceptional.[6] She was apparently able to communicate easily with businessman and politician, psychologist and community worker alike. Parker Follett evidently practised what she preached as a humanist.

Self-actualization and Personal Growth

Parker Follett in many ways was a woman before her time. Abraham Maslow, on the other hand, in the 1950s was more readily received by the management establishment as a whole.

Maslow's hierarchy of needs

In 1954 Maslow published his seminal work on *Motivation and Personality*, in which he first revealed his oft since quoted hierarchy of needs.

Maslow's Motivational Hierarchy

It is quite true that man lives by bread alone – when there is no bread. But what happens to man's desires when there is plenty of bread and when his belly is chronically filled?

At once other (and higher) needs emerge and these, rather than physiological hunger, dominate the organism. When these in turn are satisfied, again new (and still higher) needs emerge. . . . Human needs are organized into a hierarchy of prepotency.[7]

As we can see, Maslow's developmental approach is constructed not on the basis of phases of life, but on the basis of 'a hierarchy of need prepotency'. In other words, as one need is satisfied so a next, predictable need rises to the fore.

Deficiency needs

The set of needs that forms the starting point for his motivational theory are *physiological* ones. Man needs air, water, food, shelter, sleep, sex. Once physiological needs are relatively well satisfied there emerges a new set of *safety* drives. Both physiological needs and safety drives are, according to Maslow, *deficiency needs*: failure to meet either results in tangible deprivation.

Growth needs

Once both sets of deficiency needs are gratified, then *belonging needs* take over: the drive for love and affection. These are the first of Maslow's growth needs. Next in the hierarchy of prepotency is the *need for esteem*. Everyone in our society, Maslow says, needs a stable, firmly based, high evaluation of themselves. This need becomes prepotent once an individual's physiological, safety and 'belongingness' drives have been satisfied.

Esteem needs form two subsets. Firstly there are the desires for achievement, for adequacy, for mastery, for confidence, for independence and for freedom. There are *inner-directed*. Secondly there are the desires for status and prestige. These are *outer-directed*. However, even if all of these physiological, social and psychological needs are satisfied, there is still room for discontent – unless a person is doing what he or she is truly fitted for. 'What a man (or woman) can be, he must be . . . this need we call self-actualization.'[8] Self-actualization is the ultimate growth need. The full hierarchy of needs, with those attributes comprising self-actualization at the top of the pyramid, are shown in Figure 2.2.

Towards a psychology of being

The self-actualizing features that stood at the top of Maslow's hierarchy were identified by him as *being values* as opposed to *deficiency values*. In fact one of his most fundamental contributions to individual and organizational development was to focus on health rather than pathology, on so-called *peak* rather than mundane *levels of experience*.

> Man demonstrates in his own nature a pressure towards fuller and fuller being, more and more perfect actualization of his humanness in exactly the same naturalistic, scientific sense that an acorn can be said to be pressing towards being an oak tree.[9]

Maslow in fact coined the phrase *Eupsychian management*, which operates according to such 'being values'.

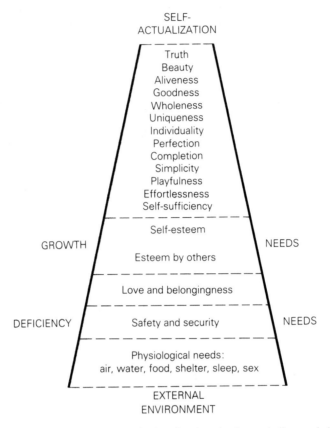

Figure 2.2 Hierarchy of Needs

Eupsychic Man

First of all, and most important of all, is the strong belief that man has an essential nature of his own. . . . Second, there is involved the conception that full health and normal, desirable development consists in actualizing this nature, in fulfilling these potentialities and in developing into maturity along the lines that this dimly seen essential nature dictates, growing from within rather than being shaped from without.

If I had to put it into a single phrase . . . we can now see not only what man is but also what he may become. That is to say we can see not only surface, not only the actualities but also the potentialities. We are now able to judge the essential nature of man according to what his highest possible development may be, instead of merely relying on external observations.[10]

Maslow therefore played a pioneering role in creating a developmental approach to management that took into account the full potential of the human being. Each human being, given a conducive physical and institutional environment in which to live and work, is naturally inclined towards self-actualization, once his deficiency needs and his more basic growth needs are satisfied. Unfortunately Maslow did not go on to relate individual to organizational growth and self-actualization.

Maslow in perspective

While Maslow's concept of a motivational hierarchy of needs has endured, his more prolific ideas on 'being values' have slipped into the managerial background. This has happened for three main reasons. Firstly his need hierarchy has been contested by contingency theorists, who believe that motivation is situationally determined, rather than absolutely prescribed. In other words, according to the contingency school of motivation and leadership, different people and situations call upon different motivations. The proponents of this view therefore accept no absolutes, no fixed motivational hierarchy or prepotencies.

Secondly few, if any, organizations have been psychologically mature enough to accommodate Maslow's 'being values' within themselves. Most of our structures and strategies have not yet evolved sufficiently.

Thirdly Maslow restricted his 'being' psychology to human behaviour within organizations. He therefore left such business disciplines as marketing and finance largely untouched – a deficiency that, as we shall see, Bernard Lievegoed has been able to overcome. In fact most of the 'growth' psychologists who made an impact on organizational development, focusing in different ways on the whole person, restricted themselves to the field of human and organizational behaviour. They therefore remain, with Maslow, isolated from the mainstream of business development and their contribution to developmental management has therefore been circumscribed.

Manager self-development

While the 'human growth' movement in general, and Maslow in particular, were popular in American and British management circles in the 1960s and 1970s, by the 1980s their influence had begun to wane. While the behavioural sciences in the broadest sense have continued to influence management theory and practice, organizational development and humanistic psychology have apparently lost their way. In their place has appeared the general field of *manager self-development*.

Most of the current theory and practice on the subject of manager self-development is very much a watered-down version of the original thrust towards human growth and development. In fact it often amounts to nothing more than self-study methods, or a smattering of self-development techniques, ranging from action learning and lateral thinking to speed reading and methods of improving one's memory.

Individual Learning and Social Renewal

Individual Learning

Learning faster than the rate of change

Reg Revans's approach is different. Revans, an Englishman, was a Cambridge physicist who turned his scientific mind to management. His early work was with managers in the coalmines and with nurses in hospitals. Individuals, according to Revans, need to learn at a speed that is greater than the rate of change if they are to survive in the long term. The same applies to organizations. Learning continues where management science leaves off. Whereas both concern coping with complexity through the appropriate use of information, the first is more personally oriented and the second more impersonal. Freedom and individuality are reflected in our questioning insight; order and predictability are reflected in our programmed knowledge. The developmental manager needs to be master of both.

Action learning is a particular branch of learning theory that not only links individual and organization, but also science and human values. How then can we make use of it, as a means of reconciling personal freedom and institutional order?

Practise what you preach

Revans's work contains innumerable quotations from the Bible and a spiritual element undoubtedly shines through it – a concern for the essence of man, and for man's moral obligations to himself and others. Revans, in fact, seems to have an almost religious commitment to action as opposed to mere learning. Unlike the Western approach, which tends to link action with outward achievement, Revans connects action with inner integrity. The implication is, to put it simply: 'practise what you preach'.

Action is also the means whereby the chiefs (managers) and Indians (workers) find common ground. Revans has tackled industrial relations problems by calling not for different forms of organization but for a different attitude to learning. Action learning is a means of linking thought and action within a single person, as well as scribe (chief) and artisan (Indian) within the nation.

Scribe Meets Artisan

It is a virtue of action learning that, like truth itself, it is a seamless garment; with its help all parties alike, scribe and artisan, manager and workman, should tackle their common foe, the external problem.

Their own opinions of each other, personal and interested, stained by the antipathies of unforgettable tradition, teased and exacerbated by every civilizing process of the educational establishment, reinforced by every decision of our industrial tribunals, may be pretty intransigent.[11]

Learning and information systems

Management and learning, for Revans, walk hand in hand. Both are concerned intimately with the processing of information and with the resolution of complex problems.

The three principal influences on management may be represented by systems based on the use of information. We call them:

system alpha – the use of information for designing objectives;
system beta – the use of information for achieving these objectives;
system gamma – the use of information for adapting to experience and change.[12]

Action learning

In the early 1970s Revans began to arrive at his grand synthesis, which he has been refining ever since. Here are what might be termed the cardinal postulates:

1 Learning is a function of *programmed knowledge* and *questioning insight.* Questioning insight involves knowing the right questions to ask in conditions of ignorance and uncertainty.
2 When the world does not change the son may follow in his father's footsteps, and programmed knowledge is sufficient. But, at the precipice, when you are climbing into a new world at every step, the primary need is for questioning insight.
3 You cannot change the system of which you are in command, fundamentally, unless you are changed in the process. The first change we call *action* and the second we call *learning.*
4 The theory of learning, whose inner logic corresponds with scientific method, suggests that the recognition of one's need to learn, the search for new knowledge, the test of that new knowledge in practical action, the critical evaluation of the results of that test, and the consolidation of the whole exercise within memory, are all essential to complete learning.
5 Those best able to help in developing the self are comrades in adversity who also struggle to understand themselves. You overcome your own fears through helping other people to face theirs.
6 Organizations best able to develop themselves are those that make best use of their existing resources. This is because a social process is calculated to help them identify internal strengths and weaknesses, to understand better their inertia and dynamics, and in other ways to make more use of their stored experiences.
7 Individual and organizational learning, development and problem-solving are all manifestations of the same process.

Social Renewal

Whereas the western European Revans emphasizes *thought* and *action*, the eastern European Rudolf Steiner emphasizes *feeling*. Both Revans and Steiner are concerned with individual self-development in the context of societal evolution; but Steiner, working at the turn of the century, had a broader cultural outlook than does Revans today.

The threefold commonwealth

Steiner, who was also an educator, agronomist and social reformer, developed the concept of the *threefold commonwealth*. The *economic*, *socio-political* and *cultural* parts of a national whole were not to be united and centralized in some abstract body: each of the three was to be centralized within itself, and then, through their cooperation, the unity of the whole society could come about.

> It will then be evident that human cooperation in economic life must be based on fraternity which is inherent in associations; in the civil rights system it is necessary to strive for the realization of equality; and in the relatively independent cultural sector of the social organism it is necessary to strive for the realization of the idea of freedom.[13]

Thus Steiner related the guiding principles of the French revolution – *liberté, égalité, fraternité* – to the social organism. The basis of economic life is, he said, fraternal. However, economic fraternity needs to be interwoven with political equality and blended with individual freedom in order to maintain a healthy social organism.

Liberty, Equality, Fraternity

> If he is to contribute his share to the well-being of the social order in modern society, if he is to add to the welfare of his community by cooperation in the production of values, he must first of all possess individual capacity, talent, ability. In the second place, he must be able to live at peace with his fellow man and to work harmoniously with him.
>
> Thirdly, he must find his proper place, from which he can further the interests of the community by his work, by his activity, by his achievements.[14]

The economics of association

Interestingly, Steiner was a great advocate of the division of labour, but for reasons that were somewhat different from Adam Smith's classical economics, or, for that matter, from Frederick Taylor's scientific management. For Steiner the specialized division of labour means that it becomes impossible to work for oneself. All one can do is to work for others and to set others to work for one.

In the other words, the division of labour makes for a social organism in which the individual lives in accordance with the conditions of the whole of the body of the community. It is simply not possible to work only for oneself. To that extent the onset of the division of labour represents a progressive step in business and economic evolution. However, economic judgements are best made in association, not in watertight, hierarchical compartments. Economic judgements cannot be made on the basis of theory alone; to be effective they must arise from the real experience and understanding of people living in association with one another, individually and as enterprises. Specialization, then, is a means to an associative end and not a separatist end in itself.

Within the economic circuit of goods and services, whose flow has been speeded up by the division of labour, associations must be formed to create the flow itself. Specifically, Steiner argues, representatives of different occupations should meet, consumers and producers should come together. The resulting contracts should then be entered into by association (and in that spirit), not purely through legal dictate.

In the economic world, Steiner maintains, everything should rest on contracts, everything should depend on mutual service rendered. Corporations should carry on business with other corporations. An association of efficiency – I shall have to be productive in my own branch of work in order to enter into contracts with other branches – will be formed by means of contract. In the final analysis Rudolf Steiner emerges as an advocate of an economic system which is neither American nor Japanese, neither conventionally capitalist nor socialist, but a unique amalgam.

Economic Life

Economic life is striving to structure itself according to its own nature, independent of political institutionalization and mentality. It can only do this if associations, comprised of consumers, distributors and producers, are established according to purely economic criteria. External planning sacrifices the free, creative initiative of the individual, thereby depriving the economy of what such initiative alone can give. At the same time the individuals who labour in industry are caught in a routine, and the formative economic forces are invisible to them.

In the associations each individual would learn what he should through contact with another. Through the participants' insight and experience in relation to their respective activities, and their resulting ability to exercise collective judgement, knowledge of what is economically possible would arise.[15]

Steiner's *associational economics* sounds less and less like Adam Smith and more and more like whoever Smith's counterpart in Japan might be – indeed, like the Zen priest Shoshan Suzuki. But before we deal with Buddhist economics we shall turn to a disciple of Steiner, the German economist Folkert Wilken, who died in 1985.

A self-determining economy

Folkert Wilken wrote a seminal work, *The Liberation of Capital*. In this book he advocates the formation of a *need-oriented economy*, which he locates at a 'higher level' than the dominant and rival private and state systems. In the private sector, he says, demand is met according to the business logic of each individual company in isolation. This means that a decline in profit and turnover causes redundancies, in both literal and social terms. The state-controlled economies try, in the name of socialism or communism, to overcome these difficulties by nationalizing the entire economy. This imposes on the state the task of determining the amount of production and consumption. Neither of these examples represents a true *self-determining economy*.

Such an economy, Wilken argues, would not replace individualism, but would make it more socially effective. People would still work for personal motives but they would have to collaborate with one another and maintain a common understanding about economic trends. The economy would then be formed on the basis of organic cooperation, in which every individual part reflects, and is in harmony with, the whole. The whole exists only to the extent that the individual parts continue to associate with one another, giving to the whole and taking from it; whereas an individual and hierarchical organization is lifeless, like a tree without leaves.

Reciprocal Economics

It is reciprocal understanding which forms the guiding social principle for the development of an economic plan and implementing it. The process of reaching this understanding must be continuous, since the economy is in constant movement, with new impetuses continuously taking place in both production and consumption, and old ones dying away. Each achievement of social harmonization represents a point of departure from a new social process.

This dynamic aspect of the economy can only be handled effectively by means of associations. The whole issue is dependent on a particular form of consciousness, and that at a level unattainable by the individual, and reachable only by joint effort. Whereas the social forms of ancient times were religious and impersonal, and based on consanguinity, society can now develop on the basis of wills of individuals who are conscious of their mutual responsibilities, and so form communities based on the spirit of brotherhood.[16]

Wilken, like Steiner, saw economic life as essentially fraternal, and capital as a means of freeing human capacities, albeit within an egalitarian social context. Their view of a need-oriented and associatively based economics was similar to that of the originators of Japanese capitalism. Yet ironically, despite the Japanese economic miracle, the views of Adam Smith, if not those of Karl Marx, continue to eclipse those of Rudolf Steiner and Folkert Wilken in western Europe and in the US.

Buddhist Economics

The Japanese Way

It was Fritz Schumacher who first popularized the idea of a *Buddhist economics* in the West.[17] Long before Schumacher, though, a Japanese writer, publisher and biblical scholar, Shichihei Yamamoto, had credited a 16th-century priest and a 17th-century clerk-turned-economic philosopher with the development of a Buddhist-based capitalism in Japan. The Zen priest was Shoshan Suzuki and the redoubtable clerk was a certain Baigan Ishida.

In 'The Spirit of Japanese Capitalism'[18] Yamamoto says that Suzuki, whose ideas were further developed by Ishida, preached that businessmen should become like 'living Buddhas'. In other words, they must travel round the country distributing goods as if they were on a pilgrimage. Any businessman who pursues his trade purely to make a profit will inevitably fail. It is only by keeping the needs of the consumers and the nation in the forefront of all thinking, planning and working that one can succeed.

Ishida's economic philosophy, in fact, drew on Suzuki's ethical base but extended his ideas in a practical and pragmatic vein. Ishida held that social order and progress could be brought into conformity and harmony with the cosmos if people followed the precepts of honesty, self-restraint and order. Ishida taught that the inner heart (the true heart of man) and the natural order (the cosmos) were one and the same.

Flexible rigidities

Interestingly, Ronald Dore, a British researcher into Japanese business and organizational practice, comes to a parallel set of conclusions, when comparing classical economics with Japanese economic tradition.

Market Morality and Social Morality

'It is not', said Adam Smith, 'from the benevolence of the butcher, the brewer, or the baker, that we expect our dinner, but from their regard to their own self-interest.'

The trouble with the Japanese is that they have never really caught up with Adam Smith. They do not believe in the invisible hand. They believe that you cannot get a decent, moral society, not even an efficient society, simply by the mechanisms of the market powered by the motivational fuel of self-interest, however clever, or even divinely inspired, these mechanisms may be.

The morality has got to come from the hearts, the wills, and motives of the individuals in it. The butcher and the brewer have got to be benevolent. They need to have a conscience about the quality of the meat and the beer they supply. They need to care.[19]

The concept of wa

It was only in the 1970s, in fact, that Japanese businessmen and business analysts accepted the idea that there was something unique in their culture, which gave them a significant edge over Western nations. And it was not until the early 1980s that they began to feel at ease in attributing their accomplishments to such traditional concepts as *wa*.

Then, suddenly, *wa* was on the lips of almost every executive who got up before any kind of audience, including his own employees. Here was a concept, sanctified by age, with which he could really get to grips. Boye De Mente, an American who has spent most of his life in Japan, describes the concept concisely.

Wa

It has been endlessly pointed out since the early eighties that *wa*, the ancient word for peace and harmony, literally means 'circle' and that the secret of Japan's economic success was based on employees and managers functioning in human-oriented circles – instead of the series of horizontal layers favored by Western management. As manager after manager explains, *wa* incorporates mutual trust and unselfish cooperation between management and labor, harmonious relations among employees at all levels and mutual responsibility for results.[20]

Small is beautiful

Schumacher had an affinity with the developing countries in general, and with the East in particular. After spending many years in industry, he wrote *Small is Beautiful*, a book that marked a watershed in business and economic thinking (though its influence in Europe and the US was somewhat different).

Western thinking was immediately captivated by Schumacher's ideas. After a period during which large and bureaucratic organizations had been holding sway, a welcome voice from the European wilderness was calling for a return to small-scale enterprise. Schumacher emerged as a new Messiah, whose way had been prepared by Adam Smith and the 19th-century Austrian political economist and champion of entrepreneurship, Joseph Schumpeter.

All three Europeans championed the cause of the entrepreneur, but each for different reasons. For Adam Smith he was the carrier of free enterprise; for Schumpeter he was the source of disruptive innovation. Schumacher's interest was different again, and in two significant ways.

Economics as if people mattered

Economics, as far as Schumacher is concerned, has to derive its aims and objectives from the study of man, rather than vice versa. Small is beautiful, therefore, primarily because it is compatible with the human being, and only secondarily because it makes economic sense.

Goods or People?

What is the meaning of democracy, freedom, human dignity, standard of living, self-realization, fulfilment? Is it a matter of goods or people? Of course, it is a matter of people. But people can be themselves only in small comprehensible groups. Therefore we must learn to think in terms of an articulated structure that can cope with a multiplicity of small-scale units. If economic thinking cannot grasp this it is useless. If it cannot get beyond its vast abstractions, the national income, the rate of growth . . . then let us scrap economics and start afresh.[21]

Business and economics, for Schumacher, are merely a means to an end: namely personal and community fulfilment. Work and leisure, the one complementing the other, he sees as means of purifying the individual character. Yet, unlike many other less practical theorists, Schumacher has, in the midst of all his theories, some very useful things to say about management and organization.

Small within large

Schumacher always draws analogies, in his economic thinking, from man and nature. In the affairs of men, he argues, there always appears to be a need for at least two things simultaneously, which, superficially at least, seem to exclude each other. Man always needs both freedom and order: he needs the freedom of many small, autonomous units, and, at the same time, the orderliness of large-scale, possibly global unity and coordination.

In any organization, large or small, there must be a certain clarity and orderliness; if things fall into disorder, nothing can be accomplished. Yet orderliness as such is static and lifeless; so there must be plenty of elbow room and scope for breaking through the established order, to do the thing never done before, the new, unpredicted and unpredictable outcome of man's creative idea.

Any organization, therefore, has to strive continuously for the orderliness of order and the disorderliness of creative freedom. The man of order is typically the accountant, and generally the administrator, while the man of creative freedom is the entrepreneur. Order requires intelligence and is conductive to efficiency; while freedom calls for (and opens doors to) intuition, and leads to innovation.

'Real' or 'Natural' Management

Like Schumacher, Agha Hasan Abedi who founded the Bank of Credit and Commerce (BCC) in Pakistan, has drawn upon laws of nature while paying heed to Buddhist economics. Unlike Schumacher, though, Abedi focuses more on interdependence than on individuality.

BCC is more widely represented in the Southern hemisphere than any other international business. It has grown from $2,500,000 to $20 billion in assets within the space of fifteen years. BCC takes what it sees as a 'natural' approach to management, and it describes the old order of the US and Europe as 'artificial'.

Natural Management

The Totality Principle   Nature operates as an integrated system in its dynamic state. The realization of these systemic properties, and of the energy generated in the processes of fission and fusion, is generic to the natural, organizational order.

The Latency Principle   No-existence, which is infinite, is the container of existence, which is finite. Nature has the capacity to be the state of existence and no-existence at the same time. From this relationship emanates the process of change.

The Flow Principle   Nature is process, nature is change. The dynamics of existence are in a state of constant flux. Flux and change create a vacuum and an opportunity.

The Integrity Principle   The moral, which is equivalent to the laws and principles of nature, governs all that is material. Hence both must be acknowledged, treated and felt as inseparable. No company can assume its ultimate identity and its pure quality without becoming at one with its moral substance.[22]

These principles are elaborated upon below, compared and constrasted with a more traditional, old-order approach. As before, we begin with the old order and proceed to the new.

Management and Morality

Visible or Invisible

For the artificial manager the processes of management and organizational planning, organizing, staffing, directing and control, can each be precisely defined and analysed.

The natural manager searches for a management truth that lies beyond conventional wisdom, both administrative and behavioural. Real truth often lies in the unseen world behind everyday perceptions, and this reflects the larger, cosmic truth that contains the smaller, conventional managerial wisdom.

Plan or Vision

The artificial manager commits his thoughts and actions to a strategic plan. Such a plan determines the long-term direction of a particular company within a competitive environment, and the allocation of its physical human and financial resources.

The natural manager commits his thoughts, feelings and actions to a business vision. He sees the organization within a larger, cosmic environment. It is unbounded, individually or geographically, and unconstrained by physical or business competition.

Management and Environment

Tangible or Intangible

The artificial manager lives in a world of objective reality. The real world is one which can be seen and heard, touched and felt – people, money, machines, materials.

The natural manager recognizes the invisible forces, or psychic energies, governing the visible world. The natural world is the interaction of the seen and the unseen in an indivisible, living system.

Part or Whole

The artificial manager sees the management process in parts, in principles, in separate processes or activities. He plans and controls, motivates and communicates. Individuals and groups are seen as separate entities, as are management and workforce, or skilled and unskilled workers.

The natural manager conceives of the management process as a whole. He believes that the managerial essence is lost in pursuit of the parts. He sees himself managing the whole process and the whole person. He integrates individual and organization, business and environment, people and things into a management ecosystem.

Management and Organization

Mass or Energy

The artificial manager visualizes the organization as a structure. He concentrates on organizational and form and managerial content. His institution is structured by means of a series of pyramidal levels, which are periodically reformed. People belong when they have a place in the amassed structure.

The natural manager visualizes the organization as a process, a vast stream of energy to which all contribute and from which all draw. He concentrates on such energy, on its quality, velocity, vitality, quantity and direction. Organizational changes are viewed as continuous and evolutionary, rather than as episodic. Moreover, he views each person as a being in progress, a self-directing source of energy rather than an inert mass.

Thought or Feeling

The artificial manager maintains that thinking is primary, and, as a result, that scientific management is the ultimate management force. Feelings have their place, but they tend to cloud the scientific process. Intuition is suspect.

The natural manager believes that thinking is important but that feelings are primary. In fact feelings energize and humanize thought. Without feelings thoughts are lifeless, they lack movement and flow. Intellect and reason have their limitations. Ideas can be developed using the thought processes but thinking alone does not originate ideas.

People and Management

Work Skills or Life Skills

The artificial manager focuses on the person's business and technical skills with a view to improving performance. His first requirement is to ensure that both he and the people he manages perform a task at a satisfactory level. Performance can be enhanced through training and development.

The natural manager focuses on life skills for the whole person, including his technical and commercial abilities. He therefore concerns himself with the individual's physical, mental and spiritual well-being. His first requirement is that both he and the people he manages should be whole, should be persons of quality. The quality of performance will then follow. Furthermore, he believes that managers must develop fellow managers to be better than themselves.

Control or Humility

The artificial manager sees control as a strength and humility as a weakness. For submission involves loss of control. As a result he tends to produce fixed positions or positions of conflict. He visualizes central headquarters as a control centre.

The natural manager sees humility as a strength. In effect natural control is achieved by taking the risk of relaxing control, by detaching one's ego from a certain position. To let go of one's need to control is to let interfusion happen. The natural manager visualizes his company as a support centre, rather than as a control centre.

Self and Management

Self-assertiveness or Self-improvement

The artificial jungle fighter of a manager believes in the survival of the fittest. The world, for him, consists of winners and losers. Even the modern search for win/win situations retains the language of winning and losing.

For the natural manager winning is a non-event, irrelevant in the cooperative pursuit of purpose. Competition is only with oneself and this takes the form of self-improvement. The natural manager commits himself to unique success in pursuit of extraordinary vision and purpose.

Time or Timing

The artificial manager tries to control time. He imposes his time schedule on others. This forcing of events may accelerate or delay achievement. While he recognizes the importance of timing, this may be subordinated to the need for power or task achievement.

The natural manager knows that one cannot control time but only the timing of one's interventions. He pursues a course of action with persistence and perseverance, exercising patience and waiting for the right moment. He intuitively perceives others' need for direction, support and inspiration, and intervenes accordingly.

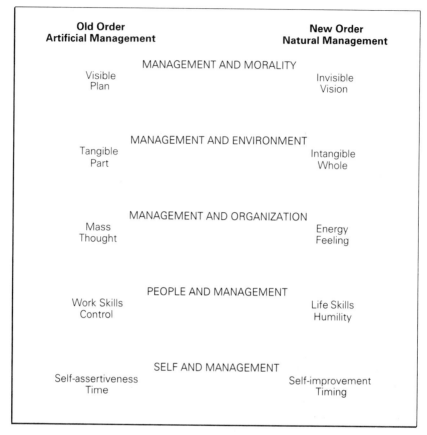

<table>
<tr><td colspan="2" align="center">**Old Order**
Artificial Management</td><td colspan="2" align="center">**New Order**
Natural Management</td></tr>
</table>

Old Order Artificial Management		New Order Natural Management
	MANAGEMENT AND MORALITY	
Visible Plan		Invisible Vision
	MANAGEMENT AND ENVIRONMENT	
Tangible Part		Intangible Whole
	MANAGEMENT AND ORGANIZATION	
Mass Thought		Energy Feeling
	PEOPLE AND MANAGEMENT	
Work Skills Control		Life Skills Humility
	SELF AND MANAGEMENT	
Self-assertiveness Time		Self-improvement Timing

Figure 2.3 Artificial and Natural Management

Conclusion

Conventional management principles, as we know them today, draw on such commonly acknowledged founding fathers as the French industrialist Henri Fayol, the German sociologist Max Weber, and the American engineer Frederick Taylor. In more recent years well-known American management theorists such as Peter Drucker and Warren Bennis have made dominant contributions. As we have seen, it is only in the last decade that this rationally based wisdom has been called into question, primarily by Tom Peters and his 'back to basics' followers.

However, neither the rational old guard nor the current advocates of primal non-conformism have paid attention to the 'developmental' school of management that has grown up over the last eighty years. Unlike its primal and rational counterparts, this developmental approach spans East and West, North and South, and is therefore cross-cultural in nature. Its originators span economics (Schumacher) and philosophy (Steiner), religion (Yamomoto) and psychology (Maslow), business (Abedi) and politics (Parker Follett).

In fact the contemporary disciplines that have most to offer developmental management are biology and ecology. These newly grown roots are establishing themselves in the fertile, though hitherto concealed, grounds with which you have now become familiar. After describing these roots, in the next section, I shall be taking you into the core of developmental management, through the ideas of the Dutch psychiatrist, Bernard Lievegoed. Thereafter we shall consider the implications of this style of management for each of the major business functions.

Notes

1   M. Parker Follett, *The New State*. Peter Smith, 1926, p. 3; 2nd edn, 1965.
2   Parker Follett, *The New State*, p. 112.
3   Parker Follett, *The New State*, p. 3.
4   Parker Follett, *The New State*, p. 75.
5   M. Parker Follett, *The Creative Experience*. Peter Smith, 1926, p. 41.
6   L. Urwick (ed.), *Dynamic Administration*. Pitman, 1941.
7   A. Maslow, *Motivation and Personality*. Harper & Row, 1964, p. 53.
8   Maslow, *Motivation and Personality*, p. 91.
9   A. Maslow, *Toward a Psychology of Being*. Van Nostrand, 1962, p. 57.
10 A. Maslow, *Eupsychian Management*. Irwin & Dorsey, 1965, p. 62.
11 R. Revans, *Action Learning*. Blond Briggs, 1980, p. 43.
12 Revans, *Action Learning*, p. 84.
13 R. Steiner, *Social Renewal*. Steiner Press, 1977, p. 81.
14 R. Steiner, *The Threefold Commonwealth*. Steiner Press, 1945, p. 14.
15 Steiner, *Social Renewal*, pp. 19–20.
16 F. Wilken, *The Liberation of Capital*. Allen & Unwin, 1984, p. 193.
17 E. F. Schumacher, *Small is Beautiful*. Abacus, 1973.
18 S. Yamamoto, 'The Spirit of Japanese Capitalism', in B. De Mente, *Japanese Etiquette and Ethics in Business*. Passport Books, 5th edn, 1987.
19 R. Dore, *Flexible Rigidities*. Athlone Press, 1987, p. 7.
20 De Mente, *Japanese Etiquette*, p. 3.
21 Schumacher, *Small is Beautiful*, p. 82.
22 H. Abedi, *Real Management*. BCC internal publication, 1984.

Section B

Developmental Management

3

The Biological and Ecological Context: the Roots

Introduction

The Laws of Growth

Developmental management is founded upon the laws of growth and change that underpin human development. It is rooted particularly in the life sciences, that is in biology and ecology, rather than the physical or social sciences. It is based neither on purely instinctive behaviour nor on wholly rational conduct, but on a process of conscious evolution.

Biologists, ecologists and some humanistic psychologists, in recent years, have uncovered such laws of growth and evolution, with a view to their being applied to the management of organizations. Unfortunately they have been largely ignored by the organizational development establishment, and have certainly been bypassed by those involved in product, market and systems development. It is my intention here to uncover the roots of developmental management and then to follow up the core concepts, as well as the branch theories and applications, that have become available to us.

Characteristics of Evolution

Inclusion

Emergent evolution describes the process of long, slow change alternating with short, rapid change and sudden transformation.

Earlier levels of life are absorbed into later levels.

Emergence

Sudden and sharp discontinuities punctuate the progress of slow change.

These rifts either signal a leap to a new, more complex level or they signal a devastating crash to some earlier level.

There is a process of building up as well as a process of tearing down.

Transition

Dominant models reach a certain peak of success when anomalies become numerous and troublesome.

A 'clash of worldliness' between perspectives creates a period of confusion and tension.

The new synthesis invariably incorporates the new apparent partial truths of the older model, provides consistent explanations for the precipitating anomalies, and opens up new territory for exploration.

When evolution gets 'stuck', it may revert to an earlier, more plastic level of order before the leap to a new synthesis.

Acceleration

Galactic change is measured in billions and millions of years, biological change in millions.

Today, change of evolutionary significance is measured in decades and years.[1]

The laws of qualitative growth, with which this chapter will be concerned, can be divided into three distinct categories. The first involves patterns of development which seem to follow a somewhat predictable form. The second involves three or four developmental stages – in individuals, organizations and communities. The third makes clear the interdependent character of developmental management.

Patterns of Development

To Grow or to Die

One of the greatest contributions to developmental management, whether of individual enterprises or of whole ecosystems, comes from the American biologist and business consultant George Ainsworth Land.

To Grow or to Die

History, in every sense, from the biological to the social, demonstrates that what we really have to fear is not so much the perpetuation of our growth failures; much more dangerous is the deliberate attempt to repeat our successes. Today's successes become tomorrow's failures. Life in its very manifestation is growth and change. Not to grow is to die.

Evolution carries with it the message of extinction. If we isolate ourselves from the 'system' of life, if we do not find a balance of trade with our environment, we face a future known in all of its frightening dimensions. The message is abundantly clear: grow or die, evolution or extinction.[2]

As an individual or organization evolves to higher levels of being, according to Land, the potential for slipping either backward or forward is always present. In other words, if an organism fails to grow with its cultural environment, for example by adopting new technologies or methods of work, then it must of necessity grow against it. People or organizations cannot actually stand still. They choose to move forward or back.

How, then, do we evolve and develop?

Developmental Thinking

The management consulting group that has done the most to promote developmental management is the NPI (Netherlands Pedagogical Institute) which operates throughout western Europe. One of its members, the English social anthropologist Martin Large, has represented *developmental thinking* very thoroughly in his book *Social Ecology*.[3] He makes the following seven major points:

1 As long as an organism continues to develop and maintain itself there is life. But as soon as development ceases the organism rigidifies.
2 The concept of development is derived originally from biology and is used to describe the life-cycle of people and things. While growth could be taken to mean a purely quantitative change, development involves qualitative or structural changes.
3 Development involves a journey from the past through the heart of

the present, into the future. Thus the process of development involves an unfolding of structure over time.

4 An organism grows, unfolding to the point where the original structure cannot be maintained. There is then a crisis, as the architectural forces of development break down the old structure. The process of breaking down is sometimes called *involution*, which is needed to prepare the way for a more differentiated structure – which can in turn undergo further *evolution*.

5 Each life crisis involves a progression from involution through chaos to evolution. Each stage of development is initiated by a structural crisis, in which the foundations are laid for a new structure.

6 Such a development is discontinuous, taking place in leaps and bounds, so that sometimes dramatic structural changes can occur – as when a chrysalis turns into a butterfly. Old structures are then reformed as a higher unity, at a more complex level of organization. This process is irreversible. Development therefore involves particular structural crises and evolutionary phases.

7 Development can be pictured as a dynamic balancing process where security needs and the need for challenges predominate in turn.

These seven points are true of any living organism, be it an individual, an organization or a whole community. The implications for each of these are significant. For one thing, crises are to be welcomed as part and parcel of the growth process, provided they are handled with a conscious awareness of evolutionary forces. For another, organisms develop in stages.

The developmental manager, therefore, should be accustomed not only to viewing crises as opportunities for conscious evolution, but also to working towards progressive and discontinuous shifts in the degree of freedom with which his people and organization function. In effect he is designing increasing amounts of complexity into his structures and processes as both he and his enterprises evolve.

Developmental Stages

The Developing Organism

It is this progressive development, through distinct stages, in the developmental manager's product, market, people or organization that mark him out as an active and even aggressive force. Such staged and conscious evolution is to the developmental manager what business entrepreneurship is to the primal manager and corporate strategy is to the rational manager. This phased development is characteristically divided into either three or four cumulative stages, each representing a degree of complexity exceeding that of the phase that preceded it. For Martin Large there are three such stages (Figure 3.1):

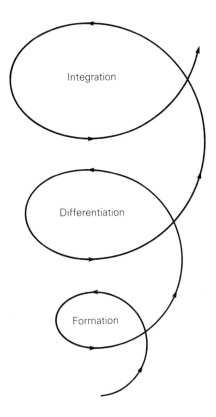

Figure 3.1 The Evolutionary Spiral
Source: B. Hubbard, *The Evolutionary Way*. Turnstone, 1983, p. 26.

1 The process of formation or growth of the whole person, product, business or organization, which only begins to split apart as skills, features or functions are separated off and allocated to emergent parts of the whole.

2 The process of differentiation and hierarchization, whereby some capacities, products or divisions become governed by others, after which initial attempts are made to relate one to the other.
3 The process of integration, involving more technical, economic and social interdependence and greater complexity of structure – production and risk-sharing, consortia and joint ventures become the norm rather than the exception.

Stages of Growth: from Accretion to Mutualism

George Ainsworth Land has written about the stages of development of individuals, organizations and whole communities. Drawing on his biological knowledge, he has concluded that there are three fundamental stages of development, which he calls:

accretive,
replicative,
mutual.

Principles and Stages of Growth

Physical, biological, psychological and social systems are growth motivated; that is, their behavior acts in the direction of development of higher levels of, and more widespread, interrelationships. Thus all systems tend to evolve more organized behavior, becoming integrated through the incorporation of diversity.

There are, in fact, three distinctly different forms of growth, each of which merges into the other on a continuum of levels of development. The first of these is purely additive – an extension of the boundaries that already exist. We shall call this form of growth accretive, that is inclusion through sameness.

The second form of growth is replicative; it is growth through influencing other people or things to take on the form of the initiator. As a cell, for example, grows and divides it takes in the environment and transforms it directly into itself. Replicative growth, therefore, is inclusion through similarity.

The third form of growth involves reciprocal interaction. Mutual growth incorporates give and take, that is the equilateral sharing or joining process. Such mutualism is inclusive of differentness.[4]

Land's stages of development affect the personal and psychological domains as well as the social and communal ones. I shall consider each in turn, covering accretive, replicative, and mutual forms.

Personal and Psychological Growth

Drives and compulsions for such things as power, possession and dominance (according to Land) are accretive in nature: they involve control of man's internal or external world. The need to manipulate and submission to manipulation – dependent and counterdependent modes of behaviour – are basically replicative: they involve both modifications of the outside world, to copy the internal, and changes to the inside world, to mimic the external. Mutualistic patterns are found in empathetic and creative behaviour, and in the drive for fulfilment and self-actualization: they are characterized by recombination and fusion, involving self-extension through sharing. Personal growth is attained through reciprocal exchange with the outside world.

Experiencing the process of creative, mutual (integrated) growth does not exclude us, however, from the manifestations of accretive (formative) and replicative (differentiated) development. Each man, each society, is an ever-changing mixture of all forms of growth, working through and with each other.

Societal and Communal Growth

A cell, person, organization or whole community that has achieved mutualistic growth has done so by building on accretive and replicative behaviour. Thus mutualism is founded on lower forms and cannot exist without them. Lower forms of growth provide the self-maintenance necessary for mutualism to be successful. Thus primal and rational management are prerequisites for the developmental or even metaphysical varieties that may follow.

The earliest human cultures were fundamentally accretive inasmuch as information and cultural forms were rigidly controlled, and passed to each generation almost unchanged. When written symbols supplemented the organic information storage and retrieval system, the shift to replicative societies began. Missionary activity and imperial conquest ensued. Worldwide travel and more sophisticated communications media have provided a broad new base of common information, and have increased the likelihood of exchange of ideas and cultures. These phenomena contribute to the mutualistic, global village.

Decay and Renewal

The demise of the British, French, Portuguese and . . . American colonial empires represents only a few examples of how evolution from accretive boundary expansion, absolute ownership and control, to that of replicative influence – 'think, act and value like us' – have both outgrown themselves. We are now being pressured to grow into a new form of mutualistic relationship between ourselves, as the previous colonizers, and themselves, as the previously colonized.[5]

A village initially comes into being as people 'accrete' and band together in small groups to form a larger, more defensible, viable organism. The same, you might say, takes place in the early stages of business formation, though usually under the influence of an entrepreneurial individual. Common pursuits, or shared values, unite everyone, whether they are engaged in farming, milling, mining or, in contemporary business terms, approaching the customer. As offspring begin to learn their parents' trades they 'replicate' the original and successful organism. However, when they overproduce their own capacity to use the products that they make (as in the steel and automobile industries today), pressures emerge to develop deeper relations with other communities. 'Mutualism' comes about through the development of specialization, trade and the exchange of information with others.

Finally, as with biological growth, so in social organisms the recapitulation of forms of growth takes place as changes in scale and complexity occur. Companies that renew themselves have not only to collaborate more intensely with their customers, competitors and suppliers, but also to create new business enterprises, both with and without them. The highest form of mutualism begins to transform into a new accretive form.

Nucleation

The three stages of growth and development, to which both Land and Large allude, can in fact be stretched to four, and the four developmental stages lead to a corresponding number of management domains. In such conditions the creative process underlying the development is included as a fourth evolutionary stage. The fourth stage represents 'metaphysical' management. The American biologist and psychologist Barry McWaters calls this stage *nucleation*.[6]

Nucleation describes the emergence of a conscious center that holds responsibility for internal regulation and self-transcendence. In each evolving being a center is formed, a center that has in mind the integrity of the organism itself, the establishment of the right relationship with the environment, and the transcendent evolution of the organism.[7]

The center, or nucleus, embodies in itself the integral pattern of the whole, the DNA, the picture of the organism in its perfect form. The nucleus also embodies the RNA, the messenger unit by which the nucleus will communicate the knowledge of its form to subsequent generations. The nucleus, in other words, is the inspiration behind the organization. It permits differentiation and calls for integration. It fosters communication between the parts, balances their relationship, and controls and transforms processes that are out of sync. 'It is the nucleus which has the capacity for multidimensional communication',[8] at all levels, with diverse cultures and with multifaceted people. It has the very special role of communicating higher intention, of transmitting vision.

In a continually evolving organism, a nucleus will form and assume a central role. The same applies to society at large as to the single individual or organization. In a business context, genuine nucleation, though rarely achieved, is required of the corporate policy-making function. In Table 3.1 I have summarized the three or four stages of evolutionary development, as depicted by Large (the anthropologist), Land (the biologist) and McWaters (the psychologist).

Table 3.1 Stages of Growth and Development

Source	Stage			
	1	2	3	4
Large	Formative	Differentiated	Integrated	
Land	Accretive	Replicative	Mutual	
McWaters		Differentiation	Integration	Nucleation

I now want to move on from the evolutionary stages, of which the development manager needs to be aware, to the interdependent outlook, which is characteristic of his operating style.

The Interdependent Character of Developmental Management

Principles of Interdependence

Progression through the three or four stages represents the developmental manager's aggressive thrust, as he powers the organization through the successively more complex layers of business evolution. At each stage he has to recognize, accommodate and harness progressively more breadth and depth in product, market, individual and organizational functioning. Therein lies the hard edge of development. At the same time the process of conscious evolution has a visibly soft edge to it, as McWaters reveals.

Conscious Evolution: a Definition

1 The emerging potential of human beings to take responsibility, individually and collectively, for a positive future, through sharing in the unfolding of creation.
2 The process by which an individual or organizational entity can transform itself from a state of fear and alienation to one of enlightened cooperation.
3 The capacity of a group to work together synergistically, that is to become a functional entity with capabilities beyond the sum of the individual parts.
4 The potential of an individual or organization to develop a resonant relationship within the parts of itself, with its environment, and with the world as a whole.[9]

McWaters identifies four so-called *principles of relationship* which underlie the interdependence that characterizes developmental management. These are:

> synergy,
> attunement,
> alignment,
> quantum transformation.

Synergy

Synergy is the release of free energy that occurs when a group of entities – be they individuals or organizations – comes together with a common aim. The resulting whole is both quantitatively and qualitatively greater than the sum of the parts.

Synergic release is often experienced at the beginning of group work. A momentary fusion may occur when individuals come together, a 'high' is experienced, and what has been called a 'honeymoon period' ensues for a time. The free energy created by the 'group high' can be used for productive and collective activity. Synergy can be created across space, between people or things – as in the case of a really successful merger – and over time. In effect the principle of synergy reflects the evolutionary process we have described – that evolutionary spiral into greater and greater levels of integration.

> Synergic release from wave/particle formations led to the creation of the atom; atomic combinations resulted in molecules; combinations of molecules resulted in organelles; combinations of organelles produced cells; etc. At each new union an attractive force is released that seeks out the next evolutionary stage of union.[10]

It is for this reason that a developing enterprise can never stand still. As entrepreneur links up with customer an attractive force is released which seeks out the next evolutionary stage, the creation of a business organization. As one employee links up with another, another attractive force is released which seeks out the formation of a human organization. As one culture after another becomes involved so yet another attractive force is released which now seeks out the development of a multinational organization. The process is unending.

Attunement

The second of McWaters's principles of relationship, or inter-dependence, is that of attunement. Attunement is an expression of the receptive will of the individual or the organization, through which a larger context of consciousness is invited and permitted to penetrate more and more deeply into self-consciousness. Thus individual energies are attuned to the wider environment just as a musical instrument is tuned to the key of an orchestral work.

By means of attunement, a businessman becomes aware of pervading market trends, a manager of human resources is receptive to the needs of employees, and an interior designer absorbs the surrounding high street atmosphere and incorporates it into his attractive shop front. An individual, an organization or indeed a musical instrument comes across as harsh and cacophonous if it is ill-attuned to its surroundings. While each may insist on a way of being that is out of resonance with its environment, such a disharmony must ultimately have serious implications for both the part and the whole. For example any retailing chain that lacks ambience is likely, over the long term, to lose clientèle.

Alignment

Whereas, through attunement, the developmental manager literally tunes into a wider organizational market or social context, through alignment he or she 'chooses to find meaning and purpose in contributing to the well-being or evolution of a higher reality'.[11] In a commercial context a developmental marketing manager in a pharmaceutical company is contributing to the physical health and well-being of individuals and nations. Such physical well-being represents a higher reality than, say, the alleviation of headaches and indigestion. In an operational context a developmental production manager in a steel mill is creating a working climate in which his workforce can fulfil their higher needs for self-actualization, as well as their immediate needs for physical health and safety.

Quantum Transformation

The principle of quantum transformation offers us hope. All the stubborn parts of oneself, and of one's organization or society, do not have to agree to change and grow all at once. It only takes a clear and definite suggestion from one small part to remind the whole of its inborn preference for evolution and development. An inner ear begins to hear the call, begins to sense the possibility.

Critical Mass

In each evolving being, the nucleus works toward turning the attention of a significant percentage of the parts toward evolutionary transformation. When this percentage is reached – critical mass – the idea is transmitted rapidly and directly to all parts of the organism, and a quantum evolutionary leap is experienced.[12]

If a small, yet critical, percentage of the organization or market-place is able to see the light, there will be intonations and ramifications for the whole human enterprise. As a result, evolution in product, market and human development takes place in unpredictable leaps. That seems to have been the case, for example, in the United States in the early 1980s, when Steve Jobs's Apple Computers began to grow like wildfire. A small, but critical percentage of the computer market-place had apparently seen the desktop light.

Mutualism in Developmental Management

Whereas McWaters has developed specific principles of relationship, George Land argues that mutualism, in general, lies at the core of human evolution. Although the mutualistic principle manifests itself particularly strongly at his third developmental stage, it underpins the whole of his developmental thinking.

Growth and Interdependence

If we reach down to the basic nature of the concept of growth we find a single fact. Growth cannot occur independently. It requires interaction and interrelation between the growing thing and its environment. The process requires a joining of things . . . .

In every natural phenomenon there is the irreversible procession from accretive to replicative to mutual growth, at which point, at a new level of organization, the process repeats itself. Growth, at this stage of our examination, is defined as a process of joining, in which the ratios of interactive effect are continually expressing higher levels of interaction.[13]

The process of joining, as an evolutionary development, is particularly apparent in the world of electronics and telecommunications. The need for computers and companies alike to talk to one another is becoming an evolutionary requirement. The world of the lone high-tech warrior, ploughing his own organizational and technological furrow, has well nigh disappeared.

AT&T, for example, as of August 1985, had developed strategic alliances with no fewer than eight companies, of various sizes and product lines, including Olivetti, Microsoft, Motorola and Amdahl. These alliances were geared towards joint development of products, markets and systems within and across national frontiers. They involve a progression from accretion and replication to mutualism.

By mutualizing our resources we can realize the latent potential of our species. To bring this about, however, will require a rapid and radical integration of the quality of human growth into the processes of planning, forecasting, and creating a future still and always highly unknown. But we can do so with the knowledge that, by and through nature's processes, we can determine the quality and form, if not the content of things to come.[14]

Conclusion

Laws of Nature

The roots of conventional rational management lie not in nature but in man-made institutions of antiquity, including the church, the army, and civil administrations. The roots of the currently fashionable primal management lie within the hunter–gatherer communities of prehistoric times. The roots of developmental management, however, lie in both physical and human nature, and in the life sciences that underpin them.

From their studies of atomic, molecular, cellular, animal and human life, scientists such as George Land, Martin Large, Barbara Hubbard and Barry McWaters have discovered underlying patterns of physical and social development. These are only beginning to enter into the management vocabulary, though Mary Parker Follett was working along the same lines some sixty years ago.

The Surge of Life

The surge of life sweeps through the given similarity, the common ground, and breaks it up into a thousand differences. This tumultuous, irresistible flow of life is our experience: the unity is but for an instant; it flows on to new differings which adjust themselves anew in more varied, richer syntheses. . . . This is the process of evolution.[15]

Stages of Growth

Individual atoms and whole societies alike evolve by creating ever-richer syntheses out of ever-increasing variety. There is also a predictable sequence to the growth process.

The sequence begins formatively. *Formation* or *accretion*, in business enterprise, is represented by the primal urge for growth through sameness, thus expanding the entrepreneur's financial base and extending the communally shared values. *Replication* is reflected in the rational orientation towards expansion through differentiation –

of functions, products, markets and territories – thus replicating business by extending standard procedures into different operations, and by adapting performance to accommodate such individual differences. *Integration* is represented by a developmental approach to creating unity out of diversity in people and things, in products and markets, as well as between the stages of their evolution, thereby combining physical and social development with organizational and economic harmony. Finally, at least as far as McWaters is concerned, a fourth stage locates the *regulative centre* of the evolving organism, which contains a picture of the enterprise in its perfect form, and enables it to engage in physical, organizational, economic and social transformation.

Notes

1 J. Lipnack and J. Stamps, *The Networking Book*. Routledge & Kegan Paul, 1986, p. 22.
2 G. A. Land, *To Grow or to Die*. Random House, 1973; 2nd edn, John Wiley, 1985, pp. 74, 127.
3 M. Large, *Social Ecology*. Published by the author, 1981, chapter 2.
4 Land, *To Grow or to Die*, p. 197.
5 Land, *To Grow or to Die*, p. 196.
6 B. McWaters, *Conscious Evolution*, Turnstone, 1983.
7 McWaters, *Conscious Evolution*, pp. 67–8.
8 McWaters, *Conscious Evolution*, p. 73.
9 McWaters, *Conscious Evolution*, p. 4.
10 McWaters, *Conscious Evolution*, p. 79.
11 McWaters, *Conscious Evolution*, p. 78.
12 McWaters, *Conscious Evolution*, p. 84.
13 Land, *To Grow or to Die*, pp. 11–12.
14 Land, *To Grow or to Die*, p. 145.
15 M. Parker Follett, *The New State*. Peter Smith, 1926, p. 35; 2nd edn, 1965.

4

The Developing Organization: the Core

Introduction

The Originators of Developmental Management

As we have seen the origins of developmental management reach back to the Austrian Rudolf Steiner in the 1920s, and link up, via Bernard Lievegoed in the Netherlands, with the modern school of *organizational renewal* in the US. The most important single influence on its formation and impact is Lievegoed.

Lievegoed: the developing organization

Bernard Lievegoed, a venerable Dutchman now in his eighties, is by far the best-known management consultant in that country, and is also a highly respected psychiatrist. Lievegoed, in turn, has drawn on Rudolf Steiner for his own source of inspiration, with respect to developing organizations.

Steiner: social renewal

Steiner, as we saw in Chapter 2, had strong views on the evolution of man and organizations, and on the processes of social renewal (on which Lievegoed subsequently drew).

> Everything that happens to man is an image, having its prototype amid those great events of cosmic evolution with which his existence is bound up.[1]

For Steiner, as for Lievegoed and his fellow management consultants at the Netherlands Pedagogical Institute (NPI) (based in the Netherlands and operating around the globe), human and organizational evolution are intertwined. Each follows a developmental pattern to which we referred in Chapter 3.

Lippitt, Schmidt and Greiner: organizational renewal

In this core chapter on developmental management I want to unravel the implications of this pattern for organizational development. I shall begin with Lievegoed's seminal work, and then enter into the American thinking that derives from it. The leading Americans in this developmental context are Gordon Lippitt, Warren Schmidt and Larry Greiner, all of whom were students of organizational renewal.

I shall start by comparing and contrasting the developmental manager with his primal or rational counterpart.

The Characteristics of Developmental Management

Qualitative growth

Whereas both primal and rational managers are concerned with growth in quantitative terms, the developmental manager, as George Ainsworth Land has intimated (see p. 63), focuses on its qualitative attributes. So the questions a developmental manager asks are concerned not with the prediction of physical quantities but rather with the forecast of future socio-technical structures. Such a manager requires special insight into the qualitative development of individual human beings and products, and of collective organizations and industries, over time.

Parallel development

Whereas primal and rational managers view business and organization entities as discrete phenomena, the developmental manager views individuals, organizations, products and markets as parallel phenomena, each governed by similar laws of structural evolution. In all living organisms, growth continues within a certain structure until a limit is reached. Beyond this limit the existing structure or model can no longer impose order on the larger mass. The consequence is either disintegration or a step up to a higher-level order.

This phenomenon can be observed in a single living cell or in a complex business organization. A cell does not grow indefinitely, but at a certain moment it divides into two new cells, which in turn grow only to their limits, and so on. The same can be observed, according to both Land and Lievegoed, in higher organisms, which pass from one phase of development to the next. This phasing occurs both in individual development and in the evolution of whole species. By analogy it affects the development of individual companies, over time, as well as entire product lines, industries and economies.

Developmental Laws

Development of all kinds conforms to a series of laws, which are true equally of a living organism and a business. We shall here concentrate on Lievegoed's interpretation of them as they apply to developing organizations.

- Development occurs in time, in a series of stages.
- Development is principally discontinuous.
- Within each stage a particular structure tends to dominate.
- The stages become progressively more complex.
- A new structure is not added to the old; rather a shift occurs to a whole new pattern of relationships.
- Development is irreversible.

Let us take a look now at this developmental process as a whole.

A picture of development

Development can be depicted diagrammatically as a flight of steps or as a process of spreading, whereby the emphasis shifts from old to new centres (Figure 4.1). A stepwise picture of development represents total transformation from one step to the next, but in fact this seldom happens in organizational life. Remnants of earlier stages tend to remain in some shape or form.

Thus the ever-spreading picture is more representative of the developing organization, in that, as an organization evolves we find remnants of earlier structures. For example, a rationally managed organization will still have pockets of primal enterprise. Developmental management is full of ambiguity and unpredictability.

Social evolution

The term *social Darwinism* denotes the survival of the fittest. It befits the primal manager. The term *social engineering* denotes the con-

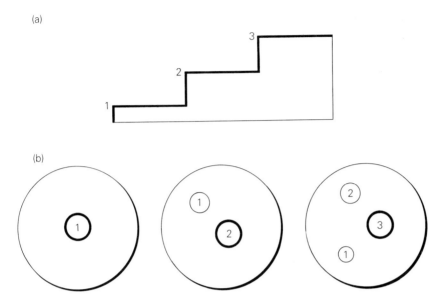

Figure 4.1 Development (a) by Step, and (b) by the Spreading Process

struction of logically determined forms of organization. It befits the rational manager. The term *social evolution* befits the developmental manager. Social evolution involves setting in motion organizational changes in the direction of a stage of development that is more advanced but of which only the barest outlines are known. The final form and content of the next stage can thus arise out of the potentialities of the people involved. Let us now investigate these stages. For Lievegoed, as for Land, there are three of them.[2]

The Developing Organization

Three Phases: Pioneering, Differentiated, Integrated

As an enterprise develops, according to Lievegoed, its structure changes from an undifferentiated general beginning to successive stages of ever-increasing complexity. At each successive stage of development a different subsystem is dominant.

First comes the so-called *pioneer phase*. The dominant influence is the pioneer himself. He takes the initiative within the economic subsystem of society. He finds the pioneering answer to a consumer need which he recognizes. This phase reaches its limit when the organization has grown so much that the pioneer no longer knows everyone personally, when the technical equipment needed has become so complicated that specialists are required, and when the market has grown so large that the pioneer finds himself working not for the customer he knows but for an anonymous public. At this point the pioneer organization either becomes 'overripe' and begins to disintegrate (decrease of profits, increase of customer complaints), or it has to be restructured so that it can start on the next phase of its development.

In the second, *differentiated phase*, the pioneer with his economic achievement is no longer the dominant factor. The requirements of the technical subsystem in the enterprise become pre-eminent. With the help of scientific management techniques, the structure based on personal relationships is transformed into one based on an impersonal and logical division of functions. The man has been replaced by the system. The limit of this second phase is reached when the neglect of the social system in the enterprise begins to make itself felt. The progress achieved through technical improvements is slowed down by a decrease in the motivation of the people involved. Feelings of powerlessness against the 'system' creep in.

The third, *integrated phase* can be established successfully only if the social subsystem is interwoven with the economic and technical ones. This cannot be achieved simply by maintaining the existing structure and adding 'human relations'. What is required is rethinking the whole organization. The dominant factor now is the community of people working together, as a combined source of innovation and enthusiasm, towards the common goal.

Comparative Phases

Lievegoed's pioneering, differentiated and integrated phases relate to our primal, rational and developmental aspects of management. These three phases have been neatly summarized by Martin Large as shown in Table 4.1.[3]

Table 4.1 Lievegoed's Development Phases

Characteristic	Phase 1	Phase 2	Phase 3
Approach	Personal	Impersonal	Individual
Leadership	Primal	Rational	Developmental
Goals	Directive	Purposeful	Inspirational
Structure	Simple/flat	Complex/pyramid	Open/hexagon
Response	Improvised	Planned	Evolved
Style	Active	Authoritative	Adaptive
Orientation	Outward-oriented	Inward-looking	Outer/inner balance
Emphasis	Economic	Technical	Social

The Pioneering Phase

Characteristics

The first stage of Lievegoed's developing organization is the pioneering one. At this point an owner–manager is primarily interested in answering a need at a price that his customer is willing to pay. He is economically driven. In its pure form a pioneer enterprise is run by its founder. It comes into being as a result of a creative act by an individual person. This person is an entrepreneur. He has a realistic imagination.

The pioneer runs his firm with an autocratic style of leadership, which is based on the prestige he enjoys in the eyes of his people. In other words, he has their trust. If there is trouble he can be relied upon to find a way out. He can typically be relied upon in this way because he knows all his employees and their family circumstances. He engaged them himself and they are 'his' people; he knows all their jobs, having performed all of them himself at one point or another.

Communication is direct. The pioneer communicates straightforwardly and directly with all his employees. At least in the early years he has worked in very close contact with them. He speaks their language. The organizational form is simple. So there is no need for formal communication channels, or for job or task descriptions to regulate employees' rights and responsibilities.

The working style is therefore improvised. All problems are solved by improvisation rather than by planning. This style makes for flexibility. Production or service can be rapidly adapted to demand, and the special requests of individual customers can be met.

The workforce functions as one big family. In many cases, particularly before women's emancipation, the wife of the pioneer functioned as a kind of welfare worker for her husband's employees and families. 'We're all one happy family' is a favourite phrase of many a pioneer until the first company strike gives him an unforgettable shock. The pioneer is not only close to his employees but is also close to the customer. He does not know what it is to operate in an anonymous market-place. He works in a limited geographical area and knows each customer personally.

The limits of the pioneering phase

The healthy pioneering enterprise that Lievegoed has described has rightly motivated staff within and loyal customers without. Objectives are simple and clear, and success or failure can be witnessed by all. Such an organization remains healthy as long as:

the pioneer himself knows all his employees and his customers;
the production process or services rendered remain relatively simple;
the accumulation of experience is an asset because technology and
    the market remain relatively stable.

Close-knit character

The close-knit character of a pioneering enterprise is both its strength and its weakness. As long as influences from outside do not disturb the system, the firm can grow and even be taken over by the next generation without much difficulty.

The advent of change

However, if the 'external' world starts to move, if a new technology becomes available to satisfy needs, if market conditions change and competitors break into the pioneer's field with brand new sales techniques, if the market grows so that personal contacts with customers are no longer possible, if extensive changes take place in the social structure so that a patriarchal style is no longer acceptable, then the pioneering phase has reached its limits.

Loss of confidence

The first thing that happens once the pioneering company has become 'overripe' is that the employees begin to entertain doubts about 'the boss'. His prestige begins to decrease and his autocratic style becomes intolerable. Mistakes then begin to creep in. Once single mistakes begin to turn into overall failures to adapt, once the negative impact of particular instances becomes so great that the whole ethos and structure of the organization is affected, the pioneer enterprise has reached the threshold of a new development.

Symptoms of decline
The symptoms of such a crisis, heralding a period of transition, are decreasing profits, increasing customer complaints, communication blocks, decreasing manœuvrability and decreasing motivation.

In pioneering limbo

In practice the transition from a pioneering enterprise to the next stage of a business's development can be forestalled in one of three major ways: by forming a *cartel*, a *conglomerate* or a *family business*.

Cartels
Historically, the formation of cartels – groups of companies that club together to fend off competition and curb the impact of fundamental changes – has been one way of inhibiting development. However, such arrangements, particularly in today's volatile and highly inter-nationalized business environment, are extremely vulnerable to breakdown.

Conglomerates
More common today are conglomerates. The original enterprise is split up into a number of smaller units, each of which is run in the pioneer style. The central holding company becomes a kind of financing body. The pioneering approach, albeit somewhat adapted, can thus be maintained across a large, diversified organization. However, such conglomerate holdings, because they lack a coherent corporate image, are unduly dependent on one pioneering character for their underlying identity.

Family businesses
A third extension of the pioneering style is that represented by the family business, in which a close-knit family-based structure may be retained from one generation to the next. Such features as staff

loyalty, goodwill towards the company, integrity of management and social responsibility are more likely to prevail than in a straight-forward pioneering enterprise, or in a conventionally managed organization. It is the blend of enterprise and community that characterizes the family business form. This blend is more likely to endure, over both time and space, than a one-sided, 'masculine' enterprising approach. Inevitably, though, if a family business is to grow and develop into a large business, it has to move on to a newly differentiated phase.

The Differentiated Phase

The historical answer to the problems of the overripe pioneer enterprise came in the form of scientific management. Frederick Taylor in the US, Henri Fayol in France, and Max Weber in Germany were the early proponents of the scientific, administrative and bureaucratic responses, each of which was based on rational principles of management and organization.

The main principles of the differentiated phase, according to Lievegoed are:

> mechanization
> standardization,
> specialization,
> coordination.

Each principle has been formulated to deal with production and distribution on a large scale. For as we move out of the pioneering phase into the differentiated one, single products and markets are replaced by mass production and marketing.

Mechanization

The principle of mechanization is that technical resources must be used wherever possible, in place of increasingly costly, unpredictable and relatively inefficient human resources. Mechanization – or automation, in this context – is concerned not only with labour-saving machinery on the factory floor but also with enhanced information-processing facilities in the office.

Standardization

The principle of standardization is concerned with interchangeability and uniformity. Standardization means that every aspect of production, every process, every working method can be whittled down to an exactly prescribed standard. From a number of alternatives one possibility is chosen and is declared to represent the norm for reasons of expediency.

In addition to interchangeable standard parts and quality standards, the differentiated organization has standard job descriptions, performance appraisals, wage and salary scales, and so on. Business and organization therefore become, at least to a much larger extent than in the pioneering days, predictable and controllable. Individual departments become concerned more directly with meeting their own budgeted requirements than with the satisfaction of customer needs.

In the early stages of standardization, the production function leaps ahead of sales. The firm, and its scientifically based management, have initially become technically minded and inward-looking, rather than economically minded and outward-looking. While methods and techniques for controlling and developing the internal organization become increasingly scientific, the sales department continues to function anachronistically in the pioneer style. On the one hand the elaboration of norms and standards has led to a thorough knowledge of production costs and output, but on the other hand much less is known about sales costs and the benefits obtainable from alternative sales techniques. This development leads to an aggressive sales mentality; the firm's products are forced into the market.

As management evolves through its second stage, however, standardization spreads into mass merchandizing and marketing. Marketing plans and strategies are developed to complement production and distribution planning and control. The composite and highly specialized marketing function, including sales and distribution, then overtakes production and finance at the leading edge of the differentiated organization.

Specialization

Mechanization and standardization lead as a matter of course to specialization. Mechanization requires an ever-increasing perfection of equipment, as well as a growing concentration of knowledge and experience of every part and component technology. Standards can be met only if all the causes and effects that could influence the object to be standardized are controlled in minute detail. All of this can be best achieved through specialization.

Three kinds of specialization, according to Lievegoed, appear in the phase of differentiation:

Functional specialization Similar activities are concentrated in a single department under one specialized department head, who in turn engages further specialists. Purchasing, operations, marketing, finance and human resources become separate departments in place of the all-powerful, all-competent pioneer. These core departments, in their turn, are subdivided so that, for example, marketing is broken down into distribution, sales, advertising and public relations.

Hierarchical specialization Managerial authority is established and contained in and by vertical layers. The top is concerned with long-term policy-making; in the middle these policies are converted into medium-range strategies and structures, through strategy-making; and at the bottom of the hierarchy immediate direction and control are exercised through implementation.

Specialized management processes The three interrelated management processes – planning, execution and control – are recognized as being distinguishable, and are duly separated. Execution may be subdivided further into the specialized management processes of organizing, staffing and directing.[4]

Coordination

The principle of coordination serves to counterbalance the forces of differentiation, which tend to pull people and things apart. Such coordination is brought about, directly or indirectly, through:

Unity of command To avoid the issuing of contradictory instructions, each person is allocated only one superior.

Manageable span of control The number of subordinates that a given superior has to control is limited by the number of people about whom he is able to retain detailed knowledge.

Reliable communications Clear objectives and direct channels of formal communications are installed to ensure that management remains informed about the activities of its personnel, and that they are informed of the plans of management.

Systematic training Systematic transmission of knowledge and skills ensures that people will do their work in the way prescribed by the formal plan. Higher levels of management coordinate the training of lower levels in the formal hierarchy.

The limits of differentiation

The phase of differentiation, in sum, is the very antithesis of the pioneer phase. It is rational as opposed to instinctive, impersonal rather than personal, and is based on organizational rather than situational principles of management.

Differentiation is an essential phase for a company if it is to operate over the long term on any scale. Clearly differentiated functions have to be developed. However, the laws of development are relentless. As growth continues well into the second phase, new crises emerge and call for a second major reorientation.

Rigid bureaucracy

Formalization and bureaucratization reduce the flexibility of the organization, so that it fails to respond to market and social changes. Through specialization, divisions and subdivisions are formed which draw further and further apart. They lose their understanding of one another's tasks and can no longer speak the same business language. Small functional kingdoms arise, with their own objectives and standards, and communication breaks down.

Excessive control

Problems of communication increase not only across divisional boundaries but also up and down the ever-extending hierarchy of control. At the top less and less is known about what is happening at the base of the hierarchy, and vice versa. As the lack of coordination and responsiveness reaches crisis proportions there is a call for strong leadership, which represents a step back into the pioneering phase. Similarly the call for a new style of 'management by wandering about', made in the 1980s by Tom Peters and Bob Waterman, arises from the nostalgic desire to return to the days of the pioneer.[5]

Alienation

One of the most serious problems to occur is the steady fall in personal motivation. As the scale and impersonality of the organization increases, so the individual's perceived impotence, *vis à vis* the system, grows relentlessly. People feel that their work has become devoid of meaningful content and therefore experience a kind of qualitative underemployment. They feel reduced to a number, a mere extension of the system. To identify with the objectives of the whole organization becomes well nigh impossible. Customers, as well as employees, gradually become part of the same alienating process.

In the early days of differentiation, the move away from personalized customer relations to mass marketing was a necessary and useful development. It was the only way to make goods or services available at affordable prices to a mass market. Automobiles (historically) and personal computers (currently) are good cases in point. However, a highly differentiated company can become so distanced from its market-place that it begins to push products and services at people rather than adapting to their changing needs. Its customers, as Lievegoed vividly portrays, thereby become 'used' rather than 'served'.

> Advertising and persuasion techniques place the consumer under pressure. He is seen just as much as an instrument as the internal workforce: he must not think or judge or choose for himself; he must just reach for the branded product at the command of his influenced subconscious. A new commandment appears: in the sweat of thy brow thou shalt consume![6]

While the workforce intensify their disruptive practices within the firm, consumer organizations are founded to mastermind attacks from without. Industrial and external relations become important, though reactive, functions within the company. Tensions and inevitable crises mount.

Differentiation in limbo

Regression

It is always easier to go back towards the known than forwards towards the unknown. Many differentiated companies in the 1970s and 1980s responded to crises of falling profitability, productivity and motivation by regressing. They slimmed down their headquarters, decentralized operations and installed a tough man at the top, in order to 'turn the company around'. Lee Iacocca of Chrysler is a legendary example in the US, and Michael Edwards, former Chairman of British Leyland, is a good example in the UK.

All of this represents a return to a pioneering outlook. The advent of *intrapreneuring*, spearheaded by Gifford Pinchot in the US,[7] and the trend towards *privatization* in Thatcher's Britain also herald the return of phase-one thinking. Moreover, the growth of franchising, management buyouts and subcontracting have all positioned the differentiated company in a state of limbo, between phases one and two.

Progression

In addition to this process of regression, however, some of the very same companies observed by Lievegoed in the 1970s are undergoing a progression in the 1980s. In fact they are differentiating their production, marketing and personnel functions more distinctly. The advent of flexible manufacturing systems, increasingly individualized products and services, and ever more flexible work patterns marks a notable change of emphasis from the mass to the individual.

Alvin Toffler, in his book *The Third Wave*, refers to this phenomenon as *demassification*.[8] It heralds a development from the personal and communal (phase one), to the functional and organizational (phase two), to the individual and social (phase three).

The Integrated Phase

Emergence of the social subsystem

For Lievegoed, the third phase – integration – is centred on the development of the organization's social system, and its integration with the already developed economic (phase one) and technical (phase two) subsystems.

> If we start with the entrepreneurial initiative of the pioneer as our thesis, then scientific (differentiated) management is in a certain sense the antithesis, and a third step will have to be the synthesis of the positive elements of the first and second phases with the addition of a new element which makes this synthesis possible – the mature social subsystem.[9]

Lievegoed's third phase is based on the premise that every individual can and wants to develop. Real fulfilment at work can be attained only if the individual need for ongoing development is satisfied. A mature social subsystem is required to facilitate this. To accommodate it a new form of organization is required.

The pioneer phase has a shallow, broad form of organization; the phase of differentiation has a deep, pyramid form, with the directing and controlling board of directors at the top. The phase of integration demands a form that Lievegoed terms a 'clover-leaf' organization.

The clover-leaf organization

In the clover-leaf organization the board no longer stands at the apex of a pyramid. It is now situated at the center of the organization, at the crossing point of all the channels of information and communication. The function of the board is to integrate the four subsystems or management activities outlined in Figure 4.2:

> relations management,
> process management,
> resources management,
> information management.

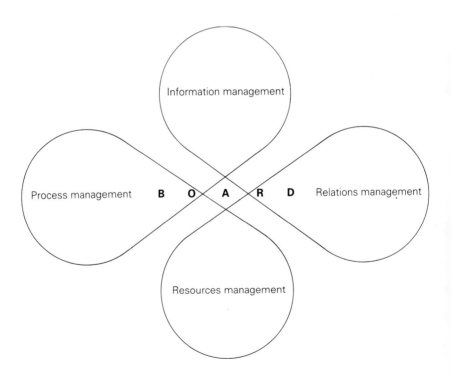

Figure 4.2 The Clover-leaf Organization

Relations management
The management and cultivation of relations involves both external and internal contacts. The most important external relations are those involved in marketing. In marketing the true task of the pioneer reappears: the discovery of a consumer need and the answering of this need by solving problems for others. Everything else is derived from this primary task and serves the exclusive purpose of realizing it.

Other external relations are, historically, those with suppliers and distributors, with trade unions and shareholders, and with local and national government. More recently there has been a spate of associated ventures between companies themselves in preproduction research, in joint marketing ventures and in international consortia. These are becoming an increasingly important part of relations management.

Internal relations form the second part of relations management. This subfunction involves discovering the needs of people working within the company, including their desire for ongoing personal development, and catering for these individually and collectively. These needs are economic, psychological and social. Internal relations, moreover, involve the stimulation of innovation as a continual activity of all employees. Such innovation takes place as a process over time.

Process management
Between the inputs and the outputs of the company there are many activities of a material nature (production flows) and a non-material nature (information flows), which follow one another over time. Within these flow processes human beings are used, or become superfluous, and therefore process management is the crucial test for the genuine integration of the social system.

In the second, differentiated phase, people are organized vertically in a structure that is superior-oriented. In the third phase emphasis is placed on a horizontal orientation of workers within the process flow. In these horizontal consultation groups, people are oriented towards those who precede them and influence their work, and towards those who are next in the process flow and whose work is influenced in turn. In process management there is a close interaction between the technical and the social subsystems. Only through integrating the technical 'hardware' and the social 'software' can a truly functional process flow be guaranteed. Such a flow is also determined by the availability and allocation of resources.

Resources management

Resources of different kinds are necessary to make possible the process flow, which is determined in turn by external relations. The procurement, management and disposal of these resources at the right place, in the right amounts and at the right time constitutes the third of the four clover-leaf functions. 'Resources', in this context, include both material components – capital and facilities – and non-material components – people and know-how (so-called *intellectual capital*). In the third phase the non-material resources are more important than the material ones. Thus the board must be primarily concerned with the procurement, allocation and development of its non-material resources.

Information management

Information processing has grown quantitatively and qualitatively to such a degree, in large-scale enterprise, that it warrants – in the third phase – a completely separate subsystem. It is therefore given a place as one of the leaflets of the clover-leaf organization. Like a nervous system that permeates the whole organism but has its own center, the information system receives its policy direct from the board. Its task is to send every piece of information to the place where it is required so that those concerned can act intelligently in the interests of the whole company, and to distribute information in a form that is useful for everybody as regards content, frequency and intelligibility.

> It is the task of the information centre to use the assembling, processing and distribution of information to enable people individually and in groups to adjust and control, independently, within the framework of the defined standards. In this way it becomes possible for everyone to act intelligently within the context of the overall objectives.[10]

The information-processing centre will have a department concerned with external functions, primarily market research and intelligence, and an internal department serving the administrative, financial and management functions. The section of the internal department serving process management will need to collaborate with engineers. In fact collaboration, mutual consultation, and an attitude of service, are the necessary characteristics of the information-processing subsystem.

The board

The board is situated at the centre, in the heart of the clover leaf. Instead of being at the top of a pyramid, in splendid isolation, it is now at the point where all the channels of communication cross. Its members, therefore, must have sufficient proficiency and interest in the four main subsystems to ensure that they can make balanced judgements and take corrective action, as well as initiate and innovate. The role of Chairman of the Board, accordingly, changes fundamentally.

Chairman of the Center – Board

- Instead of seeing himself at the top of a pyramid, he shifts to the center of the organism, at a point where all channels of communication meet. Ideally too the chairman would shift geographically, as well as organizationally, away from a parochial and national center.
- Instead of making heavy-handed decisions and exercising ultimate authority, he selectively guides, encourages, envisages and harmonizes, asking questions, giving support, recognizing potential, and inspiring confidence. He also needs to publicly and imaginatively distinguish between these enabling and envisioning functions and the more established ones of entrepreneurship and management.
- Instead of primarily focussing on efficiency and effectiveness, progressive corporate chairmen have concentrated on the management of change, on an ongoing basis. What remains to be done is to shift the focus from change – which has no direction or higher purpose to it – to an evolutionary path of interdependent development, serving to link past, present and future.
- Instead of necessarily competing with companies outside, and resolving conflicts amongst people inside, the third stage chairman strives for association with enterprises and institutions and reaches decisions through mutual agreement. What remains is to accentuate this shift of emphasis, particularly externally, away from an autonomous corporation towards an interdependent corporate architecture.
- Instead of pursuing business, technical and organization development as separate goals, the new chairman strives to integrate all three within a transformed technological, commercial and social vision. What is required is for that transformed vision to percolate its way through the organization, by a process of cultural evolution, stimulated by powerful images and suitably heroic figures.

- Finally, instead of insisting that individual goals and aspirations should be subordinated to those of the organization, the new corporate chairman should adapt the organization to the needs of the individual. What he needs to do is to model the organization to the needs of the individual's growth and development from youth to adulthood and maturity, and to identify and accommodate diverse forms of individuality within it.[11]

In the final analysis the primary task of the chairman and his board is to manage innovation and development.

The limits of integration

It is difficult to assess the limits that the integrated, clover-leaf organization might come up against because so few companies have yet become, in Lievegoed's terms, fully integrated. However, problems have emerged with 'self-managed' companies (particularly in Yugoslavia) that have attempted to enter the third, socially oriented phase, without undergoing a proper economic and technical development. In other words many a socially oriented and cooperative enterprise will find itself struggling to survive because it has not built up the economic or technical resilience to compete aggressively and effectively in the market-place.

The Developing Organization in Perspective

Bernard Lievegoed, together with his mentor, Rudolf Steiner, and his fifty or so disciples at the NPI, has attempted singlemindledly to introduce developmental management into organizational life. The concept of the clover-leaf organization, transcending functionally based management, is quite unique and, probably for that reason, somewhat difficult to grasp. It represents a fundamentally new departure in managerial thinking.

The notion of phases of development, however, is a little more commonplace. In Chapter 3 I described its origins in developmental biology. In the chapter that follows I shall be dealing with some of its applications in developmental psychology. However, closer to home, there have been three organizational theorists whose work on phases has paralleled that of Lievegoed. Gordon Lippitt, Warren Schmidt and Larry Greiner are three Americans who have played prominent roles within the *organizational development* movement. Their particular interest has been in the area of what has come to be called *organizational renewal.*

Organizational Renewal

Crisis and Development

Interestingly, in the US Gordon Lippitt and Warren Schmidt came independently to similar conclusions about organizational development to Lievegoed's. They referred to their phases as *growth stages* in an organization's development renewal. Instead of pioneering, differentiated and integrated phases they have adopted the terms

birth,
youth,
maturity.[12]

At a particular stage of its evolution, through birth and infancy, youth and maturity, an organization – like an individual – faces one or two issues that are crucial to that phase of its development. If those issues remain unresolved the organization will enter decline. At each stage, as revealed in Table 4.2, there are appropriate and inappropriate developmental responses.

Infant responses

With the creation of a new enterprise, if it is to survive, the pioneers must decide continually what to create, in a commercial and organizational sense, and what to sacrifice in financial and emotional terms. If the decisions made are inappropriate the enterprise will be stillborn, or will die in its infancy.

Youthful responses

If the pioneers succeed in 'getting through the knot hole', and survive into the next, youthful, phase, they will need to turn into 'scientific' managers. As such they will be seeking much greater stability, as well as a solid and enduring reputation. If management fails to plan, organize and control effectively, the company will become over-reactive to immediate stimuli, and dominated by short-term crises.

Table 4.2   Appropriate Developmental Responses

Critical issue	Correct response	Incorrect response
Creation	New organizational system comes into being.	Idea remains abstract; organization is undercapitalized.
Survival	Organization learns from experience and becomes viable.	Organization fails to adjust to realities of its environment, and remains marginal.
Stability	Organization develops efficiency and strength, and retains flexibility.	Organization overextends itself, returning to survival stage.
Pride and reputation	Organization's reputation reinforces efforts to improve quality.	Organization places more effort on image-creation than on product quality.
Uniqueness and adaptability	Organization changes to take full advantage of its unique capability, and provides growth opportunities for its personnel.	Organization fails to discover its uniqueness and spreads its efforts inappropriately, thus inhibiting growth.
Contribution	Organization gains public respect for its contribution to society.	Organization may be accused of failing to uphold its responsibility to its shareholders.

Source: G. Lippitt and W. Schmidt, *Organizational Renewal.* Prentice Hall, 2nd edn, 1982, p. 245.

Mature responses

As the differentiated and youthful organization enters its integrated and mature phase its critical concerns duly evolve. It aims now to achieve uniqueness and adaptibility, on the one hand, and to contribute to society, on the other. The managers' focus is now long-term as opposed to medium- or short-term. The key issues to be resolved are how to change and adapt, and how to share business and management with others. The lack of such a developmental orientation leads to unnecessarily defensive or aggressive attitudes, to a narrowness of approach and to an ultimate failure to adapt.

Evolution and Revolution

Stability and change

Lippitt's and Schmidt's three growth stages, then, encompass creation and survival; stability, pride and reputation; uniqueness and adaptability; and contribution to society. They are in fact very similar to Lievegoed's three phases: pioneering, differentiated and integrated.

A final source of knowledge on development phases comes from a researcher at the Harvard Business School in the early 1970s, Larry Greiner.[13] Unlike the others, however, Greiner maintains that growing organizations move through five distinguishable phases of development, each of which contains a relatively calm period of growth that ends with a management crisis. The calm period of growth he describes as *evolutionary*; the period of crisis and turmoil he terms *revolutionary*. The critical task for management in each revolutionary period is to find a new set of organizational practices that will become the basis for managing the next period of evolutionary growth. Interestingly, these new practices eventually sow their own seeds of decay and lead to another period of revolution. Companies therefore find, ironically, that a major solution in one time period becomes a major problem at a future date.

The extent and duration of a stage of development is not only a function of the age and size of an organization, it is also related to the market environment of its industry. For example, a company in a rapidly expanding market will have to add employees rapidly. Hence the need for structures and systems to accommodate these changes is accelerated. While evolutionary changes tend to be relatively short in fast-growing industries, much longer evolutionary periods occur in mature or slowly growing industries.

Five stages of growth

Although Greiner conceives of five growth periods (Figure 4.3), three of them consist merely of subdivisions of the youthful or differentiated phase.

It is important to note that each stage is both an effect of the previous stage and a cause of the next one. When we consider, with Greiner, each stage of development, we find that he is not fundamentally at odds with Lippitt and Schmidt, or with Lievegoed. In fact, Greiner's phases one (*creativity*) and five (*collaboration*) correspond with Lippitt's *birth* and *maturity* and with Lievegoed's *pioneering* and *integration*, respectively.

The three intermediate stages represent *youth* (perhaps including adulthood) but involve a more detailed breakdown: *direction*, *delegation*, *coordination*. Let us now investigate Greiner's *evolutions*, or stages, and *revolutions*, or crises, in more detail.

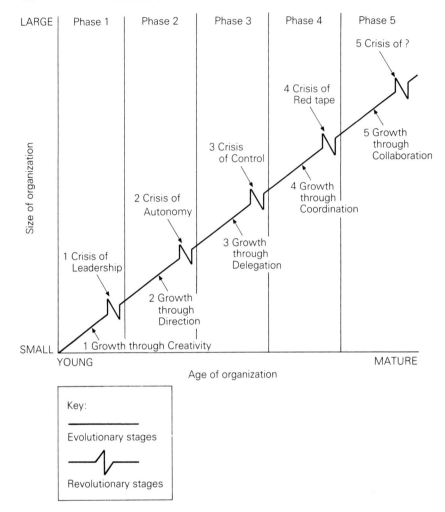

Figure 4.3 Evolution and Revolution as Organizations Grow
Source: L. Greiner, 'Evolution and Revolution as Organizations Grow', *Harvard Business Review*, July–August 1972, p. 41.

Phase one: creativity (pioneering/birth)
In the birth stage of an organization the emphasis is on creating a product or service, and a market:

● The company's founders are usually technically or entrepreneurially oriented, and they disdain management activities; their physical and mental energies are absorbed in producing and selling a product or a service.

- Communication among employees is frequent and informal.
- Long hours of work are rewarded by modest salaries and the promise of ownership benefits.
- Control of activities comes from immediate market-place feedback; the management acts as customers react.

. . . Up comes the leadership crisis.

All of this enterprising activity is essential for the company to get off the ground. But therein lies the problem. As the company grows, larger production and distribution runs require the founders to acquire knowledge about operational systems and structures. Increased numbers of employees cannot be managed exclusively through informal communications. New employees are no longer motivated by an intense dedication to the product or organization. Additional capital must also be secured and new accounting procedures implemented for financial control.

Thus the founders find themselves burdened with unwanted management responsibilities. A leadership crisis occurs, which, for its resolution, requires a managerial revolution.

Phase two: direction (differentiation/youth)
Those companies that survive the first phase by installing capable management usually embark on a period of sustained growth under able and directive leadership. This is the youthful phase, involving the early influence of scientific management.

- A functional organization structure is introduced to separate operations from marketing activities, and job assignments become more specialized.
- Incentives, budgets and work standards are introduced.
- Communication becomes more formal and impersonal as a hierarchy of titles and positions builds up.
- The new management take on most of the decision-making responsibility.

. . . Up comes the autonomy crisis.

While the new management policies and techniques channel employee effort more efficiently and effectively into growth, they eventually become inappropriate. They become ill-fitted for the control of an increasingly complex and diversified operation. Lower-level employees find themselves stifled by a cumbersome and centralized hierarchy. Because, moreover, they have become more in touch with the grass roots than the senior management, they begin to feel torn. Should they take responsive initiative or stick to seemingly outmoded procedures?

Thus the second revolution is imminent. There is increasing demand for autonomy at lower levels. However, while the lower levels may be ill-accustomed to making decisions the higher levels may be ill-disposed to surrendering power. The crisis needs to be resolved through appropriate delegation.

Phase three: delegation

The next organizational evolution results in a more decentralized structure:

- Much greater responsibility is given to managers of individual operations and territories.
- Profit centres and bonus systems are used to stimulate motivation.
- Top executives at the centre confine themselves to managing by exception, based on periodic reports from the field.
- Senior management may acquire new companies or enter into joint ventures, to supplement the existing, decentralized units.

. . . Up comes the crisis of control.

A serious crisis eventually looms as top management begins to sense that it is losing control over a highly diversified operation. Freedom breeds not only autonomy but also parochialism.

Revolution gets under way as management seeks to regain overall control. However, an attempt to reassert centralized control is bound to fail, given the emerging complexity of the operation. Those companies that resolve the crisis discover a new form of coordination.

Phase four: coordination

This next evolutionary phase therefore calls for a new and subtle form of coordination.

- Previously decentralized units are merged into newly formed product groups.
- Formal planning procedures are installed.
- New staff personnel are hired at headquarters to initiate company-wide technical, commercial and organizational review programmes.
- Stock options and company-wide profit-sharing schemes are

introduced to encourage individuals and divisions to identify with the company as a whole.

... Up comes the crisis of red tape.

Gradually a lack of confidence builds up between line and staff, between headquarters and the divisions. The proliferation of systems and procedures begins to turn into too much of a good thing. Such procedures take precedence over problem-solving. A red-tape crisis looms.

The next revolution is under way. A new form of collaboration is required to resolve it.

Phase five: collaboration (integration/emerging maturity)
The last observable phase, according to Greiner, emphasizes strong interpersonal collaboration to overcome the red-tape crisis:

- Focus is now on problem-solving through group interaction.
- Teams are combined across foundations; a matrix structure is often created, linking up temporary projects and permanent functions.
- Headquarters staff are reduced in number, and combined into interdisciplinary teams.
- Experimentation is encouraged throughout the organization.

Greiner is unsure at this point what crisis will emerge next. He hints at the prospect of 'psychological saturation', whereby employees 'burn out'. Perhaps at this stage, he argues, they need more time for reflection. The fact is, Greiner himself has reached an evolutionary cul de sac. He is unable to come fully to grips with the challenges of, and opportunities for, genuine integration and maturation. His final phase fails to have a ring of true maturity about it because he is not completely in touch with the emerging technological and social developments of our time, nor with his own emerging maturity.

New Patterns of Work and Organization

Dispersed organizations

While Greiner alludes to a succession of revolutions, characterizing each crisis of transition, only the managerial one assumes genuinely revolutionary proportions. The step up from a pioneering enterprise to managed organization does appear to be a revolutionary one: the rules of the business game change fundamentally; a science of management replaces the art of entrepreneurship. Thereafter, his 'revolutions' seem to go off at half cock.

The problem is that in the 1970s, when Greiner, Lievegoed, and Lippitt and Schmidt were writing, structures of organization and management, employment and self-employment were little changed from those that had existed fifty years before. In the 1980s, though, we have had a very different situation. With the rapid emergence of new communications technologies the *dispersed organization* has become a practical reality. Such organizational dispersion reinforces individuality and independence. At the same time collaboration between businesses, as well as within them, is increasing at a very rapid rate.

Interorganizational cooperation

Interorganizational cooperation enhances commonality and inter-dependence. It takes the form of consortia, joint ventures, risk-sharing, countertrading, piggy-backing and several more such colla-borative arrangements (Table 4.3).[14]

Table 4.3 Interorganizational Collaboration

Collaborators	Mode	Operation
Eurotunnel	Consortium	This Anglo-French group is a consortium of major construction and finance companies, assembled to build the Channel Tunnel.
Barclays/De Zoete	Joint venture	Clearing bank and stockbroker have combined forces to create a whole that is greater than the sum of its individual parts.
Rolls Royce/GE (USA)	Risk-sharing	These two major companies, on opposite sides of the Atlantic, have become partners in the development and manufacture of high-powered aircraft engines.
Ford Levi Strauss Pierre Cardin	Countertrading	Ford trades its cars for Uruguayan sheepskins; Levi Strauss sells a turnkey plant to Hungary and gets jeans in return; Pierre Cardin gets oriental skills by providing consultancy services to China.
Pitney Bowes/small business	Piggy-backing	Pitney Bowes markets, through its nationwide marketing and service network, innovative products of small businesses.

The enabling company

Whereas the birth phase in a company's development is represented by the independent enterprise, and the youthful phase by a holding or parent company, I have argued that the maturer phase is represented by an *enabling company*.[15] The enabling company is the instrument through which independence and interdependence are combined with dependence. The new enterprise and the managed organization are not eclipsed; rather a rival – the enabling company – appears in their midst.

While the role of 'enablers' has been visible in the training world for years, the enabling company's role is much more wide-ranging. Whereas the enabler develops people's potential, the enabling company harnesses the potential not only of people but also of products, markets and whole businesses.

Moreover, and this is the key, enabling involves:

- not so much holding down but more *holding together*;
- not so much employing people and their skills but more *deploying individuality and its potential*;
- not so much competing but more *cooperating*;
- not so much overpowering people and institutions but more *empowering staff, suppliers, customers, associated companies and whole societies.*

The model of a maturing, developmental organization is therefore one of linked rather than hierarchical structures (Figure 4.4). It thereby accommodates both independence and interdependence.

Conclusion

Developmental Management

As an organization evolves so its structures and functions are transformed. The transformation from a new enterprise into an established organization is well substantiated both in theory and practice. We are generally familiar with the conventional business entrepreneur and administrator.

The so-called *developmental manager* is something of a new breed. His emphasis is social rather than technical or economic. His style is supportive and enabling, rather than dynamic or authoritative.

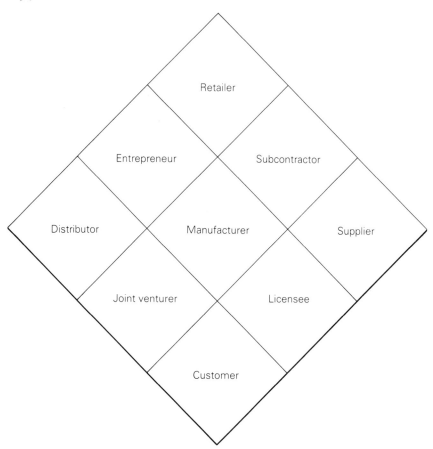

Figure 4.4 The Enabling Company

He fosters both independence and interdependence, rather than independence on its own or dependence as the predominating and employed mode of being. Greiner, Lippitt and Schmidt, and most other proponents of organization development go this far but no further. The form of organization does not fundamentally change, though the style of management does. This new style is less mechanistic and bureaucratic, more organic and democratic.

The New Corporate Architecture

But for Lievegoed and for the practising businessman in a dynamic company or industry today, the pattern of work and organization has changed. The boundaries not only between different business functions but also between home and work and between one company and another are dissolving. It is as if a new *corporate architecture* is unfolding.

Development and Renewal in the Chemical Industry

The evolutionary perspective in chemistry is rich in deep-seated and significant innovations. The tendency is to break up the industry, to split it up into subsectors which are, increasingly, closely linked to the solution of specific problems, and to rearrange it into new industries, born from an interdisciplinary perception of the contribution of innovation.

This does not necessarily mean that the major chemical companies will disappear, but in order to evolve they will need to rebuild themselves around specific problems, explicit markets and societal demands. During this process they will be combining with industries which traditionally were buying their products or supplying them with raw materials.

Finally they will no longer be unistrategy companies. They will manifest strong intersectoral synergy.[16]

Organic development, in that emerging context, overlaps conventional boundaries between home and work, between one company, discipline or department and another, as well as between public and private enterprise. As organizations continue to grow and evolve in the future, therefore, they will undergo evolutions and revolutions of which Greiner has not yet dreamed.

Developing Business Functions

I now want to turn from the organization in general to the major business functions in particular. As I portray the unfolding of these functions you will notice that, aside from the three evolving stages, there are also soft and hard edges to each. In that sense I am following in Tom Peters's footsteps.

Notes

1 R. Steiner, *World Economics*. Steiner Press, 1979, p. 266.
2 B. Lievegoed, *Organisaties in ontwikkeling*. Lemniscaat, 1969. Eng. trans. as *The Developing Organization*. Tavistock, 1973; new edn, Basil Blackwell, 1990, chapter 5.
3 M. Large, *Social Ecology*. Published by the author, 1981, chapter 6.

4 H. Koontz and C. O'Donnell, *Principles of Management*. McGraw Hill, 5th edn, 1972.

5 T. Peters and R. Waterman, *In Search of Excellence*. Harper & Row, 1982.

6 Lievegoed, *The Developing Organization*, p. 75.

7 G. Pinchot, *Intrapreneuring*. Harper & Row, 1984.

8 A. Toffler, *The Third Wave*. Bantam, 1982.

9 Lievegoed, *The Developing Organization*, p. 79.

10 Lievegoed, *The Developing Organization*, p. 86.

11 R. Lessem, *The Roots of Excellence*. Fontana, 1986, p. 209.

12 G. Lippitt and W. Schmidt, *Organizational Renewal*. Prentice Hall, 2nd edn, 1982.

13 L. Greiner, 'Evolution and Revolution as Organizations Grow', *Harvard Business Review*, July–August 1972, p. 41.

14 R. Lessem, 'The Enabling Company', in *New Problems at Work*, ed. D. Clutterbuck. Gower, 1986, p. 92.

15 Lessem, 'The Enabling Company', p. 94.

16 U. Colombo, 'Industrial Development and Renewal in the Chemical Industry', *Futures*, 18(2), April 1986, pp. 170–91.

5

The Developing Business Function: the Branches

Introduction

In this chapter we shall explore the implications of developmental management for the basic functions of business. Such functions, in this context, are not planning, organizing, directing and controlling, but financial, marketing, operational and human resource management.

At this stage of the development of management theory and practice we can do no more than explore the functional implications, for although they may have done so implicitly, functional theorists have not yet made explicit the evolution of their disciplines, at least beyond the rational stage. Moreover, it is important to mention that each business function may not necessarily evolve, in linear fashion, from a primal to a developmental state: for example, although human resource management is theoretically probably the furthest advanced of the functions, the primal domain has taken a very long time to emerge.

In this chapter, then, we shall be investigating the four domains of management – both hard and soft:

> finance,
> marketing,
> operations,
> human resources.

We start with finance because many see money as the essence of business, and conclude with human resources because the function is, theoretically, the most developed.

Finance

Money and business have never been very far apart. In fact, particularly for those who have not been involved in business themselves, the two appear to be inextricably connected.

Finance: the Primal Domain

Money, though, is actually an abstraction. People who are instinctively adept at making money start off from some other place, deep within their own subconscious. In fact, there is a whole range of 'inspirational' American business literature, which helps managers tap those subconscious motives – that is, should they wish to grow rich.

Secrets of success

By far the best-known of these books is by Napoleon Hill, written in the 1920s and entitled *Think and Grow Rich*.[1] Still a bestseller today, the book declares on its front cover: 'This could be worth a million dollars to you.' Hill in fact spent some twenty years with such business geniuses as Andrew Carnegie, Henry Ford and Nelson Rockefeller, uncovering their secrets of success.

The starting point for all great men of business, Hill concludes, is desire. The means by which a desire for riches can be satisfied, he says, involves six practical steps:

1 Fix in your mind the exact amount of money you desire.
2 Determine exactly what you want to give in return – there is no such reality as something for nothing.
3 Establish a definite date by which you want to possess the money you desire.
4 Create a definite plan for carrying out your desire, and begin at once to put your plan into action.
5 Imprint on your heart and mind the amount of money you intend to acquire, the time limit for its acquisition, and what you intend to give in return for the money.
6 Remind yourself twice daily of your intentions, once before you go to sleep, and once when you wake up in the morning. As you

remind yourself, see and feel yourself already in possession of the money.

As you can see the primal approach to finance starts with the person, and his or her concrete desires, rather than with money, which is abstract. Although Napoleon Hill's work is the best-known of this kind there are at least a hundred other such books, albeit not as well researched.

Moneylove

Hill's primal approach and a hundred other similarly toughminded ones focus on the desire to succeed, and hence to make a fortune. Jerry Gillies's tenderhearted approach, and several other American ones like it, are oriented towards *moneylove*.

> One of the major premises of moneylove is that one of the best things you can do for your own prosperity consciousness is to lift someone else's. Every dollar you help someone else to earn will come back to you multiplied, along with large helpings of love.[2]

The theme of moneylove is echoed by Mary Kay, American founder of Mary Kay Cosmetics. Money is not only a means to a personal end, that is self-love, but it is also multiplied by the love of others.

> I suppose I'm like a mother who wants to give her children – my salesladies – the things they didn't have. The first thing they need is to hear 'you can do it!' Sometimes nobody has ever told them that in their life. But we also make sure they learn the necessary skills, as beauty consultants. And when they do that they begin to improve in other ways too. Their confidence builds.[3]

It is clear, then, that a primal approach to finance, whether hard or soft, builds on personal desires not only for success and achievement but also for love and self-value. Whereas the literature in this primal area is largely American, other toughminded primal sources exist – in Japan, for example, in descriptions of the art of oriental warfare.[4]

Finance: the Rational Domain

Whereas the proverbial entrepreneur or animator, like Andrew Carnegie or Mary Kay, sees personal psychology and business finance as intimately linked, for the rational manager they are worlds apart. This is the case, particularly, within the rigid field of management accounting. As we shall see, it is less strictly the case in the looser realms of business finance.

Management accounting

The entire discipline of accounting has grown up – double-entry book-keeping having originated in seventeenth-century Italy – as an abstract and impersonal tool of business.

> Book-keeping is the systematic recording of business transactions in a manner which enables the financial relationship of business with other persons to be clearly disclosed, and the cumulative effect of the transactions on the financial position of the business itself to be ascertained. Business transactions comprise the exchange of value, either in the form of money, or of goods and services which are measured and expressed in terms of money.[5]

Double-entry accounting, then, enables a businessman or financial controller to gauge at any time his company's financial position, and its 'financial relationship with other persons'. Thus an abstract relationship takes over from a personal one. Precise, rationally derived measurements overtake emotionally laden bonds of trust, or mistrust. Stable financial accounts and corresponding managerial accountability supplant 'back of the envelope' records of transactions. Similarly, an accountant may overtake a craftsman, technician or salesman at the head of the company.

Subsequent developments of the financial function, often mathematically based, have extended its rationality and impersonality. Discounted cash flow, capital budgeting, portfolio analysis, and financial model-building and simulation, have added further degrees of intellectual sophistication to an already analytically refined discipline. In that analytical context its primal origins are all too often lost. However, in the last few years, a combination of primal instinct and intellectual wizardry has produced a financial revolution.

The financial revolution

In the words of Walter Wriston, head of Citicorp (the world's largest bank) between 1970 and 1984:

> The information standard has replaced the gold standard as the basis for international finance. Communications now enable and ensure that

money moves anywhere around the globe, in answer to the latest information or misinformation. There now exists a new order, a global marketplace for ideas, money, goods, and services that knows no national boundaries.[6]

In the financial heartlands of London, New York, Hong Kong and now Tokyo, the primal nature of money-making, however, has retained its underlying identity. Brokers, jobbers and floor traders have continued to draw on their primal instincts, particularly those of the tougher variety. The drive for personal gain has maintained its influence on every deal. But with the onset of computerization and the internationalization of the world's stock markets, there has been a new twist to the financial tail.

An intellectual superstructure has been build directly upon a primal substructure, resulting in great fluidity and instability. Fixed and archaic primal instincts have become intertwined with a flexible intellect, contained in both people and technology.

'Soft' Markets

For generations (centuries in the case of many of the great financial capitals of the world) the principles guiding the financial markets have been specialization and control. The Chicago commodity markets concentrated on futures in pork bellies, the Baltic Exchange in London developed the markets for freight rates by sea. Markets for short, medium and long term funds were separated and the whole structure buttressed by central authorities that controlled interest rates and currency movements.

In the nineteen-eighties, however, technology has made it possible to trade huge volumes on screens and on the exchange floors. What is more, it has made it possible to develop increasingly sophisticated and complicated products such as options (when the investor takes out an option to buy or sell a share, bond or commodity at a future date), swaps (when the borrower can swap, for example, his fixed rate debt, raised in one country, with the floating rate debt raised by a company elsewhere).

In summary, as both investors and borrowers grow more sophisticated, so new products are developed that enable companies to swap their obligations, investors to convert their bonds into equity shares or different currencies, and banks to take advantage of their spread of customers to organize flexible instruments that could be made short term or long term, moved into one currency or another, and switched from floating to fixed interest rate at will.[7]

The shift from gold, through coin, paper money and credit to information as a unit of exchange progressively removes finance from its primal origins.

Finance: the Developmental Domain

As finance evolves from its position as a vehicle and outlet for personal ambition or social generosity, to a channel for organizational effectiveness or commercial flexibility, to a medium for personal, organizational, industrial and economic development, so its role and perspective changes.

Finance for development

Ever since the formation of joint-stock companies, in the nineteenth century, finance for business development has been acknowledged. More recently, as international economic awareness has increased, the need for finance for national development has also become recognized. However, such recognition has been at best, partial, in that a genuinely developmental outlook has seldom been adopted. One of the earliest to take a developmental approach, albeit perhaps in a more philosophical than practical vein, was Rudolf Steiner at the turn of the century. Disciples of his, such as the economists Folkert Wilken in Germany and Christopher Budd in Britain, have adopted the term *capital economy* to describe Steiner's theories.

Capital Economy

A 'capital economy' is distinguished from other forms of economy by the emancipation of capital within it. It is a mode of economy in which the economic process has more or less freed itself from inclusion within the cultural and political spheres. It has, as a concomitant, the emancipated consciousness of the individual. A capital economy only finds its true setting in the social order when capital finds its way to the individual, solely on the basis of his capacities.

The social order appropriate to capital will never be discovered unless men realize that it is the evolutionary task of capital to call forth from man a new social order, based on self-knowledge and self-initiation, not high authority.

Without capital, in fact, self-expression and individual development are impossible. Capital, in this sense, may be a paint brush or a machine; it can be the stock for a shop or the right to mine a vein of ore. What turns nature into capital is the fact that it is used to unfold the capacities of man.[8]

For Budd, then, capital is a financial means to a psychological end, the unfolding of the capacities of man. The same developmental outlook applies, for Folkert Wilken and indeed Fritz Schumacher (see Chapter 2), in relation to the unfolding of the capacities of a whole nation.

Financial and economic reciprocity

As the capacities of a nation unfold, so that nation becomes ever more closely intertwined with other nations. Mary Parker Follett's pairing of individuality and interdependence works on both an individual and a national plane.[9] We therefore see – as in Kenichi Ohmae's *Triad Power*[10] – the advance of economic interdependence across a worldwide stage.

In fact interdependence and reciprocity are built into the underlying nature of double-entry book-keeping, for basic book-keeping recognizes the twofold aspect of every transaction – namely the receipt of something of monetary value by one person and the parting with it by another. In essence, assets and liabilities represent two sides of the same coin. On the one side we have some outstanding demand or expectation awaiting satisfaction and, on the other, we have the potential or sufficient support to produce such satisfaction.

Recognizing this fact, in the mid-1970s, I developed a double-entry system, covering not only financial transactions, but also physical, social and psychological ones within a business enterprise.[11] This system was used to audit the *social performance* of companies.[12] One such account is shown in Table 5.1.

Table 5.1 Psychological Balance Sheet

Assets/psychological supports	Liabilities/psychological demands
Total years experience: managerial clerical skilled manual	Accrued demands for work experience
Accumulation of knowledge	Accrued demands for utilization of knowledge
Investment in training: skill-based knowledge-based self-development-based	Accrued demands for utilization of capacities developed

Marketing

While business is generally identified with money and finance, its origins lie closer to marketing. As Peter Drucker has emphasized, in a modern business context:

> The purpose of a business is not to make a profit. . . . Rather a business exists for its economic contribution. Its purpose is to create a customer.[13]

Marketing: the Primal Domain

Barter and trade

If we look for the primal origins of marketing we shall find them in the market-places of antiquity. For wherever there is buying and selling, marketing of the most basic kind is going on. In fact, trade by way of barter preceded by thousands of years economic exchange mediated by money. When, on my last trip to the Victoria Falls in Zimbabwe, the affable sculptor by the roadside offered me a wooden elephant, which he had carved, in exchange for a tee-shirt or 'something like that', he was continuing a tradition that stretches back to prehistory. Having sensed that my need for his carving was not all that great, and that British-made tee-shirts were easy for me to come by (but difficult for Zimbabweans), he made his proposition. In the event, my little boy accepted on our behalf!

Young children acquire experience of *primal marketing* long before they learn how to handle money. When my ten-year-old son 'sells' his friend Jim the idea of playing monopoly, having previously ascertained that Jim is bored and needs stimulus, he is already marketing – in a primal way. Indeed, a Canadian management consultant, Jean Marc Chaput, has written a book called *Living is Selling*,[14] in which he elaborates on this primal theme.

Salesmanship

Primal marketing, in a contemporary business context, is best represented by *salesmanship*. Hundreds of books and courses on the subject remind us that marketing is as much to do with 'touch and feel' as it is to do with 'intelligent perception'.

A veteran salesman himself, Harry Turner, in his book *The Gentle Art of Salesmanship*, indicates that a good salesman has two particularly dominant personality traits, *ego drive* and *empathy*. These, incidentally, correspond very nicely with the hard (ego drive) and soft (empathy) traits that feature in all our management and functional domains.

> Ego drive is the urge to succeed. If it is not balanced by empathy it can be a destructive force. Empathy is about sensitivity to the reactions and feelings of others. Very few people have both these qualities in equal proportions. Strong empathy and reduced drive means less cutting edge, which will make the closing of sales difficult. Too much ego drive and too little empathy produces the killer instinct.[15]

Another authority on salesmanship, Heinz Goldman, has gone on from where Turner left off, introducing us to the *AIDA* rule, which is well known in salesmen's circles!

The AIDA Rule

> the successful salesman needs to arouse the attention of the customer, make him personally interested in the offer, and increase his desire to buy the product, in order to stimulate him to the action of buying.[16]

Marketing: the Rational Domain

From sales to marketing

The transition from primal salesmanship to *rationally based marketing* has been described, in picturesque fashion, by Harry Turner. Years ago, he says, larger than life characters like 'King Gillette' created products which they virtually willed into existence. Such men followed hunches, took breathtaking chances and finally conquered the world with their determination to succeed. They had charisma, and buccaneering style. Their business talents were as much instinctive as academic.

Modern Marketing Man

> Modern marketing man is different. Charisma? He thinks charisma is an Indian restaurant in suburbia. Buccaneering? That's in old black and white movies on TV. Modern marketing man is often dull, studious, careful, safe. He does everything by the book. But although this type doesn't get my adrenaline flowing, I won't condemn him out of hand.
>
> Big business is now exceedingly complex; there is a compelling need for high volume sales, and the degree of competition is so keen that only

the most economical methods of design and production or distribution will maintain profitability.

It is therefore blindingly obvious that marketing – as it is now understood – embraces a whole lot more than simply selling the product. It must identify what product should be made, how, when and where it should be sold, how much it should be sold for, and to whom?[17]

However, the high priest of modern marketing is not the British salesman Harry Turner but the American academic Philip Kotler.

Analytical marketing

Marketing is the analyzing, organizing, planning, and controlling of the firm's customer – impinging resources, policies, and activities with a view to satisfying the needs and wants of chosen customer groups at a profit.[18]

As we can see, the abstract world of resources and customer groups replaces the concrete world of people and things. The science of analytical marketing may be diagramatically represented as shown in Figure 5.1.

By the 1960s rationally based management had come a long way

Figure 5.1 The Marketing Manager's Framework
Source: J. McCarthy, *Basic Marketing: a Managerial Approach.* Irwin, 1968, p. 22.

from its primal origins, substituting analytical cut and thrust for the emotionally based ego drive. And by the 1970s marketing had become the most intellectually demanding of the business disciplines.

Relationships marketing

Kotler's approach to analytical marketing remained undisputed, at least within the mainstream of corporate life, until well into the 1980s. Recently, however, a new marketing orthodoxy – equally rational but more flexible in its approach – has begun to emerge.

As long ago as the late 1960s Bernard Lievegoed came up with the notion of *relations management*.[19] Supplanting marketing and personnel management, this function, as the organization moves out of the differentiated phase, combines both internal and external relations, that is relations with both employees and customers.

The Nordic School of Services, based in Finland and Sweden, has gone a step further, replacing the old concept of analytical marketing with a new *interactive* one.

Developing Long-term Interactive Relationships

Marketing can be seen as relationship management: creating, developing, and maintaining a network in which the firm thrives. Such a network is interactive, that is involving bilateral and multilateral supplier–customer relationships, to produce goods and services. These relationships, finally, are long term, stressing that relationships need time to be built and to be maintained.[20]

The interactive approach to marketing, then, stresses the building of relationships rather than the promotion of products or the satisfaction of individual customer needs. Moreover, these relationships extend beyond customers to suppliers, distributors and investors.

A company can be viewed as a node in an ever-widening pattern of interactions, in some of which it is a direct participant, some of which affect it indirectly and some of which occur independently of it.[21]

The cut and thrust of tightly bound analytical marketing is being supplanted – though not replaced – by the fluidity and interactivity of loosely bound *relationships marketing*. This development parallels the shift from fixed hierarchies to changeable organizational networks, and from the rigidly based financial systems of yesterday to the more flexibly based financial instruments of today. The interactive approach to marketing requires as much intellectual acumen as the analytical approach, even though there is a shift from conceptual sharpness and rigour (hard, vertical thinking) to fluidity and flexibility of perception (soft, lateral thinking). It is in the context of the deepening relationships to which the Nordic School refers that a fundamentally new management domain is called into being.

Marketing: the Developmental Domain

The primal salesman both warms up and warms to his customer, responding to his visible wants. It is a personal involvement.

The rational marketing manager both provides for and interacts with the market-place, generating intangible customer benefits. It is an impersonal involvement.

The developmentally minded marketeer becomes intensively involved with his institutional customers in an interdependent and evolving relationship, responding to their invisible inner needs.

Synergistic marketing

As relationships marketing turns into its synergistic equivalent so the boundaries between supplier and customer are dissolved. The customer, in fact, becomes a coproducer. In Figure 5.2 we can see a range of interactive and synergistic connections between seller and buyers. In some instances, involving joint ventures, the division between the two parties dissolves and in its place there is fusion.

Within these intensive relationships there is both the time and the scope to uncover potential needs that were previously invisible and fulfil them as actual wants. In Mary Parker Follett's terms, the meeting of individualities within an interdependent context leads to creative opportunities for mutual development. This has obviously been the case, for example, in the intense relationship between Marks & Spencer and Psion Computers in the UK: new hardware and software, hitherto undeveloped, has been created to meet a mutual need.[22]

Evolutionary marketing

The harmonious and interdependent relationship that characterizes synergistic marketing is not an isolated phenomenon. It emerges out of an *evolutionary perspective*. Just as a developing individual matures,

Figure 5.2 Interactive and Synergistic Marketing
Source: E. Gummersson, 'The New Marketing', *Long Range Planning*, 20(4), 1987.

or, in Maslow's terms, moves towards self-actualization, so may a marketing relationship.

For example, David Potter of Psion started out by packaging game software, on a one-off basis, distributing each product as widely as possible. His primary, and primal, concern was to sell a lot of product and to generate quick profits. However, once Psion had the time and space to think, it turned its rational attention to matching the knowledge and skills of his growing software house to the evolving needs of the market-place, and Psion's attention turned to more intellectually demanding products.

This process is reminiscent of the *product stretching and proliferation* that Philip Kotler and his colleagues introduce in *The New Competition*, describing one of the strategic competencies of the

Japanese.[23] No sooner had Psion achieved its intellectual upgrading than it began to become involved in an ongoing relationship with Sinclair Research: Psion provided the software for Sinclair's hardware. The relationship was interactive, without being synergistic – it was not a joint venture involving a genuine fusion of people and ideas.

In the Marks & Spencer case, however, such interfusion has taken place (see Figure 5.3). Psion has enabled M & S to solve problems, in the course of its systems development, that neither had foreseen. In the process, as David Potter says, Psion has acted as a 'stalking-horse' for M & S, while M & S has helped Psion to become a more professionally run organization. As their interdependence intensifies,

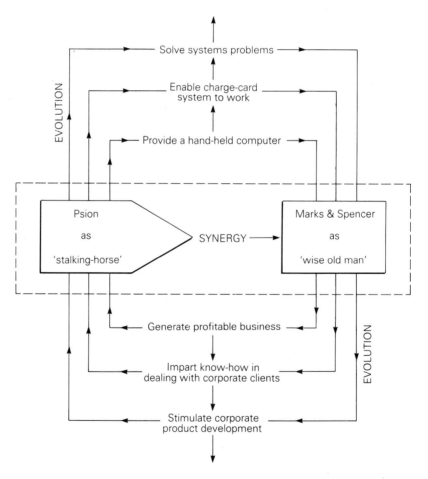

Figure 5.3 Evolutionary and Synergistic Marketing

moreover, mutual benefits will arise of an increasingly invisible, extensive and long-term nature.

Operations

Production and operations management is the poor relation of the business functions in the US and the UK, though not in Japan and West Germany. On the one hand it is considered too close to engineering to be a business discipline in its own right; on the other, it has become too mathematical to be accessible to the average manager or business student. However, the emergence of communications technology in the past ten years has given operations management, together with management services (computers and data-processing), a new lease of life.

Operations Management: the Primal Domain

Homo faber

Man is a technological animal, thus he is sometimes called *homo faber*, man the maker. Other animals have technologies (beavers construct dams and birds build nests), but only for man are tools a central factor in his existence; only man has evolved culturally to the point where 'he consciously can alter radically his physical environment and his own biological make up'.[24]

One of the reasons that Britain was the first country to undergo an industrial revolution was its innate (primal) affinity with technology. Such a primal drive, to tinker with physical things and physically to fashion one's environment, is more of an innate than an acquired skill. However, skills of craftmanship, with wood or metal, textiles or plastic, can indeed be acquired. Nevertheless, conventionally they lie outside the business and management curriculum.

Product quality

Craftsmanship
West Germany has a particularly strong reputation for craftsmanship, which is reinforced by its solidly based apprenticeship schemes. Production and engineering skill is acquired on the job, backed up by personal example. It is the immediate and tangible experience at this

primal level, reinforced by personal supervision, that counts. Zen Buddhist traditions have had a similar affect on the working population of Japan, inculcating a desire for perfection that has been largely absent in the US and the UK in recent years.

People – Technology

Quality, or its absence, doesn't reside in either the subject or the object. The real ugliness lies in the relationship between the people who produce the technology and the things they produce, which results in a similar relationship between the people who use the technology and the things they use.[25]

Quality circles

The major vehicle in Japan for maintaining quality production has been the *quality circle*. Interestingly, rationally based techniques for quality control were imported from the US after the war, and, combined with primarily Japanese features, were woven into a unique form. Kagu Ishikawa, a Japanese production engineer who has written a book on the subject, defines the quality circle as

a small group, performing quality control activities, voluntarily within the same workshop, carrying on continuously as part of a company-wide program, focussing on mutual development, with all members participating.[26]

The basic ideas behind quality control, Ishikawa says, involve:

- contributing to the improvement of the enterprise;
- building up a worth-living-in, happy and bright workshop;
- exercising human capacities fully.

Quality management

Ishakawa has an interesting way of looking at management as a whole, which in many respects offers a primal approach to operations management.[27] It contains three elements:

People The first concern of management is the happiness of the people who are connected with it. If the people – employees, subcontractors, consumers – do not feel happy, and cannot be made happy, the company does not deserve to exist.

Quality Defective products will not only inconvenience consumers but will also hinder sales. If a company makes too many products that cannot be sold, it will waste raw materials and energy. This waste will be a loss for society. A company must always supply products with the qualities the consumer demands.

Price, cost and profit The consumer's main demand is for a just quality at a just price. No matter how inexpensive a product, if its quality is poor no one will buy it.

Operations Management: the Rational Domain

Operating systems

Although Ishikawa has begun to move into the rational domain, once we fully make the transition the tone changes completely. As probably the best-known professor of operations management in the UK, Ray Wild, puts it: 'An operating system is a configuration of resources combined for the provision of goods or services.'[28]

The Nature of Operating Systems

Bus and taxi services, motels and dentists, tailors and mines, fire services and refuse removers, retail organizations, hospitals and building contractors are all operating systems. They all, in effect, convert inputs in order to provide outputs that are required by a customer.

Physical inputs will normally predominate, hence: operating systems convert, using physical resources, to create outputs, the function of which is to satisfy consumer wants, that is to provide some utility for the customer.[29]

The bulk of new operations management text will contain mathematical and statistical techniques for such functions as:

> facilities location,
> materials handling,
> work study and management,
> activity and project scheduling,
> inventory control.

However, there is a rationally based and qualitative logic that underlies it all. This can be divided between overall *function* and *structure*.

The functions of operating systems
Four principal functions can be identified:

- *Manufacture*, whereby something is physically created. *Process* or *mass production* involves the continuous manufacture of a commodity in bulk. *Batch production* occurs where the number of discrete items to be manufactured is insufficient to enable mass production to be used. *Jobbing manufacture* is intermittent.
- *Transport*, by which the location of someone or something is physically moved, within or outside the organization.
- *Supply*, by which the ownership or possession of an item is physically changed.
- *Service*, whereby (as at a hospital, launderette, or welfare department) something or someone is treated or accommodated.

The structure of operating systems
The nature of the operations manager's job will to some extent depend on the nature of the system he is managing. However, in a rational context all such systems may be seen to comprise:

inputs,
processes,
outputs.

This basic analytical model (Figure 5.4) underlies the 'hard', rational approach to operations management. In the last few years, in the wake of what Bill Abernathy at Harvard called an 'Industrial Renaissance' in the US, a softer approach has emerged.

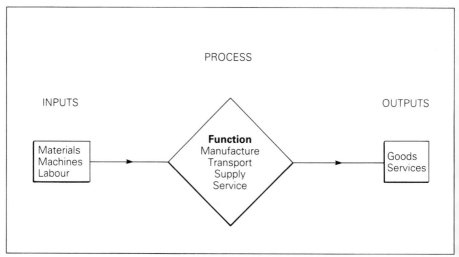

Figure 5.4 A Simple Operations System

The technology of learning

Abernathy, and his production-minded colleagues at the Harvard Business School, have called for the kind of renaissance in manufacturing technology that effectively *de-matures* such large and mature companies as General Motors and General Electric. With a different view of maturity from the one adopted in this text, Abernathy calls for technology-based revitalization of large-scale manufacturing enterprise. In the process he exposes the limitations of the conventional analytical approach to operations management.

The Possibilities of De-maturity

Our task today is to incorporate particular new technologies and heightened product variety into high volume manufacturing systems and to do so without the luxury of long lead times.

What is therefore needed is a view of production as an enterprise of unlimited potential, an enterprise in which current arrangements [as those set out above by Wild] are but the starting point for continuous organizational learning. No omniscient engineer ever handed down a design for product or production that could not stand improvement.

We do not mean, of course, that learning should proceed while schedules and shipping deadlines get ignored; competent management requires simultaneous attention to both current tasks and future possibilities. What gets lost in the shuffle, however, is the intimate connection between the two.

Only when grafted on to a production system dedicated to ongoing learning and communication, only when used in tandem with a skilled and responsible workforce, can new technologies realize their potential as competitive weapons. Only when such a workforce is truly engaged in the enterprise, and encouraged to learn and excel, can a company hope to introduce competitively successful new products in a timely fashion.[30]

The 'Industrial Renaissance' takes the US, if not other nations, a long way from the world of machines, materials and labour towards one where it is *human capital*[31] mediated through information technology that will make the difference between success and failure. Koji Kobayashi, Chairman of the Japanese semiconductor company NEC, makes a similiar point.[32]

In order to respond to the shift from mass orientation towards product diversity and individuality, and to meet a wider variety of customer needs, Kobayashi believes that very large amounts of information will need to be generated. The transfer and processing of the information will be done at the plant. And if sudden changes in the market occur it will be necessary rapidly to adjust the design and manufacture of products accordingly. Computer and communications technology has already begun to provide the basis for such manufacturing, and as the technology evolves the sophistication of manufacturing will grow.

The argument is taken a step further, into the developmental domain, by two technologists from Berkeley, California, S. Cohen and J. Zysman.

Economies of Scope

A new vocabulary has emerged. Programmable automation permits an automated machine to perform a range of tasks. This permits a single range of equipment to produce a variety of components or to assemble a variety of products, creating flexibility. Economies of scope stand alongside economies of scale.[33]

Operations Management: the Developmental Domain

Evolutionary operations

In a recent and illuminating book Cohen and Zysman argue that 'manufacturing matters' in a way that simplistic arguments about post-industrial societies fail to reveal. For them, services are not a substitute for, or successor to, manufacturing. One needs the other. The process of development is not one of sectoral succession but one of increased sectoral interdependence, driven by an ever more extended and complex division of labour.

Manufacturing, in days gone by, was conducted by individual craftsmen, or by small groups of workers engaged in cottage industries. This was the era of primal production. For the last hundred years, though, in industrialized countries, mass production has taken over as the rationally dominant mode. It is only recently, with the advent of flexible manufacturing systems facilitated by the microprocessor revolution, that this stable model is being overturned.

Interdependent operations

As manufacturing enters the developmental domain so the acknowledged interdependence between manufacturing and services, as well as between one manufacturing sector and another, becomes commonplace. In fact technological innovation depends on a series of subtle and complex interconnections. Knowledge of automobile or aeroplane manufacturing, for example, promotes innovation in machine tools.

The more advanced or modern the production process, the longer and more complicated the chains of linkages.

> A primitive farmer has his wife scratch the ground with a stick. He also has a very low productivity. A modern American farmer is really the pivot man in a long, elaborate chain of specialists. Everything is linked to everything else, in a way that is similar to – but surely different from – the Hare Krishna view that everything is one.[34]

It is interesting to find that this kind of industrial and technological perspective was shared, at least in part, by Henry Ford. The fact that Ford's reputation as a technological innovator was marred by his despotic, and sometimes even bigoted, character should not deter us from appreciating his unique philosophy of industry.

At least part of the man – Henry Ford was a hugely paradoxical character – was steeped in a metaphysical world that underpinned his technological breakthroughs.

> The function of the machine is to liberate man from brute burdens, and release his energies to the building of his intellectual and spiritual powers for conquests in the field of thought and higher action. The machine is the symbol of man's mastery of his environment.[35]

For Henry Ford, then, who created the automobile industry as we know it today, industrial advancement was not some depersonalized, technocratic process, but the realization of an individual's vision.

Technological Vision

> Every advancement begins in a small way and with the individual. The mass can be no better than the sum of the individuals. Advancement begins with the man himself, when he advances from half interest to strength of purpose; when he advances from hesitancy to decisive directness; when he advances from an immaturity to a maturity of judgement; when he advances from apprenticeship to mastery; when he advances from a mere dilettante at labor to a worker who finds a genuine joy in work, why then the world advances.
>
> As far as individual, personal advantage is concerned, vast accumulations of money mean nothing. But if one has visions of service, if one has vast

plans which no ordinary resources would possibly realize, if one has a life ambition to make the industrial desert bloom like the rose, and the work-a-day life suddenly blossom into fresh and enthusiastic motives of higher character and efficiency, then one sees in large sums of money what the farmer sees in his seed corn – the beginning of new and richer harvests whose benefits can no more be contained than the sun's rays.[36]

So, as operations management, like the financial and marketing functions, evolve they become less concerned with the immediate and primal and more with the remote and metaphysical. The same applies to human resources.

Human Resources

Elements of the human resource function first began to appear in Europe and the US at the turn of the century, in reaction to the harsh behaviour of autocratic businessmen like Henry Ford! It was not until the 1940s and 1950s, though, that like most of the business disciplines it began to acquire fuller shape and form. In fact, owing to its peculiar origins – a reaction against unscrupulous entrepreneurial behaviour – *personnel management* missed out on its primal origins. It has been suffering ever since, relative to the other major functions, from a lack of power and influence. It is only in the 1980s, swept along by the powerfully primal wave, that a more instinctive (less intellectual) approach to managing people has been widely documented and disseminated.

Human Resources: the Primal Domain

In 1964 Orville Collins and his fellow sociologists at the University of Michigan concluded that entrepreneurship involves, most essentially, 'the bringing together of people into new and profitable combinations'. Although the book they wrote, *Enterprising Man*, was a classic in its time, it completely bypassed the human resource establishment.[37]

It was not until the redoubtable Peters and Waterman appeared on the primal scene, almost twenty years later, that the penny began to drop.[38] *Business is people*, either in the shape of employees or as customers and suppliers. That was the primal conclusion. There was both a tough and a tender approach to this argument.

Winning friends and influencing people

The tough, 'macho' approach to influencing people was introduced to us many years ago by the American doyen of public speaking, Dale Carnegie. Although his book *How to Win Friends and Influence People*[39] is not normally incorporated into a management curriculum, it is a classic in its own right.

More recently the active sports promoter Mark McCormack has written the definitive, primal antidote to the rationally based management of human resources, *What they Don't Teach you at Harvard Business School*. For McCormack, in truly primal vein, the management of people, as insiders or as outsiders, involves the same basic approach:

> Whether I'm selling or buying; whether I'm hiring or being hired; whether I'm negotiating a contract or responding to someone else's demands, I want to know where the other person is coming from. I want to know the other person's real self.[40]

Of course McCormack is merely putting into words what thousands of entrepreneurs around the globe may have been thinking for centuries. However, not only has he taken the trouble to articulate his thoughts so that they are now codified knowledge, but his focus on the self gives it a particular Western and Northern flavour. It is also important to point out that the tough and primally oriented McCormack is naturally self-interested. He is neither philanthropic nor paternalistic. He is a businessman who knows that business is people. He is also a man.

P&L is for people and love

It is interesting to note that business entrepreneurs have traditionally been viewed as men, and thus in some cases paternalistic. Yet Mary Kay in America has developed a $300 million cosmetics company in thoroughly maternal fashion.

People and Love

> No matter how much profit a company makes, if it doesn't enrich the lives of its people it will have failed.
>
> To me P&L doesn't only mean profit and loss – it also means people and love.

When all our people come to understand one another, a familylike atmosphere remains intact and the customer is better served.

The most important justification for being in business is to fulfill a need.[41]

For Mary Kay, who had no need of a personnel manager, idealism and realism go hand in hand. For the genuine animator the source and destination of business is people – both within the company and out in the market-place. For her it is the tender side of people management that takes hold.

Ironically many human resource managers are not innately 'people people'. The reason is that they are cut off from their primal selves. Having acknowledged their heritage, via such influential practitioners as Mark McCormack and Mary Kay, they are in a more powerful position to move on to the rational domain.

Human Resources: the Rational Domain

As businesses grew in size and scope during the early part of the 20th century, entrepreneurs or even animators were no longer able to cope on their own. While some fell by the wayside others were astute enough to take 'scientific' advice. The evolution of a rationally based personnel function can be traced historically. It develops similarly with the growth and evolution of an individual firm.

Again, the development of a rational approach to human resource management can be divided into *harder* and *softer* orientations, respectively *analytical* and *behavioural*. The first we term *human resource management* and the second *management of change*.

Human resource management

Bureaucracy
In the early days of management's evolution, attempts to rationalize production and organization were tentative and *ad hoc*. However, in the first decades of the 20th century businessmen came under the influence of engineers. *Social engineers* sought to substitute rational, 'scientific' management for the highly personalized, idiosyncratic style of the owner/manager.

Some of the earliest efforts at substituting rational procedures for intuition and family traditions simply involved better record-keeping, for which purpose many personnel departments were first established.

Personnel records tracked such information as when the employee was hired, educational background and succession of jobs, and provided a record of time and production for payrolls. These were relatively routine clerical tasks.

The concern with methods was one precursor of personnel's current concern with training. It also represented an irrevocable and powerful drive towards increasing specialization.

Industrial psychology

In the last years of the 1920s *rationalization* and *efficiency* were the watchwords. The need to rationalize production arose from the new kinds of problem created by competition and demand, and from inventions in machinery and techniques.

Many jobs were broken down. In order to rationalize manufacture, combines were formed and amalgamations took place. Planning and efficiency in all aspects of a business became essential. Rationalization brought complexity with it. Because of the requirements of efficiency and the demands of complexity, selection assumed increasing importance during the 1920s.

As a result of government experience of classifying recruits during World War I, psychologists were brought into industry to help pick out the most able workers. They developed testing techniques for assessing individual differences, and personnel managers began concentrating on selection methods.

Industrial relations

The influence of personnel management expanded during the 1930s and 1940s. With their title changed to 'Industrial Relations', many personnel departments began to take charge of hiring, firing, wage determination, handling union grievances and deciding who should be transferred and promoted.

The personnel department suddenly gained so much power, partly because of management's widespread recognition of the importance of the human element, but chiefly because of the threat of unionism. Personnel managers were now called upon to be negotiators, drawing on tough, primal qualities of stamina and risk-taking. Unfortunately, though, the industrial relations manager's foe was not the external competition but the internal labour force.

Professionalization

By the end of World War II the functions of a personnel department could be clearly differentiated as employment, wages, joint consultation, health and safety, and education and training. By 1939 the range of personnel activities was fairly clearly perceived by the boards of larger, more highly organized companies, but the specialist sectors of the work were not always well coordinated.

Nevertheless, all this resulted in a much fuller functioning of human resource management. Within a few years half a dozen of its component parts were distinguished, each with its own theory forming behind it and its own skills becoming defined. Recruitment, training, performance appraisal, industrial relations and personnel administration each became subdisciplines in their own right. As a profession *human resource management* was coming of age.

The management of change

Human relations

By the 1950s and 1960s human resource management was seen to be relevant to the whole work situation, to the interrelationship between the work to be done and the individuals and groups carrying it out, and to the environment in which the whole activity took place.

A new phase of professionalism began in the mid-1950s, with specialists developing in depth certain elements of personnel management and with the help of the social sciences, identifying new approaches. Of course, the application of sociology, as well as psychology, to the management of organizations, had been initiated by Mary Parker Follett,[42] Elton Mayo[43] and Chester Barnard[44] in the US in the 1920s and 1930s.

Towards organizational development: the planning of change

The origins of what came to be called *organizational development* lie in the 1950s, when John Manning, the director of the UK Institute of Personnel Management, was beginning to identify two distinct aspects of the personnel function. At a European conference on personnel management in 1956 he said:

> On the one hand there are processes of analysing the existing conditions and resources in the light of the requirements of the enterprise, of diagnosing and defining its problems, of prescribing and executing the

appropriate action to bring about change. This may be regarded as a predominantly creative and dynamic aspect.

On the other hand there are the routine administrative duties involved in the execution of established policy, the solution of minor problems as they occur, the maintenance of healthy relationships, and the provision of personnel services.[45]

As Warren Bennis said in the 1960s:

> Bureaucracy was a monumental discovery for harnessing muscle power via guilt and instinctual renunciation. In today's world it is a prosthetic device, no longer useful. For we now require organic/adaptive systems, as structures of freedom, to permit the expression of play and imagination and to exploit the new pleasure of work.[46]

Some large companies, like Texas Instruments in the US and ICI in the UK, tried to introduce Bennis's ideas in the 1960s and 1970s. However, those early attempts were often only half-hearted, partly because organization development had not yet come of age.

In fact during the 1970s some very interesting developmental work was going on in the Netherlands led by Bernard Lievegoed, whose book *The Developing Organization*[47] has influenced many people, including myself. For Lievegoed has a much more thorough understanding of development than his better-known American counterparts.

Human Resources: the Developmental Domain

We glibly talk about personal, organization or business development and yet few of us are familiar with the intrinsic nature of it. Development is:

> qualitative,
> discontinuous,
> irreversible,
> interspersed with evolutionary crises,
> dynamically balanced.

A good human resource manager and organization developer needs to be able consciously to work within this evolutionary framework. Such an approach leads in two directions:

> *vertically* towards *manager self-development*
> *horizontally* towards *organizational harmony.*

Manager self-development

The subject of manager self-development has become very popular in personnel circles. In most cases, however, no more than lip service is paid to it. The idea that a manager should take responsibility for his own learning is built in, but no conscious path of development is established. However, an evolutionary perspective was built into Abraham Maslow's work some twenty years ago, when he traced a personal and managerial path towards *self-actualization* through the fulfilment of a hierarchy of needs.[48] More recently Daniel Levinson, in *The Seasons of Man's Life*, has indicated that we evolve through alternating *structure-building* and *structure-changing phases*, during our lifespan.[49]

In my own work *Intrapreneurship* I have related seven kinds of individuality to the four structure-building phases:

> youth,
> adulthood,
> mid-life,
> maturity.[50]

Each intrapreneur or individual manager develops in a unique way but passes through similar phases and transitions.

Organizational harmony

A developing organization not only consciously enables the individuals within it to evolve, but also evolves itself, as a whole. *Vertical development*, whereby one stage is interwoven with the next over time, is accompanied by *horizontal development*, whereby one part of the organization is interwoven with the next across space.

In fact, during such integration the protective membranes isolating one function or business from another, are broken down and reformed into open filters. An exchange of energy between personnel and marketing, or between human resources and information technology, thus becomes possible. Each becomes part of a continually re-emerging whole.

This horizontal developmental perspective has been made to work most successfully in Japan. The ability of the Japanese to interweave individual and group, group and organization, and public and private enterprise, as well as to interrelate large companies and small ones, banks and manufacturers, and industrial and trading companies, is all part of the same harmonious phenomenon.

Japanese Harmony

One's sense of self is enhanced by being selected to join a group, and the standing of that group is enhanced by its ability to attract individuals of quality and achievement.

Once taken in, however, powerful sanctions – of which the threat of ostracism is only the most severe – are brought to bear on the individual, who is expected to pursue personal interests only to the extent that the other members of the group agree that such a course does not contravene principles of harmony and effectiveness.[51]

The management of human resources outside Japan has yet to reach a point where it truly harmonizes with the other disciplines. To that extent the rational domain, recently counterbalanced by the primal one, eclipses the developmental domain – notwithstanding claims that might indicate otherwise. Indeed despite the fact that organization development has never really had its day, *organizational transformation* has now arrived on the American scene.

Conclusion

Functional Evolution

Financial, marketing, operations and human resource management each occupy all of the management domains, potentially if not actually. To the extent that the potential has not yet been realized, management in general and developmental management in particular have not yet fully asserted themselves commercially, organizationally and (specifically here) functionally.

Functional Reconstruction

However, as we have seen from this chapter, the building blocks are available for a thorough reconstruction of the business functions, though such a reconstruction can come about only through processes of personal and cultural as well as business and managerial reorientation. We need to rediscover and recombine the *hard* and *soft* within ourselves, the *youthful* and *mature* within our businesses, and *East* and *West, North* and *South* within our cultures. I can only hope that, through the developmental principles set out in this book, a start has been made for the business functions in general, and for the management of organizations in particular.

The Wider Environment

Now I want to move out from inside the organization and its business functions to the wider environment in which it operates. The evolution of individual business functions and of whole organizations can also be applied to entire societies. I shall focus first on Europe, with a view to 1992, and then on all four quarters of the globe.

Notes

1 N. Hill, *Think and Grow Rich.* Fawcett, 1960.
2 J. Gillies, *Moneylove.* Warner Books, 1978, p. 23.
3 M. Kay, *Mary Kay.* Harper & Row, 1987, p. 8.
4 R. L. Wing, *The Art of Strategy.* Aquarian Press, 1988.
5 W. Bigg, H. Wilson and A. Langton, *Bookkeeping and Accounts.* London: HFC, 1963, p. 19.
6 W. Wriston, quoted in A. Hamilton, *The Financial Revolution.* Viking, 1986, p. 31.
7 Hamilton, *The Financial Revolution*, pp. 15–54.
8 C. Budd, *Prelude in Economics.* Published by the author, 1979.
9 M. Parker Follett, *The New State.* Peter Smith, 1926; 2nd edn, 1965, p. 114.
10 K. Ohmae, *Triad Power.* Macmillan, 1985.
11 R. Lessem, 'Accounting for an Enterprise's Wellbeing', *Omega*, 2(1), 1974.
12 J. Dauman and J. Hargreaves, *Business Survival and Social Change.* Associated Business Programmes, 1975, part 4.
13 P. Drucker, *Management: Tasks, Responsibilities and Practices.* Heinemann, 1979.
14 J. Chaput, *Living is Selling.* Habitex Books, 1975.
15 H. Turner, *The Gentle Art of Salesmanship.* Fontana, 1985, p. 137.
16 H. Goldman, *How to Win Customers.* Pan, 1971, p. 173.
17 Turner, *The Gentle Art of Salesmanship*, p. 140.
18 P. Kotler, *Marketing Management: Analysis, Planning, and Control.* Prentice Hall, 1965; 2nd edn, 1968.
19 B. Lievegoed, *Organisaties in ontwikkeling.* Lemniscaat, 1969. Eng. trans. as *The Developing Organization.* Tavistock, 1973; new edn, Basil Blackwell, 1990.
20 E. Gummersson, 'The New Marketing', *Long Range Planning*, 20(4), 1987, p. 11.

21 D. Ford, H. Wakaanan and D. Johnson, 'How do Companies Interact?', *Industrial Marketing and Purchasing*, 1(1), 1986.
22 Discussed in detail in R. Lessem, *Managing Cultural Change*. Gower, 1989.
23 P. Kotler, *et al.*, *The New Competition*. Prentice Hall, 1985.
24 V. Ferkis, *Technological Man*. Heinemann, 1969, p. 27.
25 R. Pirsig, *Zen and the Art of Motorcycle Maintenance*. Corgi, 1976, p. 284.
26 K. Ishikawa, *What is Total Quality Control?*. Prentice Hall, 1985, pp. 139–40.
27 Ishikawa, *What is Total Quality Control?*, pp. 99–100.
28 R. Wild, *Essentials of Production and Operations Management*. Holt Business Texts, 1980, p. 3.
29 Wild, *Essentials of Production and Operations Management*, p. 3.
30 W. Abernathy, K. Clark and A. Kantrow, *Industrial Renaissance*. Basic Books, 1983, p. 125.
31 R. Reich, *The Next American Frontier*. Penguin, 1984.
32 K. Kobayashi, quoted in S. Cohen and J. Zysman, *Manufacturing Matters*. Basic Books, 1987, p. 179.
33 Cohen and Zysman, *Manufacturing Matters*, p. 156.
34 Cohen and Zysman, *Manufacturing Matters*, p. 14.
35 H. Ford, *My Philosophy of Industry*. Harrap, 1929, p. 167.
36 H. Ford, *My Life and Work*. Heinemann, 1924, Doubleday, 1922, pp. 277–9.
37 O. Collins, D. Moore and T. Unwalla, *Enterprising Man*. University of Michigan Press, 1964.
38 T. Peters and R. Waterman, *In Search of Excellence*. Harper & Row, 1982.
39 D. Carnegie, *How to Win Friends and Influence People*. 1962.
40 M. McCormack, *What they Don't Teach you at Harvard Business School*. Collins, 1984, p. 15.
41 M. Kay, *On Managing People*. Pan, 1985.
42 Parker Follett, *The New State*, p. 186.
43 E. Mayo, *The Human Problems of an Industrial Civilisation*. Macmillan, 1953.
44 C. Barnard, *The Functions of the Executive*. Harvard University Press, 1938.
45 John Manning, unpublished paper, 1956.
46 W. Bennis, *Changing Organizations*. McGraw Hill, 1966.
47 Lievegocd, *The Developing Organization*, see n. 19.
48 A. Maslow, *Motivation and Personality*. Harper & Row, 1964.
49 D. Levinson, *The Seasons of Man's Life*. Knopf, 1978.
50 R. Lessem, *Intrapreneurship*. Wildwood House, 1988.
51 R. Smith, *Japanese Society*. Cambridge University Press, 1983, p. 90.

Section C

The Developing Business Environment

6

Europe 1992

Introduction

1992: the Conventional Economic Wisdom

Europe, if not also the US and Japan, is buzzing with bewilderment and excitement over '1992'. The prospect of a *unified market* or a *United States of Europe* has set businesses and governments alike into frenetic motion. What is the excitement all about?

The Prize Within the Grasp

For all the complexities, the essential mechanism is simple. The starting point for the whole process of economic gain is the removal of non-tariff barriers. They will fall into three broad types:

- *Physical barriers* like intra-EC border stoppages, customs controls and associated paperwork.
- *Technical barriers* for example, meeting divergent national product standards, technical regulations and conflicting business laws; entering nationally protected public procurement markets.
- *Fiscal barriers* especially differing rates of VAT and excise duties.

The release of these constraints will trigger a supply-side shock to the Community as a whole. The name of this shock is 'European market integration'. Costs will come down. Prices will follow as business, under the pressure of new rivals on previously protected markets, is forced to develop fresh responses to a novel and changing situation.

The expectation may be that a dynamic European market, trading with the world of revamped competitivity, will provide a much needed shot in the arm for other markets and economies in less buoyant shape.[1]

Paolo Ceccini, who chaired the recent Europe-wide study on the impact of breaking down non-tariff barriers, presents all the conventional economic arguments for integration: the value of economies of scale and the virtues of increased competition feature strongly in his case. Ceccini's rationale may be represented diagramatically as shown in Figure 6.1.

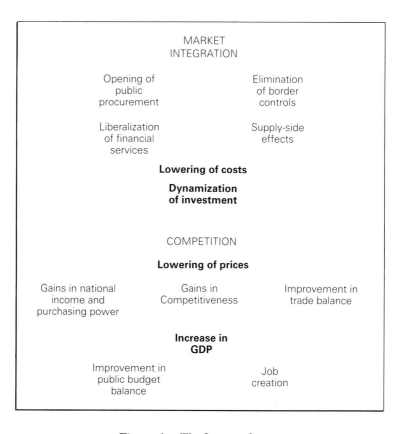

Figure 6.1 The Impact of 1992

Unfortunately too many people, like Ceccini, seem to be missing the real point. They are looking back instead of looking forward. They are harking back to the US, instead of seeking a distinctly European way forward.

Incontestably, the vision of a great European internal market grew out of admiration for the American version. . . . Yet the ingredients of America's internal market are seldom analysed to see what messages they hold for Europe.[2]

Looking Back, looking Forward

The British journal *The Economist* is much less bullish than Ceccini about the immediately beneficial effects of 1992. There is no Big Bang in prospect they say. Borders will continue to reinforce Europe's natural differences of language, taste and habit. As a result *The Economist* places more store by evolving trans-European organizational forms than by conventional economic logic. The magazine cites the case of two little-known companies to support the argument.

Trans-European Collaboration

B. V. Safari is a Dutch private company making dried food for livestock and pets. Continentale de Conserves is a French private company that makes up market tinned foods and petfoods. Both companies are the same size with annual sales of something over FFr 300m ($50m).

Their 1992 plan has a nice symmetry to it:

- Each will take a stake of about one third in the other.
- Each will have the exclusive right to market its own products, and the products of the other, in its own country.
- They will jointly own a marketing subsidiary which will sell the products of both across the rest of the European Community.
- They will jointly run a Research and Development Unit.

Europe must be full of companies that have a fine brand position at home and that want to 'Europeanize' themselves rapidly without losing their independence. For such enterprises, a 'twinning' formula of this sort would seem to have much going for it.[3]

The Economist is on the right track, empirically speaking, but conceptually it has not caught up with the times. To catch up with our times we need, paradoxically, to go back into European history. The evolutionary thread we need to follow is the one that links unity and diversity over economic, social and political time.

Unity and Diversity

The Developing Organism

As a company, or a country for that matter, grows and develops, the alternating currents of *unity* and *diversity* assume different proportions.

At a first, *parochial stage* of economic and political development –
Europe in the 17th and 18th centuries – diversity is characterized by
loosely independent and *maverick characters*, while unity is reflected in
visibly and *communally shared values*. And *competitive attitudes* rule the
individual and organizational roost.

At a second, *national stage* of development – Europe in the 18th and
19th centuries – diversity is reflected in individual and institutional
specialization, and unity in corresponding forms of *integration*. Political
and economic coordination therefore takes pride of policy-making
place.

As we can see, then, current thinking about Europe 1992 is marked
by stage one and stage two attitudes, harking back a few centuries.
For the more evolved and third, *transnational stage* of development –
Europe in the 20th and 21st centuries – diversity is characterized by
individual learning and *self-development*, and unity by *economic and social
synergy*.

Each stage, therefore, acquires added degrees of complexity, by
way of breadth and depth. We now need to investigate how this state
of affairs has emerged in Europe.

Stages of Development

European civilization has developed over 2500 years, but its all-
pervasive economic and political advance has been most rapid over
the past 200 to 300. Over that period there have been innumerable
crises and transitions, but we shall pick up the story in relatively
recent times in France. We can then trace the development of Europe
from its recent *parochial origins* to its present *international orientation*.

The greatest political crisis of all, in recent times, was occasioned
by the French Revolution and the rise of Napoleon, which ultimately
concerned the whole of Europe. By the 1780s France had attained its
modern frontiers, but it did not altogether resemble a modern state.
Although it was a monarchy, it is difficult to say where the powers of
the king either began or ended.

Stage One: Parochial

Some French provinces retained a special kind of independence in
the shape of provincial estates, which were assemblies representing

the privileges of the local aristocrats. Local laws and loyalties still existed, as did local variations in the systems of weights and measures. So France looked more like a loose, patchwork assembly of provinces and classes than a uniformly organized state.

Similarly at the beginning of the Napoleonic Wars there was no unified German nation and the Germanic peoples thought chiefly of the interests of the state in which they lived. Many were frightened of Prussia and were glad when Napoleon defeated the Prussian army. There were German writers who welcomed the Revolution and Napoleon, and there were German governments who disapproved of both, but neither had any thought of forming a unified Germany.

Before 1815 Europe was too diversified and fragmented, and the changes within it too uneven, to provide many common denominators other than those of war and peace. But after 1815 the movement of money, goods, labour and technology was in conflict with local boundaries and frontiers.

Stage Two: National

Crisis and transition

1792–1815 was a period of upheaval for Europe. Great powers were defeated, ancient royal families overthrown, frontiers removed. The Revolution claimed to represent a new conduct of human affairs. Questions were no longer to be regulated by the personal desires of kings or the force of arms. The 19th century was undoubtedly a period of *nationalism*: people began to express themselves in a national way, as Frenchmen, Germans or Italians.

In 1871 there occurred an important development: Germany, which had consisted of a number of sovereign states, was united in the German Empire. The British statesman Disraeli claimed that this change had more far-reaching implications even than the French Revolution. A new element had entered Europe: a powerful state with a fast-growing, successful economy, accompanied by political malaise and uncertainty.

The Era of Expansion

By the end of the nineteenth century Europe had distinguished itself in three ways. There was trade, there were towns, there was travel. The trader, the banker and disburser of goods had gradually become more important than the king, the priest or the seigneur. The town had become the norm and centre of European life. Travel meant the exploration of the world, the conquest of the rest of the world and the attempt to impose European civilization and culture upon it.[4]

The national state, then, became the master institution of the modern world; it played a vital part in transforming the economy of western Europe and in revolutionizing the role of Europe in the world. There grew up national banking systems, national markets, even a national drive to succeed. National rivalries increased the tempo of change.

National self-determination

In 19th-century Europe nationalism emerged as a movement to provide people with democratic self-government, free from internal disunion and external oppression. Far from having an aggressive or hostile attitude, the 19th-century Italian nationalist and patriot Guiseppe Mazzini wanted to free his people from the rule of despotic kings and privileged classes. He wanted to create a national state that would live in harmony and fraternity with other countries, believing that every country, with its own special qualities, had a mission to fulfil towards humanity. His intentions, however, were never realized.

The very fact that nations fought each other meant an acceleration of technological innovations as each strove to have weapons that were better than the others'. It meant too that as each state had to raise money to pay for war, taxation systems became more sophisticated. And, as the easiest way to raise money is with the consent of the governed, gradually citizens began to gain political rights.

The national community thus developed its own sense of kinship, replacing tribalism, feudalism, the pre-eminence of the Church and the dominance of the absolutist ruler. From being responsible for the defence of the territory against invasions, the State became the authority that resolved internal conflicts and imposed order; and it developed into an organization that recorded tradition and provided education, information and welfare.

Nationalistic fervour

Thus the nation state, as Hoggart and Johnson recognize, has been a huge success. Men have gone to their deaths in its name. People have made immense sacrifices because they are patriotic and believe in their national flag, their national ritual and rhetoric. National heritage has been enshrined in museums, commemorative dates and ceremonies. Educated and sophisticated people will weep with joy if their national team wins a sporting event. However, particularly in recent years, the success and reputation of the nation state has become tarnished.

Firstly the frontiers of the state's territories and the boundaries of a homogeneous ethnic community hardly ever coincide. This is highlighted by unrest in the Soviet Union, Great Britain, Belgium and Spain, for example. Outside Europe, the frontiers established by the former colonial powers seem to have been drawn by a ruler in straight, meaningless lines, so that they do not contain people of a common culture.

Secondly, with the powerful discipline and conformity which the modern nation state has been able to impose, and with the destructive power of weapons in the 20th century, warfare has twice brought Europe to the edge of destruction. Therefore, in 1945, it was felt that some alternative to the nation state had to be found.

Thirdly, and perhaps most important of all, it became apparent that the nation state could not remain the master institution in economic terms. There was a new economic universe, in the context of which national markets were pitifully inadequate.

The Distorted Shape of Nationalism

The nationalism which was to mean co-operation with other nations in a common service to the highest aims of human civilisation has come to mean an aggressive attitude . . . a latent hostility prepared to break out into open warfare against neighbouring countries. This is the tragically distorted shape of nationalism which now prevails, most vigorously and conspicuously no doubt in the totalitarian countries, but quite definitely, even if less obtrusively, in so-called democratic lands.

But there is hope. On the surface the nationalist political myth still rules, but when we penetrate to the economic realities developed beneath, the myth is seen to be meaningless. There is no longer any possibility of isolation in the world and the isolationist nation does not belong to our time.[5]

Stage Three: Transnational

The individual, the community and the nation are all changing their relationships and are forming new patterns. The most dramatic such new pattern is that of the European Economic Community.

The unification of Europe has been advocated by philosophers and statesmen for centuries. The Quaker William Penn, founder of Pennsylvania, called for the establishment of a European parliament as early as 1650. In 1929 the idea was first mooted of a European Federal Union. It was vigorously pursued by the French foreign minister of the time, but opposed by nearly every other European nation, each of which was too heavily involved with its own national interests.

The League of Nations, the Permanent Court of International Justice and the International Labour Office were formed after 1918, and the United Nations and its fellow organizations after 1945. Membership of these national bodies would, it was thought, lessen the self-assertiveness of the states and promote cooperation between them.

In May 1950 the French foreign minister, Robert Schuman, again put forward an idea for combining national interests. This time he proposed uniting French and German iron and steel production under a common authority. Schuman's motives in seeking to form economic alliances of this kind were ultimately to prevent the outbreak of another war and to merge the civilizations and cultural values of Europe.

The pragmatists saw Europe becoming the world's greatest trading power, the area where capitalism could thrive and make money for its followers. Within each national state there were many, probably a majority, who saw nothing visionary or idealistic in the Community, only a means of institutionalizing wealth. The idealists, though, suggested a revival of the Europe of Charlemagne, a Europe that would be Christian, anti-communist, cultured, peaceful, humane.

The European Economic Community came into existence on 1 January 1958, with France, Germany, Italy, the Netherlands, Belgium and Luxembourg as founder members. Its institutions soon included the European Parliament, the Council of Ministers, the Central Commission and the Court of Justice, as well as a number of agencies concerned with transport, investment, social funding and labour.

The Community did not number Norway or Britain among its members, and in the view of Hoggart and Johnson these two countries intended to 'torpedo' the EEC by setting up the European Free Trade Area, consisting of Britain, the Scandinavian countries, Portugal, Switzerland and Austria. But whereas EFTA was an *ad hoc* creation, the EEC had a political rationale.

Always within the EEC the idea has been present that Europe will, in one way or another, unite. It might even become a federation, crowned by a supra-national authority. This would mean the end of western Europe as a collection of nation states, and the emergence in modern times of the first unified European government. There would be such a thing as a European identity: a *homo europeanus*, a United States of Europe.

Individuality and Interdependence

The United States of Europe are unlikely to be modelled on the USA. For Europe prides itself on its diversity. European unity needs to be born out of difference. This argument is also adopted by Salvador de Madariaga, the Spanish ambassador and an Oxford don in the 1920s.[6]

Action, Thought, Passion

In a brilliant piece of analysis, upon which I shall unashamedly draw, Madariaga aligns the English, in particular, with *action* or doing; the French with *thought* or intellect; and the Spanish with *passion* or feeling. Madariaga selects these three from among the European nations because he believes they represent the purest form of each of those attributes. Other major European countries, such as Germany and Italy, can be placed in appropriate positions in between. Madariaga is not suggesting that the English do nothing but act, the French nothing but think, and the Spanish nothing but feel: it is merely a question of emphasis. In the final analysis we are all unified beings, capable of action, thought and passion.

Character Quality and Attribute Quantity

One character differs from another not so much in the tendencies it contains as in their relative strength and mutual interplay. For stronger or weaker, all tendencies are probably in all men – hence the unity of the human race.

Yet, when composed in one living total, all these differences in the quantity of the particular tendencies produce that difference in quality which we call character; just as quantitative differences in hardness, weight, and sensitivity to acids make up the qualitative difference between copper and gold.[7]

Now it is time to follow Madariaga's line of argument. As illustrated in Table 6.1, the predominant tendency of each nationality influences, in turn, its other tendencies.

Table 6.1 Predominant Tendencies

	Action	Thought	Passion
Action	Action in the man of action	Action in the man of thought	Action in the man of passion
Thought	Thought in the man of action	Thought in the man of thought	Thought in the man of passion
Passion	Passion in the man of action	Passion in the man of thought	Passion in the man of passion

We shall start, then, with a complete assessment of the Englishman before moving onto the Frenchman and finally to the Spaniard.

Englishman

English action

The Englishman is preoccupied, mainly, with taking appropriate action. With this end in view he organizes, disciplines and controls himself. In fact, for Madariaga's Englishman, *self-control* is an essential requirement.

Self-control is easily transplanted from the individual to the group. Such group control manifests itself in two ways. The first is in a strongly internalized tendency towards *social discipline*. The second is in the sense of *social service* that is deeply ingrained within the English psyche. (It is not surprising, given these attributes, that voluntary organizations proliferate in the UK.)

The individual lives in an atmosphere which is therefore imbued with moral and social responsibilities, divided into zones of different obligations. He is closely watched by his own social self and acquires *self-consciousness*, through the combination of freedom constrained by responsibility. Finally, through the interlinking of his innate insularity with his moral stance, the English man of action is prone to a sense of *self-righteousness*.

English thought

The *alogic* of the pragmatic Englishman means that between one action and another the basis of his thinking may have changed. Why?

Practical Wisdom

The line of conduct of the man of action is winding because the topography of action, like that of physical nature, avoids the straight line. At every moment, the man of action instinctively seeks and finds the line of least resistance which skirts arounds the obstacles and adapts itself to them. Hence the continuous and winding rhythm of thought and action.

The complex and vital character of English thought demands a standard more complicated and at the same time more elastic than mere reason. This standard is wisdom. Wisdom is reason saturated with irrational knowledge and with stored up experience, continually adapted to the moving waters of life, inseparable from action, which it guides and fertilizes, and so reasonable that it knows, whenever necessary, how to sacrifice reason.[8]

Thinking implies a separation from the things thought, a distance which enables us to dwell on the ideas of things and not the things in themselves. *Experience*, on the other hand, is a stream of life which bathes us at every moment.

In this stream the Englishman swims with the same pleasure wherewith he bathes in the cool waters of his rivers and shores.[9]

Empiricism, to which the English are singularly prone, is the *continuous mixture of thought and action*, or, rather, the blending of each instant of action with the minimum of thought needed for putting it into effect. Empiricism comes in two guises. One is *instantaneous*, a direct result of the feeling for the complexity of life. The other is *accumulated*, a kind of stored up treasure house of experiences, which an individual applies subconsciously at the moment it is required; it functions as a substitute for the principles the man of action rejects under the influence of the feeling that life is unforseeable.

In summary, *English thought endeavours to remain as close to life as possible.* From life it borrows its complexity, its elasticity, its alogic, its detailed shading. It does not worry beforehand about form. When the outcome in hand, therefore, is inspiration, the neglect of form allows a greater freedom on the part of the creative spirit. For the poet or innovator – as for the inventor of *action learning*, Reg Revans – a kind of internal inspiration seems to guide the work, like the force that guides the root towards the rich layer of earth.

English passion

The men of passion of England are its great poets and adventurers – Byron, Shelley, Shakespeare, Francis Drake. These inspired individuals tower over the quiet levels of the English soul as testimony to the profound passions hidden under the crust of the nation's apparent calm. Properly observed, in fact, the English calm is by no means phlegmatic; on the contrary it gives signs of an almost imperceptible vibration, which shows that its immobility is due, not to the absence of forces, but to a continually renewed equilibrium between the contrary forces of a powerful passion and a usually more powerful self-control.

In essence, the Englishman's lifestream is canalized in order to be utilized. Passion becomes polarized. Certain passions can be utilized and are therefore sources of power. Others cannot, and must be considered wasteful, or, worse still, antagonistic.

The English way of life

Spontaneous organization

How, then, does the Englishman's pragmatic approach to life and work manifest itself in the social, economic, political and cultural life of the nation? In every nook and cranny of English collective life cases will be found of *spontaneous organization*. Charitable enterprises are the most obvious example, whether in the traditional form of the Salvation Army or in the contemporary form of special appeals for the victims of natural disaster or endemic poverty.

The strongest feature of English social and political life is *liberty*, for liberty is the absence of political constraint, and such constraint is unnecessary and undesirable for a people gifted with the powers of spontaneous organization.

The English gentleman

In this atmosphere of liberty, which is, significantly, accompanied by inequality, the English nation naturally adopts a *hierarchical structure*. Empirical in their approach, the English base their hierarchical structures on continuity and tradition rather than upon principles of organization design. English society is not homogeneous, but is naturally divided into classes and subclasses, each of which plays a distinct part in the work of the whole.

The dominant feature in English educational life is the privately financed, but so called 'public' school, which substitutes itself for the family as a character-moulding agency, introducing a powerful element of standardization at the top of the social pyramid, in the shape of the English gentleman.

Fair Play

The most important items in the curricula of the public schools are undoubtedly the sundry types of sport which they cultivate. Their heroes are the captains of their cricket, football and rowing teams. Their true competitions are those in which those teams are pitted against each other.

Here, through the play of his muscles and not by any brainwork, the Englishman cultivates the sense of fair play, the spirit of cooperation, the self-denial for the sake of the community to which he belongs, the capacity for fighting with grit and determination, yet with detachment and good humour – in a word, all those virtues in action which are those of his race. In the immense majority of cases this education is completed by education in classical languages, history and English . . . a general study of the roots of European culture . . . facts about human nature . . . information about human character. The man of action is now ready.[10]

Self-control

The virtues that characterize English collective units – *stability*, *continuity*, *cooperation* – are those of the national group, as of the family. Whatever is stable and strong in the English family group is stable in the Civil Service or banking community. The father, in one word, is the governor.

People of action are always on the move as a people, knowing that they have a collective existence and that it goes forward. They want, therefore, to be led. The people of action therefore train their leaders for this important task. It develops in them *resolution, self-discipline, authority, knowledge of the law of things* and *knowledge of men.*

The empirical spirit of the English manifests itself in the unpopularity of the 'brainy' fellow. Self-control develops rapidly in this closely watched environment so strongly dominated by group influences; and self-consciousness follows self-control. Like its public schools, we find England organized around an unwritten constitution that rests on *tradition, convenience* and *rule-of-thumb practice.* Local government is a spontaneous local growth, owing to the same virtues that can be observed in central and national institutions.

Social consciousness

English, according to Madariaga, is a monosyllabic language, suited to the man of action. The tendency to action no doubt explains the aptitude of the English language for turning anything into a verb. We know that the present is the tense of the man of action, and therefore we are not surprised to find that it is on the present that the English verb is built.

English literature is social literature: the novel is a direct reflection of the life of the people, woven with all the threads which cross and re-cross in so evolved a society. An English artist is a man in whom there is a permanent conflict between action and passion. Interestingly, the Royal Society of Arts includes the 'arts of manufacture' within its overall remit. Similarly religion, for the Englishman, is very much concerned with things of this world. 'Here and now' is his motto in religion as in everything else. Religious bodies therefore take a strong interest in collective and social tasks.

World philosophy

England's world philosophy, in conclusion, is that of the *will*. The Englishman lives in action. He is busy. He moves. For relaxation and rest he moves again, passing from business to sport. He mixes with people and things.

The Frenchman is very different.

Frenchman

French action

The man of action expects practical results from his activities. The thinker, on the other hand, wants to create *order*. Order is the intellectualized outcome of action. It is the idealized projection of the world along the plane of intellect. This explains why the Frenchman is likely to excel in the preliminary stages of action, as well as in the routine stages that follow implementation. But he is likely to experience problems in the thick of activity. For the intellect is a faculty that wants space and leisure, while the present is but a point and an instant.

While the Englishman applies his thinking to the solution of practical problems, the Frenchman sees, in practical problems, the opportunity to exercise his mind. In fact, the *intellectual* in action tends to force a situation into categories pre-established by his intelligence. His attitude in action is one of continuing *protest against the illogical behaviour of life*. Whereas English organization tends to be simultaneous with action, French plans and structures often precede action, and involve a complicated system of written laws that aim to foresee all possible eventualities. This *network of principles* is 'le droit', the right way to proceed.

French thought

French thought is strongly *analytical*. It likes to burrow into ideas, find out their elements and classify them. While the Englishman seeks to safeguard the rights of life by surrounding his thoughts with a blurred outline, the Frenchman seeks to guarantee the clearness of his intellectual vision by defining the knowledge with the neatest possible edge. French knowledge is *cold, scientific, precise.*

All the Frenchman's qualities combine to give him that sense of form, which is one of the manifestations of his *instinct for clearness*, and a kind of *discipline* for his creative and representational mind. For *form*, in the eyes of the Frenchman, is not merely outward elegance, ornament and grace; it is a kind of inward elegance that results from the true balance of the parts, their harmonious arrangement, and the clearness and beauty of the whole.

In fact, there is an element of spontaneous collaboration that distinguishes French intellectual life. For in France intellectualism is general. The taste for things of the mind resides especially in the middle class. The French are acknowledged leaders in the *art of method,* and it is not by accident that their greatest philosopher gave to his principal work the title *Discours de la méthode*. It is not surprising that the French are the leading European producers of computer software!

French passion

The intellectual, instead of coming nearer to life, tends to move away from it by virtue not of a decision of his conscious mind but of an instinctive desire to draw apart from that which he wants to understand. The Frenchman, in fact, deeply feels the *dignity of reason*.

And his respect for reason dictates the way in which he supervises his lifestream.

In the Frenchman, unlike his English counterpart, passion is not the enemy that is feared and watched, but a natural phenomenon that is foreseen, and has its place. Passion has free access to the surface of the Frenchman's thought. What characterizes his pleasures, therefore, and his love of life is their intellectual appeal, their *refinement*. Whether it is food, wine or art, it is the shades of difference, the nuances – intellectually derived – that count. In the final analysis, then, the life of passion leads the French towards *beauty*.

> Ideas and sensations can feed off it, and even that light that irradiates from beauty is, though irrational, of a kind to appeal to this people eminently fond of clarity.[11]

No wonder French window displays are such an art form!

The French way of life
Intellectual order
It is not surprising to find that the social structure of France is more *rigidly framed* than its English counterpart. Custom is an element of lesser importance, and *law*, or 'droit', is the more potent force. The framework of society has been and is constantly thought out, deduced from general principles.

The main ingredient of French social life, according to Madariaga, is not liberty but *equality*. Equality is a geometrical plane made up of human rights: it is beautifully level. It is also an intellectual, rather than an instinctive construct that must be deliberately conceived. The order that prevails rests upon an assumption of equality that has been established intellectually. Therefore the multifarious activities that are carried on in England by the free and spontaneous growth of private initiative must in France rely on the help and the leadership of the State. The movements of collective life must be prearranged, laid down beforehand by some mind well trained to foresee moves on the chessboard of possibilities.

French élites
The dominant feature in the French family is perhaps the 'mariage de raison'. The atmosphere of a French home is cordial in its calm. Family traditions are rich and complex to a degree sufficient to stamp the individual with a family seal. The family in France, like the public

school in England, is the field in which social and individual tendencies come to terms with and compensate for each other. Through it an acceptable standard of collective behaviour is maintained in the nation as a whole. A French member of an *élite* may find himself in the same position as an English *leader*. But whereas leadership implies movement, an élite is static; its members are the selected few, and therefore occupy the highest ranks in the hierarchy of the established order.

The French system differs from the British then, in two respects: it is directed towards the cultivation of the intellect and it is organized by the state. French secondary education specializes in the development of the brain; the education of the will and character is no special concern of the school. Thus the family has a stronger formative influence than in England. Beyond the secondary school, the 'Ecole Polytechnique' promotes a highly specialized education of the mind, developing in its students a love of knowledge, culture and ideas.

Shades of opinion

The political evolution of France stands in contrast to that of Britain. In Britain political institutions evolve slowly and empirically, with strong continuity. In France the political mould of the country has been broken now and then, and a new cast made from the old mould. France is the specialist in constitutions among nations. Whereas the British constitution is always changing, and yet is always fundamentally the same, French constitutions follow one another through sharp turns or revolutions in the political life of the country.

The place that efficiency occupies in England is taken in France by *intellectual honesty*. Thus the working of the French parliament differs profoundly from the British model, for it is divided into interest groups representing a considerable number of *shades of opinion*. The French people, moreover, are interested in politics from an intellectual standpoint.

Not surprisingly the French language is carefully written and pronounced. Every letter receives its value and remains in its place. The French do not tolerate the elastic attitude that makes English spelling the grammarian's despair. French pronunciation is accurate and precise, and follows its own rules so precisely that it might even be viewed as a deductive science in its own right. In fact, turning from science to art, if you want to seek in France the equivalent of those popular manifestations of artistic life that are so abundant in Spain and Italy, you must turn – in Madariaga's view – to 'the almost universal ability of French men and women to arrange material for life's use with refinement and taste'.[12]

The analytical mind

The person responsible for such artistic productions, is no longer himself the raw material of his art – at once the channel and flow of his emotion – but the *artificer*, who, from the outside, works on the material and gives it shape. Thus one finds that a sense of *objectivity* forms the keynote of French art, as well as of those '-isms' – symbolism, romanticism, classicism – which the critical intellect assigns to a period of French artistic life. The analytical mind, so closely associated with French art, also characterizes the French attitude to religion, which is both Catholic and *sceptical* in its approach.

World philosophy

France's world philosophy is that of the *mind*. The Frenchman wants to understand reality. Living, for him, consists in the development of his intellect and of the five avenues that lead to it, namely his senses. Refinement and enjoyment of his faculties are what life and work are all about.

For the Spaniard, that man of passion, as for the English man of action, the situation is very different.

Spaniard

Spanish action

What is essential, immovable, evident for the Frenchman is the idea; for the Englishman the act. Just as the Frenchman seeks in action and in passion an intellectual result, the Englishman seeks in thought and in passion a practical result. The Spaniard, however, seeks in action and in thought a result in terms of passion, that is *experience of life*. Just as the Englishman selects his passions and allows the release of those that are useful to the group, the Spaniard selects his actions and engages only in those that enrich the experience of the individual.

Letting Off Surplus Energy

No longer the supple and continuous curve adapted to all forms of nature, which we have observed in the man of action of England; nor the series of straight lines successively correcting each other by sudden turns, as in the intellectual of France; but a kind of rest followed by a sudden explosion of conquering will, which, soon exhausted, falls back to the first indifference – a series of horizontal lines of action cut by abrupt peaks of over-activity.

The first struggles in order to do things; the second in order to possess them in knowledge; the third to let off his surplus energy.[13]

The individual philosophy of the man of passion implies a nature that *rebels against* the chain of *collective life*. Such collective life is seen by the Spaniard as the connecting of individual lives to a system of gears. In such a gear, at every moment, only a small sector of each wheel is actually connected and playing an active role, while the man of passion is at every moment present with his whole self wherever he is.

The man of passion lives and works in a highly personalized world. In fact the importance of personal contacts is a well-known characteristic of the Spanish. Whether the question at issue is a trivial affair or the most important business, a relation between man and man is indispensable if results are to be obtained.

Spanish thought

We have seen the Englishman in thought, taking from the object of which he thinks all that is useful at the moment; and the Frenchman in thought, looking at the object systematically with initiative and premeditation. The Spaniard thinks by *contemplation*. He waits in apparent passivitity for the object to reveal itself to him. He lets the continuous stream of life pass through him until chance will suddenly imbue it with new light.

The Spaniard thinks by *intuition.* By intuition the object contemplated reveals itself all at once in its essence, with all its internal connections and all the connections that attach it to the rest of life. Hence the *inseparability of body and spirit*, which is one of the deepest features of Spanish thought. For it is at the moment when it emerges out of the subconscious that Spanish thought is strongest, most vigorous. It has all the vital freshness of natural facts. Free from all preparatory argument, independent of all dialectical plan, Spanish thought appears on the surface of the intellect still warm from the innermost folds of the soul in which it is formed.

The very essence of the Spaniard's psychology, then, sets *passion* and not knowledge as *the ultimate aim*. It follows that if the fire of passion deforms his intuition, knowledge in the Spaniard becomes irretrievably warped. It fosters his tendency to arbitrariness and further curtails the efficiency and effectiveness with which his intellect works on the rich intuitive raw material conferred on him by nature.

Spanish passion

While the psychology of the man of action develops mainly in the plane of his conscious will, and that of the intellectual may be easily observed in the sphere of the mind, *the psychology of the man of passion is mostly subconscious* since its first impulse reactions arise from the lifestream that reaches him straight from nature. At every moment subjective vitality flows over the social will. With the same spontaneity with which we have seen the English man of action adapt himself to 'the law of things', we see the man of passion in Spain *force things to follow the law of the person*, personalizing nature and obliging it to follow the lifestream that circulates in his blood.

The popular language of Spain abounds in expressions of a strikingly synthetic nature, which sum up in a few words taut with sense, not the idea but the *passion for wholeness* that is the true substance of the soul of Spain. It is precisely when he is most egotistical that the Spaniard is most universal. He seeks universality without meaning to do so. For his egotism functions precisely in letting the lifestream pass through him, in all its spontaneity and integrity.

The Spanish way of life

A man of the people

It is not surprising, from what we have seen, that Spain is lacking in all hierarchical sense, whether in the natural, instinctive form that it takes in Britain; or the outward, political form that it assumes in France. The sense of *equality* that permeates all collective life in Spain is different from the French idea of it. Spanish equality, being a living sense, is unconsciously assumed; French equality, being an idea, is aired and asserted. Just as every Englishman, in Madariaga's opinion, fashions himself after the aristocracy, and every Frenchman, whatever his station, is, in his heart of hearts, a petit bourgeois, the Spanish, no matter what his class, is a *man of the people*.

Thus the Spanish attitude to equality cannot foster a hierarchy of the English type which implies a spontaneous recognition of inequalities; nor does it provide the basis for the erection of a state hierarchy after the French pattern, since the sense of equality is subconscious, and does not level people down to a flat plane of citizenship. Spanish collective life counts on *superimposed cohesion*, through, for example, the Church or Army.

Family cohesion

The Spanish Family

Whereas the family in England is just one of the many forms which the spirit of co-operation takes in the people of action, and, in France a kind of State writ small, in Spain the family is but the first collective sphere which the individual meets in his expansion as he travels out from his egocentric self. It is therefore the strongest of the group units in Spanish life.

While in England the nation is stronger than the family and in France the family is the meeting ground between individual and collective tendencies, in Spain the family is stronger than the wider forms of community.[14]

Personal influence

If revolutions in France are instigated by intellectuals, Spanish revolutions are dramatic crises, in which the moving forces are not principles but personalities. The Spaniard is held by the vicissitudes of continual battles for power. *Political allegiance is more personal than objective.* For the Spaniard, therefore, the constitution is like an act in a play. It can be brushed aside.

Whereas at first sight the political structures of these three peoples of western Europe are the same – they are three democracies organized under a parliamentary system – in reality they are as different as the three national characters would lead us to expect. In Britain, political institutions are the outcome of an empirical evolution. In France they resulted from a constitution carefully planned beforehand. In Spain politics is in a plastic state.

In contrasting the English idea of leaders to the French idea of élites we passed from movement to stasis, but retained the idea of hierarchy. In contrasting the French élites with the Spanish *minorias*, even the concept of hierarchy goes by the board. The *minorias* are a small number of people who happen to have reached a higher plane of development than the rest. That is all.

When a Spaniard speaks convincingly of medicine, according to Madariaga, the chances are that he is an artist. If he shows an above average knowledge of painting he may be a colonel. Each individual seeks ideas and sensations by his own unaided efforts, both because his own character as a man of passion requires him to do so, and because the environment itself provides scanty food for wholesale educational consumption. Exceptional men in Spain rise, as it were, from sea level, they do not step across from the high lands of an already established social culture.

Individual passion

The Spanish language is the one of the three that draws most on the inner man.

> You may drawl English; you may pronounce French trippingly off the tongue; you must speak Spanish fully and frankly and fill up with your own life's breath the ample volume of its words.[15]

Its words are not like English monosyllables, snapshots or acts; nor like clear French polysyllables. They are the objects themselves, full square, with all their volume, mass and colour.

World philosophy

Of the three countries Spain is the only one, at least in Madariaga's opinion, in which an *aesthetic attitude* is *natural, spontaneous, innate* and *general*. Hence the exceptional wealth of popular art. According to local climate, occupation and economic conditions, the aesthetic approach manifests itself potently in all areas of life, directly influencing the house, the dress, the language, the ceremonies and religion. Indeed, in Spain religion is above all an individual passion, like love, jealousy, hatred and ambition, consisting in a personal relationship between the individual and his Creator.

Conclusion

The European Triangle

Historically speaking, then, Spain was the leading country in the world during the era when the wealth at stake was the kind that lived in man's souls. France became the leader of a world turned intellectual by the Renaissance. England took its turn in the lead when the world became concerned with the conquest of things and trade became its main activity. In every period of history, mankind found its national protagonist and representative nation. The interesting question is: Which nation represents mankind today? Judging by the 1970s and 1980s, the answer would now have to be Japan; in the 1950s and 1960s the answer would have been the US.

Interestingly, it was the English, the French and the Spanish together who made America. The Spanish – the people of passion – discovered it. In the economic organization of America the active hand of the Englishman and of the Anglo-Saxon American can be seen. France intellectualized America.

England, France and Spain are the three points of Europe through which the European spirit flows towards the West. However, as is all too apparent, there is much more to Europe than these three nations: The Germans combine French thought with English action; the Italians combine Spanish passion with French thought; and so on. As a nation evolves, from a parochial to transnational state, so it is more able to accommodate difference. In other words, to actualize oneself – as an individual, an organization, a business function or a whole society – one needs to communicate with difference.

I now want to turn from Europe to the four quarters of the globe.

Notes

1 P. Ceccini, *The European Challenge*. Wildwood House, 1988, p. 7.
2 Ceccini, *The European Challenge*, p. 17.
3 'Europe's Internal Market'. *The Economist*, 1988, pp. 84–114.
4 R. Hoggart and S. Johnson, *The Idea of Europe*. Weidenfeld & Nicolson, 1987, p. 34.
5 H. Ellis, *The Genius of Europe*. Macmillan, 1950, p. 86.
6 S. de Madariaga, *Englishman, Frenchman, Spaniard*. Howell, 1922, p. 14. All subsequent references in this chapter are to this publication.
7 Madariaga, p. 27.
8 Madariaga, p. 34.
9 Madariaga, p. 48.
10 Madariaga, p. 86.
11 Madariaga, p. 243.
12 Madariaga, p. 161.
13 Madariaga, p. 112.
14 Madariaga, p. 214.
15 Madariaga, p. 212.

7

Global Reach

Introduction

We have so far placed developmental management in a European setting. However, the European Community is not an isolated entity, and it is vital that we appreciate the global context – business and cultural – in which it is set. For this reason, having looked at the North, that is Europe, we need to gain an overview of the West, that is the United States of America; the East, in particular, Japan; and the South, that is the developing countries. In fact it is my conviction, based on research, teaching and consultancy around the globe, that unless we draw on the fullness of what the world's cultures have to offer, business in general, and institutional life in particular, will gradually draw to a halt.

Each quarter of the globe is trying, in the most general sense, to resolve a particular endemic problem.

- For the North the dilemma is how to reconcile *the individual and society.*
- In the West the issue is how to keep in balance *enterprise and community.*
- In the East the key question is how to reconcile *harmony with adaptability.*
- In the South the overriding question is how to maintain *dream and reality*, or *vision and action* in equilibrium.

Similarly, within the EC itself the global horizons of the western (Britain), eastern (Germany), northern (Denmark) and southern (Greece and Italy) nations will rub off, to some extent, on the Community as a whole.

The four dilemmas, in fact, also mirror the life of a business as it develops from youth to maturity.

- The crucial task that *youthful* business faces is to reconcile toughminded enterprise with tenderhearted community.
- The key concern of the *established* firm is to balance individual freedom and organizational order.
- The organization in *mid-life*, facing renewal, must reconcile commercial adaptation with social harmony.
- The truly *mature* institution needs to maintain in equilibrium spiritually based vision and physically based action.

Individuals, organizations and societies do not necessarily grow and develop over time. Evolution is a painful process, involving a series of crises and transitions. Old forms have to die before new ones can be born. And at each stage of its development an organization requires a different set of heroes to lead the way. Different parts of the globe are culturally attuned to different kinds of hero.

The West: Enterprise and Community

In the late 1970s the Americans Tom Peters and Bob Waterman went out in search of so-called 'excellence', seeking to discover what made American companies successful. In the process they overturned the erudite management theories that had prevailed in the West for some fifty years, and concluded that basically two things prevailed in successful companies in their country: *fired-up champions* and *shared values*.

Their conclusions are not altogether surprising, given America's history and identity. The American historian Henry Commager has identified four attributes that infuse the spirit of his country. The contemporary political scientist Robert Reich has, similarly, identified four pervading 'myths'.

Cultural Parables

Every culture has its own parables. Conveying lessons about the how and why of life through metaphor may be a basic human trait, a universal characteristic of our intermittently rational, deeply emotional, meaning seeking species.

Cultural parables (or myths) come in a multitude of forms. In modern

America the vehicles of public myth include the biographies of famous citizens, popular fiction and music, movies, feature stories on the evening news, and gossip. They may also take more explicitly hortatory forms in judicial opinion, political speeches and sermons.

In whatever form they are transmitted constantly, and all around us, they shape our collective judgments. What gives them force is their capacity to make up, and bring coherence to, common experience. The stories interpret and explain reality and teach us what is expected in the light of that reality. They situate us, showing us where we are in an otherwise incomprehensible sea of facts. Our morality tales inform our sense of what our society is about.

Cultural myths are no more 'truth' than an architect's sketches are buildings. Their function is to explain events and guide decisions. Thus while it is pointless to challenge myths as unrealistic, it is entirely valid to say that a culture's mythology serves it well only to the extent that it retains its connection to the reality the culture faces. Myths must evolve as the context evolves. Stories that stay rigid as realities change become ever less useful cultural tools.[1]

Enterprise

The triumphant individual

The first of Commager's attributes encompasses the never-ending *frontier* of human activity, through pilgrimage, through exploration, through experimentation and change. The second, set in the context of that vast and hostile territory, the land of America, is the battle for survival, the compulsion to *move or die*. The third and probably most important constituent of the American enterprising spirit is the theme of opportunity, individual achievement, competition, capitalism and *wealth creation*.

Reich associates these traits, altogether, with *the triumphant individual*.

The Triumphant Individual

This is the story of the little guy who works hard, takes risks, believes in himself, and eventually earns wealth, fame, and honour. It is the parable of the self-made man who bucks the odds, spurns the soothsayers, and shows what can be done with enough drive and guts.

The theme recurs in the tale of Abe Lincoln, log splitter from Illinois who goes to the White House, in the 100 or so novellas of Horatio Alger, whose heroes all rise promptly and predictably from rags to riches. It appears in the American morality tales of the underdog who eventually makes it – think of Rocky or Iacocca. Regardless of the precise form the moral is the same: with enough guts anyone can make it on their own in America.[2]

The Rot at the Top

Whereas the triumphant individual rises, as an enterprising man, from the bottom up, rot all too often sets in at the top. The second parable, then, is about the malevolence of powerful élites, be they wealthy aristocrats, rapacious business leaders, or imperious government officials. They either prevent the triumphant individual from succeeding, or may themselves be just such an individual, gone wrong! In fact there are no workers against capitalists at the heart of the American story. It is rather a tale of corruption, decadence and irresponsibility among the powerful.

Experience with the arbitrary authority of the English Crown had produced in America's founding fathers an acute sensitivity to the possibilities of the abuse of power. A century later America responded to mounting concentrations of private economic power through antitrust laws. The theme recurs in the tales of humble folk, like the Joad family in John Steinbeck's *The Grapes of Wrath*, who struggle valiantly against avaricious bankers. The moral is clear: *power corrupts, privilege perverts*.

The triumphant individual, then, forever crossing into new territories, restlessly on the move, and creating ever more wealth, has only the malevolence of powerful élites standing in his way. If the rot is removed, and the enterprising individual triumphs, *support will and must come* not from the bureaucrats but *from the benevolent community*.

Community

The benevolent community

Ever since the Pilgrim Fathers landed in America the notion of the benevolent community has held sway. Over the course of two centuries it was upgraded into the concept of an American melting-pot that allowed everyone to share in the American dream. In fact, as Henry Commager comments, for all the geographical and ethnic diversity in the US, there is a remarkable degree of conformity in outlook and spirit among its people.

This *family feeling* is nurtured and developed by American companies and communities alike.

> We have employee clubs, intramural sports, travel clubs, and a choral group. With the breakdown of traditional structures certain companies have filled the void. We have become sort of mother institutions, but have maintained our spirit of entrepreneurship at the same time (Lehr).[3]

The benevolent community, then, so much a part of the American heritage, has been the tenderhearted counterpart to toughminded and triumphant individualism. But it has had to struggle to evolve.

Rebirth of Neighbourhood

> Compassion and generosity are still sentiments that Americans endorse and act on when it's a matter of concerts, cake sales, and other such voluntary activities. But when it comes to government welfare programmes the consensus has dissolved. As new waves of immigrants from Latin America and the Caribbean swarmed into the nation's cities in the 1970s and 1980s, the ideal of community seemed to be enfeebled. To many Americans, there seemed no principled difference between poor Hispanics – some of them illegal immigrants – living in Los Angeles, and those living in Mexico City.
>
> By the 1980s, accordingly, a not insubstantial proportion of the American public was ready to hear a new story about the Benevolent Community, one that defined benevolence as voluntary charity, and defined community as the local neighbourhood rather than the nation. It was to be a renaissance of America, a 'rebirth of neighbourhood', according to Reagan.
>
> This vision was emotionally appealing, mythically resonant, and powerfully out of sync with changing American reality. These ersatz neighbourhoods contained no shared history, no pattern of long-term association. What had been small towns or ethnic sections within large cities had given way to economic enclaves, whose members had little more in common with one another than their average incomes.[4]

What Reich impresses upon us is that cultural parables or myths need to evolve by accommodating current realities if they are to continue to exercise positive power and influence. This certainly applies to the fourth and final one of his American tales.

The mob at the gates

On the negative side of both the triumphant individual and America's strongly communal tradition is a 'them' and 'us' attitude that Reich has labelled the tale of 'the mob at the gates'.

'Them' and 'Us'

This mythic story is about tyranny and barbarism that lurks out there. It depicts America as a beacon of virtue in a world of darkness, a small island of freedom and democracy in a perilous sea. We are uniquely blessed, the proper model for other people's aspirations, the hope of the world's poor and oppressed.

The parable gives voice to a corresponding fear: we must beware lest the forces of darkness overwhelm us. Our liberties are fragile; our openness renders us vulnerable to exploitation or infection from abroad. The American amalgam of fear and aggressiveness toward 'them out there' appears in countless fantasies of space explorers who triumph over alien creatures from beyond.[5]

Community and enterprise

The challenge, Reich argues, is to create settings in which obligation and trust can take root, and to support them by myths that focus our attention on discovering possibilities for joint gain, and avoiding the likelihood of mutual loss – stories of *collective entrepreneurialism* and *social solidarity*. In this way he attempts to reconcile enterprise and community, not through a return to the fired-up champions or even shared values of yesteryear, but through a new form of *social ecology* befitting today's global economy.

Mythical Renewal

The problem comes when a changing environment outpaces the political culture. When we become so enchanted with our fables that we wall them off from the pressures of adaptation, the stories may begin to mark reality rather than illuminate it. Instead of being cultural tools for coming to terms with the challenge we face, they become means of forestalling them.

A living political mythology, while retaining its roots in the same core themes, is constantly incorporating new stories that manifest basic values and beliefs in new and more fruitful ways.[6]

In the same updated vein Reich argues that *competence, dedication* and *pride in accomplishment* – those traditional American virtues – will continue to matter a great deal, but, to an increasing extent, in the context of collective endeavour. Triumphant individuals are being replaced by *collective entrepreneurs*. Enterprise and community are being combined into a new synthesis.

On a macro level Reich maintains that America can no longer withdraw in fear and distaste from 'the mob at the gates', for America's interests are too intimately bound up with theirs. Nor can it boldly assert its will; for control over the rest of the world is too contingent and tenuous. Rather America must recognize the interests of others, appreciate their power, and seek out possibilities for mutual gain. The most important of 'the others' is probably Japan.

The East: Adaptability and Harmony

Both America and Japan hunger for success, which is what makes them such powerful economic rivals. But whereas in America the *passion for excellence* is conventionally fuelled by *personal enterprise* and *materially shared values*, in Japan it is the result of *communal enterprise* and *spiritually shared beliefs*. The extraordinary diligence and ambition of the Japanese is now universally recognized. What is less well known is how the Japanese come to have these qualities. Japan's seemingly frenetic drive for economic success appeared suddenly in full bloom in 1868 when the feudal government fell.

The need for achievement, in whatever part of the globe, seems to arise out of a mixture of superiority and inferiority. In the US this manifests itself in a unique blend of assertiveness and rootlessness. In Japan a similar combination of superiority and inferiority exists, but in a different form. The Japanese *superiority complex* is *mythologically founded* rather than materially founded. It is probably derived, originally, from the notion that Japan was created by divine beings.

> Shinto is an ancient body of beliefs, without a bible or other written work, which tells the Japanese that they are descendants of a group of heavenly beings.[7]

This internalized feeling of superiority has been externally reinforced, over the centuries, by a combination of insularity and nationalism. The inferior side of the Japanese 'face' may be traced back to Japan's originally close relationships with China and Korea. In the 3rd century Japan was divided into numerous competing clans with primitive lifestyles, while China was at the height of one of its great dynasties. The impact that this cultural disparity had on the Japanese mind is still very much apparent today.

In summary, then, the tension between the internally evoked feeling of superiority and the externally reinforced sense of inferiority, creates a field of force that generates the nation's drive for achievement. But unlike the American, the motive force of the Japanese is *social status* and *cultural adaptability* rather than personal achievement and wealth creation, and the channel for the energy transmitted is the *harmonious group* rather than the striving individual.

Cultural Adaptability

The process of kaizen

According to Japan's leading psychiatrist, Takeo Doi, the Japanese have been collectively conditioned over the centuries to feel a profound sense of dissatisfaction. This endures until they have completed whatever task they have embarked on, or whatever goal they have set themselves. When the goal is a great one, therefore, there is no end to the dissatisfaction that the Japanese feel. They set themselves to work at a furious pace to relieve the dis-ease they experience when confronted with something unresolved. The *pursuit of quality*, and the relentless *capacity for adaptation*, both stem from this collective urge for *meaning* and *resolution*.

Continuous Improvement

Under the process known as 'kaizen' – continuous improvement – Nissan seeks to create an environment in which all staff can contribute to improving quality, safety, and productivity as a normal part of their job.

In many environments management fights to introduce change whereas in Nissan (U.K.) the individual 'owns' the change and the problem is not introducing change but keeping up with the proposals.[8]

The philosophy of mu

Shigeru Kobayashi, who was general manager at one of Sony's major manufacturing plants in the 1970s, claimed that his company operated according to the Buddhist philosophy of *mu*. It had no fixed plans; it was completely open. By virtue of living, like the Zen Buddhist, totally in the present, the individual or the company is paradoxically *wholly open to the future*. The individual or collective mind is kept hollow, and therefore takes in completely what is happening around it.

The Japanese embrace a world view, therefore, in which, although there is 'no-thing', there is something. Consider this analogy. In English we often refer to a space between a chair and a table. In the Japanese equivalent the space is not empty, but it is 'full of nothing'. No wonder the Japanese businessman is so good at spotting gaps in the market, standing out within empty space!

The quality of shibui

If the applied philosophy of *mu* represents one main reason for Japan's cultural and economic adaptability, then *sensitivity to man and nature* represents another. *Shibui* characterizes a quality of beauty that has a tranquil effect. This sensitivity, be it to the market-place or to human relationships, is born out of an aesthetic rather than a primarily rational inclination. In fact one of the first things that even the casual business observer learns is that the Japanese measure most things in terms of human feelings.

Hiroshi Tanaka, in commenting on the birth and growth of ASICS, a leading Japanese company in sportswear, makes the point:

> The corporation is the precinct in which managers and workers alike search for the meaning of life. The bond that unites all personnel is this shared mission of the heart and soul. This is to be borne in mind if one is to understand the essence of managerial practice in Japan.[9]

Adaptability and enterprise

The extraordinary ability that the Japanese have to adapt to, and to adopt, new technologies and markets, emerges out of a combination of qualities that are largely alien to managers in the West. The combination of

> *kaizen* – perfectionism,
> *mu* – openness,
> *shibui* – sensitivity,

is very different, in origin if not in impact, from American-style entrepreneurship.

While protectionist Japan may share with the US fears about 'the mob at the gates', its 'triumphant individual' is different, if he even exists! In fact it is the *collective group* that triumphs. To the extent that the individual does so it is at the level of *spirit* rather than matter.

Group Harmony

The concept of uchi

The Japanese business organization is modelled on the family (*uchi*). The family system differs from the American, European, African or even Chinese models. Family ethics are not based on individual relationships between husband and wife or between brothers and sisters, but on the *collective family group*. Moreover the family group is an extended one, reaching out into the totality of Japanese society. This can be explained historically.

Society as Family

The primitive Indo-Europeans, being nomadic and living chiefly by hunting, were in constant conflict with alien peoples. Here human relations were marked by fierce rivalry. Peoples moved in great migrations; one race conquered another only to be conquered by still another. In such a society the struggle for existence was based not on mutual trust but on cunning and stratagem.

Japanese society, on the other hand, developed from small, localised farming communities. The Japanese gave up their nomadic life early on in their history, and settled down to cultivate rice fields. People living on rice inevitably have to settle permanently in one place. Genealogies and kinships of families through long years became so well known that the society as a whole took on the appearance of a family.[10]

This concept of the extended family is also reflected organizationally in contemporary Japanese enterprise. Akio Onitsuka, the founder of ASICS, viewed his company

not solely as a composite of his own employees. His concept . . . included the affiliated factories without whose involvement the company would not have succeeded. The corporation and the factories were one entity, one being.[11]

Beyond ASICS and its affiliates lay a further extension of the Japanese family – the youth of Japan, who would not only benefit from the company's sportswear but might become employees and thence 'responsible members of society'.

The idea of oyaban

Organizational life in Japan is marked by a subtle balance of *reciprocal obligations* (*oyaban*), set within an intricate hierarchy of *rank and status*. For centuries the Japanese have been told to *respect authority* and to *work cooperatively*. So, as we can see, while there is little place for the 'triumphant individual' there is ample scope for the 'benevolent community'.

The relationship between the larger Japanese employer and his employees is not, therefore, primarily an economic one. The average employer gets from his employees an inordinate degree of *loyalty*, *cooperation* and *effort*. In return, the employer feels responsible for his employees' *social*, *spiritual* and *economic well-being*. As Akio Morita, Chairman of Sony, has said:

> The most important mission for a Japanese manager is to develop a healthy relationship with his employees, to create a feeling that employees and managers share the same fate.[12]

Of course the benevolent community extends far beyond the factory gates into a *virtuous circle of corporate activity*, involving, according to Onitsuka, a process of recognizing society's needs and then serving them by marketing, product innovation, production and distribution. It is only then, he says, that you will realize sufficient financial returns to 'support the family' and to reinvest for their future.

The development of amae

The continual emphasis on the reciprocal nature of the benevolent community does serve to play down the influence of the individual. In fact the Japanese have a very fragile concept of themselves as individual entities. *Dependence and interdependence*, rather than independence, *are recognized and rewarded*. Takeo Doi, in his book *Anatomy of Dependence*, reveals that the Japanese does not feel right in any relationship if a feeling of *absolute trust and confidence* is absent. As a result the person who can safely encourage such dependence (*amae*) is the best qualified for leadership. To form a relationship of complete trust takes a great deal of time and careful nurturing. This applies not only to contact between individuals in a work group, but also to relations with customers, suppliers and associates in joint ventures.

Adaptability and harmony

Whereas Americans, then, are individually enterprising, the Japanese are *collectively adaptable.* Whereas the West shares personal values within a corporate melting-pot, the East *harmonizes group values* within an interdependent 'Japan Inc.'

The Japanese have been immensely successful in evolving a primal family feeling into an extended business community. Tales of the benevolent community, for them, have been suitably culturally adapted over time. What is beginning to prove problematic, however, is the lack of scope for the triumphant individual, particularly as contact with the West is increased. Moreover Japan, like the US, is suffering from its fears of 'the mob at the gates'. Both need to extend their respective notions of the benevolent community to encompass other nations. While for the US it is the 'melting-pot' theory that gets in the way, in Japan it is the country's inherent homogeneity.

When we move from West and East to the South, the business situation changes once again.

South: Dream and Reality

The time for the South – at least so it seems – has not yet come. While the centre of business power has shifted over the past 100 years from Europe to the US and then to Japan, Africa and Latin America have been left out in the cold. The dilemma that the South has to resolve – whether Africa, Latin America, southern Europe or even Alabama – is how to turn *dreams* into *realities*, *vision* into *action.*

Venturing South

Venturing South is a journey for explorers. It is the direction down into the depth, different from the trip into the Eastern harmonies, from the Western rush of golden boys and girls, and from the Northern ascent to cool, objective observation. Going from North to South means pairing light and shadow, conscious and unconscious, a vertical division of what is above and what is below.[13]

Business is an unfolding story, with intermittent crises, and many a fork along the road to enlightenment and success. The sense, in man and enterprise, of unrealized potential in life and time, the sense of what is now invisible but soon to emerge is a source of immense creativity.

Africa is the home of man. It has the longest inhabited history of all the continents.

> The indigenous people of Africa [are] far closer to their natural selves than we [are]. As a result they [have] become more and more of a mirror reflecting the receding part of ourselves.[14]

Laurens Van Der Post, the great southern adventurer, novelist and adviser to prime ministers and monarchs, has lamented the alienation of European man and society from their origins.

History

> I had been born with as great a passion for history as for stories – not surprisingly, as both are part of the same indivisible process. History presents the story as lived. The story presents the options and possibilities of life that might have been, and can still be lived. There are moments of crisis when the past is not an inevitability, but presents life with a creative course of new action.[15]

The spirit of an organization or society pursues its journey from creation into re-creation. The task of the visionary is to turn the creative spirit into physical energy and back again. Commercial enterprises in Africa are only beginning to wake up to this challenge. Those that lend themselves to meeting it successfully are inevitably agricultural, for African society is closer to the earth and to the so called 'spirit provinces' of the land.

The liberation struggle in Zimbabwe provides a potent illustration of this amalgam of spirit and energy, organized and directed towards re-creation.

The Management of Liberation

> It would be a mistake to imagine that the image of the world to come was based entirely on an imaginary vision of the past. True, the people were promised that they would regain the land in the name of the ancestors, but straightway they would set about making use of all the modern techniques of production and marketing that had, up till then, been denied to them.

The present world had been rejected because it worked to the peasant's severe disadvantage, but, once this ancestral interregnum was over, the rewards would be better lives lived in more comfortable surroundings, better food, better education, better health care.

Nonetheless without the powers of the ancestors to transcend the material plane, to triumph over the political sphere, these rewards would always remain out of reach.[16]

The dreamlike *spirit* of the ancestors, and the *energy* or material reality contained within the land form a potential continuum which may ultimately form the basis of successful business development in the South; but as yet they are disconnected, the two ends need to be linked.

Conclusion

The Globalization of Business

No progressive manager today will question the inevitability of the globalization of business. Yet, depending upon where he or she is coming from, the implications of this phenomenon will be significantly different.

For the primal manager globalization implies, on the one hand, ever wider markets to exploit, and, on the other, ever more intense competition. It is the quantitative change that counts more than any qualitative one. For the rational manager globalization implies greater complexity of operation, and an ever increasing need both for differentiation – of the product and the market – and for integration – of the organization and the environment. And in this context the manager's scientific knowledge and analytical skills become ever more appropriate.

For the developmental manager alone basic business instincts and generalized functions of business and management are not enough: he or she needs to be able to recognize and interrelate the attitudes, behaviour, cultures and institutions of the different parts of the globe in which he or she is operating. For the first time the differences between East and West, North and South make a significant impact on the managerial worldview. The developmental manager, then, assumes a genuinely cosmopolitan outlook. And this, as we shall see, has a crucial influence on the individual's ability to learn and to innovate.

Notes

1 R. Reich, *Tales of a New America*. Random House, 1987, pp. 7, 40.
2 Reich, *Tales of a New America*, pp. 9–10.
3 Reich, *Tales of a New America*, p. 86. The reference at the end of the quotation is to Lew Lehr, chairman of 3M in the early 1980s, who saw the business world providing 'mother institutions' that would compensate for the loss of the extended family in the West.
4 Reich, *Tales of a New America*, pp. 168–71.
5 Reich, *Tales of a New America*, p. 17.
6 Reich, *Tales of a New America*, p. 253.
7 B. De Mente, *Japanese Etiquette and Ethics in Business*. Passport Books, 5th edn, 1987, p. 12.
8 P. Wickens, *The Road to Nissan*. Macmillan, 1987, p. 46.
9 Wickens, *The Road to Nissan*, p. 92.
10 H. Nakamura, *Ways of Thinking of Eastern Peoples*. East–West Publications, 1968, p. 17.
11 H. Tanaka, *Personality in Industry*. Pinter, 1988, p. 17.
12 Tanaka, *Personality in Industry*, p. 88.
13 J. N. Hillman, *Revisioning Psychology*. Aquarian Press, 1975, p. 15.
14 Hillman, *Revisioning Psychology*, p. 26.
15 L. Van Der Post, *Venture into the Interior*. Penguin Books, 1954, p. 111.
16 D. Lan, *Guns and Rain*. Zimbabwe Publishing House, 1985, p. 75.

PART II

Developmental Management
in Action: the Fruits

Introduction

As an organization successfully evolves *formatively*, *normatively* and then *integratedly*, it applies a different bias at each stage of its unfolding operation:

> behavioural (action),
> cognitive (thought),
> affective (feeling).

It is the extent to which developmental managers are able to recognize and promote these sequences and combinations of activity that determines their potential for success.

These three human attributes characterize development in any kind of organization. They involve seven managerial and organizational traits in the overlapping sets, which, when lined up horizontally, constitute the totality of human and organizational potential (Figure II.I.1). In order to tap the fullness of this potential, developmental

Figure II.I.1 The Learning Field

managers need to instigate healthy communications across the entire spread of individuals and personalities. As such communications arise so genuine interdependence is attained across personal, departmental and cultural boundaries, and this in turn gives access to the field of *participative learning.*

The developing organization is a learning organization; it is a force field across which currents pass horizontally and vertically. The horizontal axis, already accounted for, creates a field of communication characterized by a series of managerial traits. The vertical axis creates a field of innovation and individuation characterized by a set of managerial functions. To tap the full potential for innovation, developmental managers must facilitate a full range of learning activities – involving different degrees of action, thought and feeling – in the entire field defined by the two axes of his own functions.

8

Learning and Innovation

Introduction

Participative and Active Learning

Within conventional analytical management the different business disciplines – finance, marketing, operations and human resources – all, as we have seen, undergo separate development. The general manager therefore has an arduous task in bringing them together. Within developmental management, each of the disciplines is rooted in an evolutionary process of learning, which emerges out of the progressive and cumulative interaction between

> action,
> thought,
> feeling.

The first aspect of innovative learning, *participation*, is 'horizontal' learning. It arises through communication *between individuals and institutions* within the organization and market-place. The second aspect, *anticipation*, is 'vertical' learning. It takes place *inside the individual* as he plays his role in the organization and market-place.

Personal and Business Transactions

Underlying these learning processes are the basic factors that determine the nature not only of individuals and organizations, but also of products (or services) and markets. These factors are none other than *action*, *thought* and *feeling*. Psychologically, for the individual and organization, these are made up of

behavioural,
cognitive,
affective

processes. Commercially, for the product or service and market, they
consist of the

product offer	service support
product content	service expertise
product aura	service relationship.

In other words, the basic elements of social and economic transactions,
whether between members of an organization or between customers
and suppliers, consist not of the traditional 'men, money and
machines' but of *active/behavioural, reflective/cognitive* and *interactive/
affective* processes.

These processes, in their turn, underlie *participative* and *anticipative*
learning.

Participative Learning: for Individuals and Enterprises

Individuals and Organizations

Individuals and organizations, then, as well as products and markets,
learn or adapt horizontally through participative transactions. You
grow individually by responding to me, as another individual. We
grow as a company by responding to the emerging needs of our
market-place. We grow as a society by responding to other societies.
Such psychological or commercial responses are behavioural, cognitive
or affective in their nature.

The three psychological responses

Each one of us, then, commercially and managerially, is made up of
action, thought and feeling, and each of these manifests itself in
different degrees, depending not only on the situation but also on our
personalities. Our personal transactions with other people, therefore,
will be more or less 'reactive', 'thoughtful' or 'emotional', depending
on both our own individuality and theirs. For example, if you and I are
both highly reflective people we are more likely to exchange
information and ideas than to engage in emotional or physical

interaction: that is, we are 'strongly differentiated' cognitively, but perhaps not affectively or behaviourally. We can take our respective ideas apart and put them together in new ways, but we are not so good at committing ourselves, nor at making things happen together. So we gain business knowledge (cognitively) from each other, but not personal (affective) or management (behavioural) skills.

The personality spectrum

However, the three personality constitutents are not cut and dried; rather they are fluid and overlapping, like variable mathematical sets rather than building-blocks. As Figure 8.1 shows, the three overlapping constituents produce seven composite attributes.

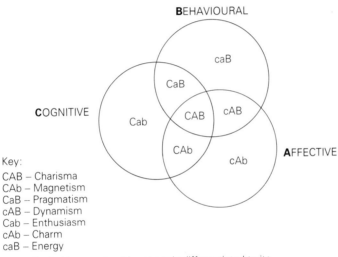

Key:
CAB – Charisma
CAb – Magnetism
CaB – Pragmatism
cAB – Dynamism
Cab – Enthusiasm
cAb – Charm
caB – Energy

Note: Capital letters stand for strongly differentiated traits.

Figure 8.1 Three Personality Constituents: Seven Attributes

The British management psychologist Kevin Kingsland, who has also worked extensively in India and the US, with individuals and organizations, argues that people are capable of engaging in a complete spectrum of interpersonal interactions.[1] Yet, individuals normally function only within a restricted area of themselves, in the same way as an organization may function only within a limited area of its corporate personality. In other words, a part of you, or your organization, is strongly differentiated and other parts are not. As a result, you will be likely to identify yourself primarily with only one or two out of the spectrum of individual, intrapreneurial[2] and managerial characters represented in Table 8.1.

Table 8.1 The Developmental Spectrum

Code	Personality	'Intrapreneur'	Transactions
CAB	Charismatic	Innovator	Images
CAb	Magnetic	Enabler	Insights
CaB	Pragmatic	Executive	Procedures
cAB	Dynamic	Entrepreneur	Deals
Cab	Enthusiastic	Change agent	Data
cAb	Charming	Animator	People
caB	Energetic	Adventurer	Actions

Interpersonal transactions

Each one of us, commercially and managerially, is biased towards one form of transaction rather than another. Similarly, we respond more easily to other people who share our behavioural, cognitive and affective learnings. Problems arise when, for example, an entrepreneurial manager tries to communicate with a manager of change, for they have no strongly differentiated attitude in common (see Figure 8.1).

Thus *participative* (horizontally based) *learning between people is most likely when they share some attributes but not others.* If they share nothing – behaviourally, cognitively or affectively – they have no basis for communication. On the other hand, if they are exactly alike, there is little in the way of added learning value.

Cultural transactions

Similar principles of differentiation apply to corporate and national cultures. The more we are willing and able to open ourselves to other cultures, the more we are able to learn. But if two cultures have no common psychological language to start with, their transactions will inevitably be severely constrained. For example, as a generalization, Japanese managers are affective, cognitive and behavioural, in that order. The English, on the other hand, are cognitive, behavioural and affective, in that sequence. While there is scope for superficial cross-cultural learning at the level of data exchange, the instincts (behavioural) and attitudes (affective) of the two nations are very much at odds. As a result, an Englishman can appreciate intellectually the Japanese approach to people management much more readily than emotionally and behaviourally. In order to acquire a deep understanding of Japanese management and culture, we have to engage in affective and behavioural transactions. They might arise through a sharing of cultural insights, social interactions or business activities.

Enterprises and Markets

A developmental approach to management is by no means exclusive to individuals and organizations. It is also readily applicable to enterprises and markets. Whereas conventional approaches to business strategy[3] and to marketing[4] are analytically based and functionally self-contained, the developmental approach[5] is adapted to different markets and crosses functional boundaries. Interfunctional management therefore replaces functional specialization.

The three psychological aspects of the market-place

The developmental approach to the market-place resembles that adopted for the individual and the organization. This is hardly surprising, for market-places are made up of people.

Table 8.2 Personal and Market Transactions

Personal transaction	Product transaction	Service transaction
Behavioural	Offer	Support
Cognitive	Content	Expertise
Affective	Aura or Image	Relationship

- The *behavioural* aspect of a product or service transaction between a customer and a company, is a product *offer* on the one hand, or a service *support* on the other.
- The *thoughtful* side of the customers is stimulated by a concept or perception of the *content* of the product, or by the *expertise* that the service offers.
- The *feeling* side of the customer in the market-place is stimulated by an attraction to and empathy with the product's *aura*, or by the breadth and depth of the *relationship* the customer has with the service.

Different behavioural (offer and support), cognitive (content and expertise) and affective (aura and relationship) combinations therefore result in a full spectrum of product and service transactions (see Table 8.2 and Figure 8.2).

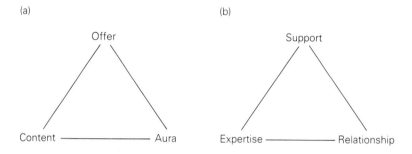

Figure 8.2   (a) Product Sets (b) Service Sets

The developmental individual and the developmental firm are able to cope, potentially if not actually, with a wide variety of differentiated market transactions, of both product and service varieties. To the extent that such diverse transactions with people and markets are successfully completed, individuals and organizations, as well as departments and companies, learn and evolve.

The market spectrum

Specifically, therefore, both product and service transactions, as perceived by the market-place, can be categorized across a full spectrum of alternatives, as shown in Table 8.3. Each department or company is biased towards some transactions rather than others. For example, an innovative systems house may be poles apart from a basic commodity dealer. The UK entrepreneur Clive Sinclair, for example, has always had trouble adapting from one to the other.

Ease in communications and hence productive transactions are, not unnaturally, associated with congruent relations between producer and consumer. If a restaurateur offers fine cuisine and personalized attention (aura, relationship), he will seek out customers who are looking for stylish food and personal service (aura, relationship). On the other hand, if a company wishes continually to evolve its product

Table 8.3 The Spectrum of Product and Service Transactions

Code	'Intrapreneur'	Managerial transaction	Market transaction	Differentiation Product	Service
CAB	Innovator	Creative	Systemic	Content, aura Offer	Expertise, relationship Support
CAb	Enabler/ Designer	Farsighted	Exclusive	Content, aura	Expertise, relationship
CaB	Executive	Integral	Specialized	Content Offer	Expertise Support
cAB	Entrepreneur	Emotional	Customized	Aura Offer	Relationship Support
Cab	Change agent	Experimental	Consulting	Content	Expertise
cAb	Animator	Social	Craftsmanlike	Aura	Relationship
caB	Adventurer	Physical	Commodity-like	Offer	Support

or service, it will want to find customers and market-places that are only partially similar to itself. For example, a specialized producer of medical equipment (CaB in Table 8.3) could gain from an association with a private hospital that was looking for exclusively designed products (CAb). As a result of such a transaction the supplier may become more sensitive to individual customer needs, from both an engineering and a market perspective.

Similarly, two companies undertaking a joint venture will need to draw on similarities and differences if each is to learn from their combined transactions. For example, an employment bureau offering a customized service (cAB in Table 8.3) to corporate clients could productively combine forces with a systems house (CAB) designing innovative personnel-based software. While the systems house might become more entrepreneurial if it opened itself to change, the bureau might become more innovative. However, if the bureau (cAB) formed a joint venture with a consultancy firm of pure boffins (Cab), it would soon run into trouble with its clients for its increasingly 'harebrained' schemes.

Summary

So much for the participative transactions undertaken by individuals and organizations, and by enterprises in market-places. Each transaction is not only made up of similar constituents, but heeds common principles of participative learning. Organizational and consumer behaviour find common cause. In fact, the transactional approach to business and management, drawing upon underlying learning processes, is essentially integrative and interdisciplinary rather than analytical and functional.

We now turn from participative to anticipative learning and from horizontal to vertical aspects of individuality and interdependence

Anticipative Learning

Individual and Organizational Development

Participative learning arises in organizational and environmental space. Anticipative learning evolves over time. However, the same attributes – individual and organizational, business and market – are involved in both. I shall begin with individual and organizational learning – the *departure* – and then investigate the process of innovation – the *return*. These terms highlight the theory that learning is an upward movement and innovation a downward one, though they involve a group of similar *transactions* (Figure 8.3).

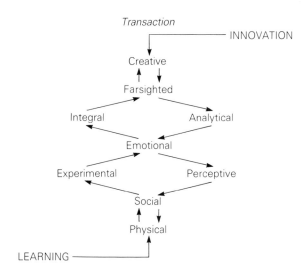

Figure 8.3 Learning and Innovation

Individual Development

Personal learning: the 'departure'

The role of adventurer: the first, physical transaction
The *call to adventure* represents the first, physical step: *without activity there is no learning.* The new-born baby learns about life through physical challenge and response. When learning ceases to be an adventure it loses its primordial appeal, for the individual and the organization alike.

The role of animator: the second, social transaction
The role of the *animator* symbolizes the supportive part to be played by a mother figure, a caring teacher, or by 'comrades in adversity'. *Without a social context, learning becomes depersonalized and sterile.* If you fail to open yourself to the supportive influence of colleagues, coaches and mentors, who inevitably cross your learning path, your journey will be in vain. Without this influence an individual or organizational entity will remain insular and insulated.

The role of change agent: the third, experimental transaction
The role of the *change agent* in the individual's or organization's development is deliberately to introduce experimentation into both life and work. The learner thereby incorporates *trial and error* and *action and reflection* in order to learn from experience. This is the period of mental alertness and youthful discovery that forms such an important part of an individual's or organization's growth and development. Any task you tackle, then, should involve some degree of exploration and experimentation before you commit yourself to a particular line of thought or action.

The role of entrepreneur: the fourth, emotional transaction
Risking the loss of your self is the inward equivalent of the outward risk-taking that accompanies business and personal enterprise. There is no real learning without such risk. Whatever ideas you evolve intellectually, you must develop the *emotional commitment* to put both them and yourself to the test. In the process you may become a different person, disassembled and reassembled, as a result of the emotional wrangles you have undergone.

The role of executive: the fifth, integral transaction

As your new self fully emerges, or a new organizational structure is revealed, a further learning step is required if there is to be continued development. An integration between the thrusting force of the newly formed individual or organization and the receptive force of an existing organization or environment is needed if the individual is to outgrow narrowly based self-interest and the institution inward-looking bureaucracy. The combined result is a *rounded business concept*, an individual with *role integrity*, and an organization with a *coherent philosophy*.

The role of enabler: the sixth, farsighted transaction

A person may have role integrity and an organization a coherent philosophy, but neither will ensure that they have *penetrated to the source of their being*. That degree of understanding of the *source and destination* of your personal or organizational existence requires a particular brand of individual and environmental insight. Such insight is developed through:

a capacity to listen
a power to observe
a willingness to be overawed
an ability and inclination to link like with unlike, actual with potential,
    visible energy with invisible spirit.

The role of innovator: the seventh, creative transaction

The acquisition of vision, finally, comes only when the insight developed through penetrating the source of the individual's or organization's being, is creatively worked through in practice. You learn about the *power of vision* only when you engage in the *creative action* that serves to bring it about. There is a lot of the chicken and egg about it, it is always difficult to tell which came first. But when you have acquired the power of vision, nothing will hold you back from transforming your environment.

Attributes of Vision

When you have found your vision you do not ask yourself whether you have one. You inform the world about it. If you're wondering whether you have a vision, then you haven't got one.

When you've discovered your vision, you abound with inspiration. Your eyes sparkle. You can see it in the atmosphere. It is pulsing with life.

When you have a vision everything you plan and do stems from it. Its all-consuming nature makes all previous attitudes and ideas seem like a training ground for the ultimate vision.

When you feel part of an overall vision you don't think of rest and reward. Total absorption removes all sense of personal effort. You cannot help but pursue the vision.

When you have a vision that is all you want to talk about. Everything people say or do is a readout of that vision. The world becomes a theatre for your visionary script.

When the vision is present in you everyone around gets included or ignored, depending on whether or not they feel associated with it. In other words, people become actors in your production or else they remain off stage.

When you find your vision nothing will be permitted to stand in its way. Obstacles must be overcome or else life won't be worth living for you.[6]

Personal innovation: the 'return'

Learning reflects the individual's or organization's *upward* journey, from the *call to adventure* on to the *acquisition of visionary power*. *Innovation* represents the journey *downward*, from *vision* to *action*.

Developing your vision: the first, creative transaction

- What is your personal mission?
- How is it going to change the world around you?
- How will its fulfilment change your life, work and vocation?
- What universal problem will your unique idea solve?
- Where does your imagination lead you?

Vision will be stillborn unless it is united with insight and understanding, and thereby with social need.

Recognizing market need: the second, farsighted transaction

- Does your idea have market or organizational potential?
- How are technology and society evolving and where does your vision fit in with such developments?
- What particular market trends or social needs pertain to your idea?
- What underlying need will you serve?
- What business partnerships and alliances will arise?

If vision is father to the innovation and need is mother, the offspring is your role in the organization.

Structuring your role: the third, analytical transaction

- What is your role in the organization?
- What product or service of yours is being designed for what market?
- How is the product created, developed, produced and sold?
- How does your role interact with others in the organization and outside?
- How are physical and human resources procured and channelled?

The product and organization, once designed, are brought to life through the commitment of your inner will and outer resources.

Acquiring resources: the fourth, emotional transaction

- What's in it for you personally and financially?
- What is your competitive advantage?
- Who will champion your product's cause?
- What is the risk and what is the likely return?
- How do you sell yourself?

Once the commitment is made, progress needs to be planned and monitored so both individual and organization can respond purposefully to change.

Adapting to change: the fifth, perceptive transaction

- How are your targets and programmes established and monitored?
- How are tasks planned and implemented, step by step?
- What systems have been installed to process information?
- What experimental forms enable you and your organization to adapt to change?
- How does the organization provide you with scope for free expression?

The next step involves people, that is, literally all those employees, customers, suppliers, shareholders and other allies who comprise the human body of the organization.

Involving people: the sixth, social transaction

- How do you foster shared values so that people feel they belong?
- What myths and rituals will bind your people together?

- How do you bring about a family atmosphere and a sense of community?
- How do you maintain closeness to your client or customer?
- How do you achieve productivity through people?

Finally and ultimately, the complex and ethereal vision needs to be embodied in simple tangible form, to inspire effort.

Taking action: the seventh, physical transaction

- What and how much per day do you physically produce?
- How do you keep the energy level up, in yourself and others?
- How do you ensure that what you produce remains constantly and physically visible both inside and outside the business?
- How do you impose a sense of urgency?
- How do you maintain a bias for action?

The same principles of learning and innovation, involving the vertical assimilation of the spectrum of transaction, can also be applied to the organization as a whole.

Organizational Development

Organizational learning

Learning, for the organization, as for the individual, encompasses:

physical adventure
communal involvement
experimentation with new technology
commercial risk-taking
organizational consolidation
assimilation of the surrounding environment
the progressive re-creation of the corporate image.

Innovation works the other way round.

Organizational innovation
Organizational innovation involves the following sequence of trans-actions between the organization and its environment:

- Uncovering the historically based vision of the organization.
  - What are the origins of your company's national culture and economy?

- What are the product and technology?
- What were the founder's underlying motives and psychology?
- What powerful and captivating vision has emerged out of your company's unique cultural, economic, technological and personal heritage?
- How can it be stated and visually represented in the word and picture language of uplift and idealism?
- How might it serve as a 'meta-vision' to embrace each of your people's own personal visions?
- Relating the acquired vision to an underlying context, thereby discovering its meaning or significance.
  - What unique cultural and economic context, in the pattern of geographical space and historical time, marks your evolving enterprise?
- Structuring and conceptualizing the link between vision and context, thereby defining the product and organization in practical terms.
  - What particularly appropriate principles and structures of management and organization have you developed in your company?
- Harnessing the will and motivation of your people to drive the company forward, committed to profitable growth.
  - How have you tapped the egotistical drives of your people?
  - How have you provided the means of channelling these self-centred motives into the common cause, commercially, organizationally and culturally?
- Adapting to change so that the forces of single-minded commitment and clearly principled management do not cause rigidity and inflexibility.
  - How do you keep your organization and resource base fluid so that strength of commitment can be linked with flexibility of response?
- Establishing a family atmosphere whereby values are shared and people feel they belong together.
  - How do you cultivate a family atmosphere in your company with a common identity and culture, reinforced by social ties and binding myths and rituals?
  - How do you nevertheless encourage individual flexibility and enterprise, so that individuals can dream their own dreams within the context of the whole?

- Ensuring that the vision is continuously manifested in action, through which the dream ultimately becomes a reality, the true power of vision is realized and the resources of the earth are transformed.
- How are you deploying energy to transform energy, so that, in turn, your vision can be refuelled, reformed and renewed?

Now that we have investigated the inverse processes of learning and innovation for the individual and organization, it is time to turn to the enterprise and market-place.

Product (or Service) and Market Development

Individuals and organizations learn, then, by cumulatively evolving from physical to creative activity. They innovate in the reverse order.

The same adaptive processes apply to products and markets. In this case, however, we substitute the terms *growth* and *decay* for *learning* and *innovation*. Creation and destruction are part of the cycle of life, one being necessary for the other. In order to build some things up, you need to break others down. Before building up a new concept of, say, developmental management, you have to break down the old analytical one.

Just as learning and innovation in the development of individuals and organizations have their sequences of transactions, so do growth and decay in the development of products and markets (Figure 8.4).

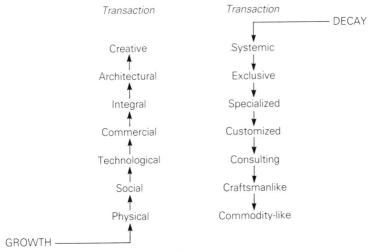

Figure 8.4 Product Growth and Market Decay

Product (or service) growth

Growing a new product or service is analogous with personal and organizational learning. The same basic elements, as we shall now see, are involved – only the context changes, from the individual and organizational to the technological and commercial. We begin again, then, with the element of physical adventure.

The role of adventurer: the first, physical transaction
The process of developing a product or service begins with the *physical manipulation of matter or energy*, whether it is in the form of chemical molecules, pieces of plywood or data on a computer screen. The outcome of such activity is generally a raw, unprocessed or semi-processed *commodity*, whether it is a roughly hewn piece of wood or a rough smattering of ideas scribbled on a piece of paper. If you fail to get to grips with the basic raw material of your envisaged product or service, be it in the form of things or information, your subsequent development will inevitably be 'half-baked', be it a cake or a new database!

The role of animator: the second, social transaction
No product or service was ever dreamed up in isolation. Not only are most new developments today the result of teamwork rather than the creativity of an individual inventor, but even the lone technical boffin has to place his invention into some social context. For *a product or service without a customer is worthless.* As you play with your new-fangled recipe, logo or keyboard, you need at an early stage to bring the customer into the picture as well as your team members. *No developer or designer can afford to be isolated.*

At this second, social stage, then, you not only maintain close contacts with colleagues and customers, but you begin to hear the right noises. People around you like what you are doing; they feel you are onto a good thing. The product you are developing has a good aura about it, or the service you are evolving seems to relate to them. There is a sense of *craftsmanlike* shared values and mutual approval between producer and product (or service), supplier and prospective customer, and members of the team working together.

The role of change agent: the third, technological transaction
The time will soon come, after five weeks or five years, depending on the kind of business you are in, when you will need to *produce*

something new that works. Whether it is a pencil or a pocket calculator, a waffle or a war movie, it not only has to *serve its projected purpose* but it also has to *do it differently* from the existing product or service.

You will not arrive at this new graphic, electronic, culinary or cinematic technology all at once. It is an *interactive* process, involving *thought* and *experiment*, data gathering and processing. In the process you build up a *flexible network of relationships* within and outside the firm. Gradually, moreover, your originally raw commmodity will begin to assume a more refined function, providing specific outputs that the prospective user perceives as beneficial. So the product you have developed has the *right content* or your service offers the *right expertise*, as far as the customer is concerned.

The role of entrepreneur: the fourth, commercial transaction

At the earlier, social stage of the product's development, a customer will have been involved, or at least envisaged prospectively. At this fourth, commercial stage, he or she needs to be convinced to buy your product or service. At this point, then, it becomes *customized* or *consumerized*. Emphasis within your company shifts from production to marketing but without losing touch with the technology, the people and the raw materials from which the new item came. A bond of unassailable trust is formed between the key players within the company and outside.

If the customized item developed is a product, like a gardening book or a machine tool, it makes a strong impact on the individual or institutional customer; it offers exactly what he or she wants and its image is pitched right. If it is a service, be it a pension scheme or an office cleaning facility, not only is the support provided strongly customized but the relationship with the client is a very warm one.

The role of executive: the fifth, integral transaction

An account executive in a top-rate computer bureau or advertising agency is responsible for offering his or her client a family of specialized products or a portfolio of specialized services, rather than a single product or service. By this stage, therefore, the product or service has evolved from a single offering or support to a *specialized product or service line*.

The account executive's function therefore is to mix and match the content of the product family with the specialized market requirements, or to mix and match the expertise contained within the portfolio of services with the customers' specialized needs. In order to do this successfully he or she has to *manage the interface* not only between product and market but also between the different departments within the organization concerned with the development, production and distribution of the product or service.

The role of designer: the sixth, architectural transaction

As the product or service is progressively developed so its complexity increases, not only in itself but also through the evolving relationship between supplier and customer. Whereas the account executive offers a family or portfolio of specialized products or services to a particular market segment, the *corporate architect evolves total environments*, combining either content and aura or expertise and relationship.

For example, the development of Habitat led to a whole new shopping experience for millions of people in Britain. Both the style of the merchandise and the aura of the shops are entirely distinctive. Seen from this perspective Terence Conran has evolved from craftsman and entrepreneur to not so much an executive as a corporate architect. He has created a *unique ambience* within which product and service, building interior and exterior, combine harmoniously with the customer's needs.

The role of inventor: the seventh, creative transaction

Whereas the corporate architect develops an exclusive environment within which his unique products or services are sold, the fully fledged *inventor* creates a *whole new system of production and marketing*, product offer and service support.

The classic case in point is Henry Ford, who spent many, many years tampering with machinery before he produced his first car; having tried it out on a few friends and then some associates, he became involved in small-scale production before aiming at a wider market. Ultimately he caused a transportation revolution, through his original system of mass production and mass marketing of automobiles. This combined new product *content* (the horseless carriage) with a new product *aura* (modern mechanized man), as well as a new manifestation of *expertise* (the assembly line) and a new customer *relationship* (dealer network). The product made a dramatic physical, economic and social impact, first on America then on the whole world, and paved the way for a completely new service industry and customer support base, through selling and repairing automobiles.

In retrospect, however, Ford's automobile degenerated from a production and marketing system into a mere commodity: 'any customer can have a car painted any color that he wants so long as it is black'. But that happened only after a prolonged and creative process of market decay. As for the man himself, while he was full of internal contradictions, he was undoubtedly a man of immense genius and creative spirit.

Market Decay

As a business learns and develops – through its products and services – so it evolves from commodity status to a complex system. Conran did not create Habitat overnight, and Henry Ford was forty-six when he set up Ford Motors. Both men spent their earlier years evolving and learning.

While personal and product growth is a positive life-force, market and environmental decay is a negative one. Interestingly, though, each needs the other: *positive* and *negative* charges are both *vital* to our physical, psychological and economic development. It is as if the anticipation of business and market decay, like that of mortality, provides the spur and challenge to commercial and psychological growth, while the prospects of economic evolution provide the support and encouragement.

Systemic market transactions

The culmination of business development, as we have now seen, is the invention of a totally new system of products and services. This system, in its turn, calls into play a unique set of market transactions. *Systemic market transactions* involve uniquely differentiated products and services, in which the overall offer and the support – that is, the product content and service expertise, as well as the product aura and service relationship – are unparalleled in the market-place.

A typical European example is the natural skin and hair care franchise, Body Shop International. Not only are Body Shop products unique but the store image is wholly distinctive and the customer service – both in the degree of expertise possessed by staff and in the personalized relationship created with customers – is unsurpassed in the business. In the USA Apple Computers in its original form was a similar case in point.

Exclusive market transactions

But the inevitable law of markets is that just as a business gains its aim of creating uniquely differentiated products and services a process of market decay has already set in. There are a number of stores now that have set up in competition with Body Shop. Each of these aims to offer exclusive products to its customers – that is, those interested in buying natural cosmetics – but none has come up with fundamentally new products or services. In other words, rivals are trying to compete with Body Shop on content and aura, on the one hand, while offering only marginal product variations on the other.

As market decay progresses, though, a range of exclusive brands will inevitably appear, each with its own differentiated *content* and *image*. Similarly, a range of exclusive services will be bound to appear, each with its own differentiated *expertise* and *relationships*. In these conditions customers no longer base their choice on all four differentiated features but only on one or two of them.

Specialized market transactions

At this point the market for, say, designer clothes or exclusive computer software becomes less differentiated, particularly insofar as *product aura* and *service relationships* are concerned. The 'feel' and distinctiveness of the offer or support become les important than its *functionality*. In relation to the psychological constituents discussed earlier, we have witnessed a movement from CAB (systemic) to CAb (exclusive) to CaB (specialized) (see Table 8.3).

A good example of such a functional transaction is that between a clothes shopper and Marks & Spencer; thirty years ago transactions with Marks & Spencer may have been viewed in a more exclusive light, and this was certainly so a hundred years ago when Michael Marks was first making a revolutionary impact on the British shopper. Today the specialized transaction between the shopper and M&S could be contrasted with the more exclusive transaction between a shopper and Benetton, which has a particular and strong aura.

Customized market transactions

As the perceived differentiation of the product or service declines even further (which may now be the case with personal computers), companies seek to differentiate the *aura* or *relationship* of their offer or support, rather than its content or expertise. This is because by this time there is such a proliferation of content and expertise that a kind of market saturation sets in. Often entrepreneurial characters such as Alan Sugar are able to take advantage of such market situations: although Sugar's Amstrad computer is perceived virtually as a commodity in the UK, a very strong aura pervades his company, and he has a powerful set of *customized* relationships with selected retailers.

Consulting transactions

In a mature market, such as that for automobiles, the perceived opportunities within the market-place for fundamental product and service innovations are limited. Moreover, there is a proliferation of specialized and customized products and services. Increasingly the customer begins to look for specific technological features such as fuel-saving devices or speedier gear transmissions. Emphasis therefore turns to specific content and expertise but within a more limited context than has hitherto been the case. Dense manuals convey to the customer the 'expert systems' built into the automobile.

Craftsmanlike transactions

Further proliferations of knowledge, taste and purchasing power among both producer and consumer lead to even finer degrees of market differentiation. The demand for personal service, in very select contexts, is accentuated. The recent upsurge in *customer care* programmes implemented by banks, railways and airlines may be seen as an attempt to raise the level of competence on this transaction level. Similarly, in the clothing industry, a resurgence of craftsmanship and the opening of craft shops, particularly in relation to knitwear, is a response to market decay.

Commodity-like transactions

Ultimately (as is now the case, for example, in the markets for computers and confectionery) the market decays towards commodity status, where intense and fierce competition is based on such tangible and immediate features as price and accessibility. At this point *the customer views the product or service in its most rudimentary form.*

Conclusion

Personal Learning and Corporate Growth

Participation

As for individuals so for business enterprises, most learning takes place across transactional boundaries. Horizontally – that is participatively – an *exclusive* producer (CAb) can learn a great deal from his *specialized* counterpart (CaB), whereas a fellow exclusive manufacturer is likely to be too similar to provide significant knowledge and insight, and a commodity producer (caB) stands too far apart.

Anticipation

Vertically – anticipatively – learning also takes place across boundaries: an enterprise will develop fully if it is able to identify with the entire range of transactions from commodity-like to systemic. However, while a *consultancy-based* group (Cab) can learn from a *systemic* (CAB), *exclusive* (CAb) or *specialized* (CaB) manufacturer, it is unlikely to be able to learn much from a mass producer of packaged commodities (caB) or from a cooperative group of craftsmen (cAb).

Innovation and Decay

Ironically, the processes of market decay parallel those of individual and organizational innovation. Specifically, the process whereby an innovator turns a vision into action or an idea into reality mirrors the process of market decay from systemic to commodity transactions. The parallel processes are illustrated in Table 8.4.

Table 8.4 Personal/Organizational Innovation and Market Decay

Personal/Organizational Innovation	Market Decay
Developing a vision	Systemic transactions
Recognizing potential	Exclusive transactions
Structuring an organization	Specialized transactions
Committing resources	Customized transactions
Adapting to change	Consulting transactions
Involving people	Craftsmanlike transactions
Making things happen	Commodity-like transactions

The implications of this phenomenon are twofold. First, it seems *the true innovator must be willing continually to undergo processes of creation and destruction.* In other words, by turning his revolutionary system into a commodity, the innovator is supplanting the very creativity that was responsible for his company's birth. As a result he is continually having to renew and replenish his creative energies, if he is to succeed on a large scale.

Second, in order to be able to transact across a multiplicity of levels, *the developing company needs to be highly sensitized both to the processes of market decay and to the full spectrum of its own transactional capabilities.* The more sensitized it is vertically – that is, behaviourally, cognitively and affectively – the more sensitized it will be horizontally, and vice versa.

The company's transactional *adaptability* will be *externally* represented by its familiarity with the *full spectrum of market-places* and *internally* by its equivalent *operational, financial, marketing* and *personnel responses*. As a result, developmental management will dominate the company's strategic and organizational behaviour. Doubtless, the company's adaptability in the market-place and its ability to evolve will be conditioned by the manager's adaptability and ability to mature as an individual.

To see this in action, we shall now review the processes of individual and organizational learning in a specific corporate context. That context is set within our economic and societal evolution.

Notes

1 K. Kingsland, *The Whole Personality.* Unpublished manuscript, 1985.
2 R. Lessem, *Intrapreneurship.* Wildwood House, 1988.
3 I. Ansoff, *Corporate Strategy.* McGraw Hill, 1964.
4 P. Kotler, *Marketing Management: Analysis, Planning, and Control.* Prentice Hall, 1965; 2nd edn, 1968.
5 S. Mathur, 'Thinking Strategically', *Journal of General Management*, June 1984, pp. 34–42. H. Murray, *Markets and Marketing.* Unpublished paper, 1988.
6 Kingsland, *The Whole Personality*, p. 86.

9

Innovative Learning at Dexion

Introduction

Introducing the Learning Organization

The 19th century was the age of *economic man*. Economic achievement, endorsed by both Church and State, became the hallmark of the industrializing societies. The 20th century, however, has seen the rise of *organizational man*. Institutional power, endorsed by both 'free' and socialist enterprise, has supplanted personal power. The 21st century is likely to herald the successor to economic and organizational man – the whole person.

The 19th century was the age of the *entrepreneur*. In the 20th century the *rational executive* has taken command: business administration has taken over from business entrepreneurship, the bureaucratic organization from the pioneering enterprise. The 21st century, as I see it, will be the era of the *learning organization*.

Within such an organization a healthy array of individual managers, institutions and cultures hold interdependent sway. In the vertical dimension, each engages in an ongoing evolutionary process of learning and development (upwards), and a continuing transformative process of innovation and creativity (downwards). In the horizontal dimension, each participates in an interactive process of learning with and through others.

The Limits to Learning

The learning project

As long ago as the late 1970s the Italian industrialist and management philosopher Aurelio Peccei set up a *learning project* to deal with the whole question of societal learning.

> Tangles of mutually reinforcing old and new problems, too complex to be apprehended by the current analytical methods and too tough to be attacked by traditional policies and strategies, are clustering together, heedless of boundaries. There is a desperate need to break these vicious circles. An entirely new enterprise is thus required. Focusing on people, this new enterprise must be aimed at developing the latent innermost capability of learning so that the march of events can eventually be brought under control.[1]

Maintenance learning

The American Jim Botkin, who headed Peccei's learning project, and two colleagues from eastern Europe and north Africa, distinguished between two forms of learning. The first, *maintenance learning*, involves the acquisition of fixed outlooks, methods and rules for dealing with known and recurring situations. This is the realm of the *analytical manager*, suitably at home when internal and external environments remain the same. Maintenance learning, therefore, is indispensable for the stability of the individual, the organization and our societies.

Innovative learning

For long-term survival, however – particularly in times of turbulence, change and discontinuity – another type of learning is more essential, one that is more compatible with development. It is a type of learning that can bring – individually and collectively – change, renewal or total transformation.

Botkin's *innovative learning* is divided into two:

- *Anticipative learning*, which corresponds to our vertical variety, involves the *consideration of trends* and the *making of plans*, so as to shield institutions from the trauma of learning by shock. Through anticipative learning, the future, for the individual and the organization, may enter our lives as a friend and not as an assailant.

- *Participative learning*, which corresponds to our horizontal variety, involves *cooperation*, *dialogue* and *empathy*. It requires not only keeping communications open but also constantly testing one's own operating rules and values against those of others. Without participation, anticipation is futile; and participation without anticipation can be misguided.

On the one hand, then, managers within learning organizations have to be able to enrich their context, keeping up with the rapid appearance of new situations. On the other hand, they must communicate the variety of contexts through ongoing dialogue with other individuals, institutions and cultures. The one is pointless without the other. Whereas anticipation stimulates 'vertical' learning in time, participation allows 'horizontal' learning across space.

The Learning Organization is Born

Comino–Dexion

A learning organization of both vertical and horizontal varieties came into existence some sixty years ago, when a Greek-Australian resident in Great Britain started up the Krisson Printing company in a basement in central London. Out of those humble origins Demetrius Comino developed his company Dexion, creating, in time, an industry for storage and materials-handling equipment that has spread worldwide.

More importantly, however, Comino created an organization geared towards innovative learning. We shall take Dexion International as our example of the learning community or organization, making due reference to Comino's pioneering thoughts and actions.

> In Dexion we believe that a company is a living organism; in order to be really healthy, it must grow and develop. We therefore regard growth as fundamental. The most important single requirement therefore laid on us is the requirement of learning, or, to put it differently, it's how it is that we can become effective systems for our own transformation, as individuals and as organizations. Such self-transformation (learning) must become a continuing process, a way of life.[2]

Participative Learning

In 1927 Comino, a qualified mechanical engineer, left his employer to set up a venture of his own. He had no idea what business he wanted to go into, but he did have some very definite intimations of the kind of organization he wanted to create. He described these later in a letter to one of his employees during the war.

> Our equipment now consists of half a dozen lathes, a couple of milling machines, a drill and diverse other small devices. Most precious of all is the experience gained, literally at the cost of sweat and blood. We don't know what kind of economic and social system we will finally find ourselves in, but it will certainly be a gain to work out our salvation as a group rather than as isolated individuals. Whatever kind of place it is, we should be able to make some sort of centre in it for ourselves (I almost said corner, but centre is the word.) It is a radiating centre we want, not a retreat.[3]

Comino went into printing because he had some Greek business friends who needed materials printed. From the outset he employed school-leavers from the East End of London for both economic and social reasons. At an early stage there was established a complementarity of managerial effort between Comino, the *visionary* and *agent of change*, and Fred Riley the *action man*, who helped Comino turn his dreams into reality. In time Norman Bailey, the one among the initial recruits who had been to a grammar school, became the *analytical manager* and George Thomson, another East End lad, who rose from floor-sweeper to production manager, emerged as the *animator*. The sales force, duly encouraged to win friends and influence people, was unashamedly American in approach, though British by entrepreneurial heritage.

Anticipative Learning

It turned out, in fact, that the printing business was an ideal learning environment for young people. It provided a training not only in production methods but also in literacy. The business was very varied, and everyone got involved in the selling and promotion of merchandise.

But Comino came to realize, soon enough, that he would not be able to devote his life to printing. He required wider product and market horizons. By 1937 he had begun experimenting with a metal construction material. In his printing works there was a space problem. As business expanded he continually had to dismantle and rebuild his storage equipment. Throughout the war he searched for a versatile system of storage construction, with the minimum of components, simple to erect and cheap to buy. His failure to find one led him to invent 'slotted angle', a 'grown man's version of Meccano'.

Slotted angle was only the beginning. Whereas Dexion (the Greek *krisson* means 'better' and *dexion* means 'right') started out as a one-component solution to a storage problem, Comino's close contact with industry led to customers' exploiting the product's versatility. Dexion, particularly in the hands of an inveterate problem-solver and agent of change like Comino, became a packet of possibilities.

Product and Market Development

We can no longer rely on the next generation learning the new things and taking the next steps forward. We have to re-educate ourselves two or three times during our lifetime. We have reached a stage where we have to keep learning and re-learning if we are not to become obsolete. It is not merely that things are changing in the sense that we now build racks with speedlock instead of slotted angled. What is important is the increase in complexity and inter-relatedness.

Products used to be things; lengths of slotted angle, speedlock components, and so on. But now products have become a system, a service. What advanced companies do is solve customer's problems. The customer can no longer say 'I want a rack'. He says 'I want the solution to a problem'. We and our customers must learn to think in terms of wholes, not parts. A product is no longer a thing, a piece of ironmongery. It is what we do in our part of [the industrial] system to take account of what is happening in some other part.[4]

Today the Dexion Group has a series of divisions that range, in their product-market scope, from the original slotted angle to electronically integrated handling systems.

Innovative Learning

Learning: the Departure

As we have already discovered, individual or organizational learning of the vertical kind involves a *departure* and a *return*:

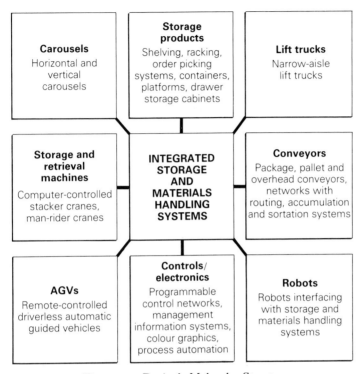

Figure 9.1 Dexion's Molecular Structure

- the departure begins with adventure and ends with creativity;
- the return begins with vision and ends with action.

Both involve successively different combinations of behaviour, thought and feeling. I shall illustrate these learning processes through references to Comino, as the individual learner, and to Krisson and Dexion as models of the learning organization.

The adventurous role: the physical transaction

Comino responded to the *call to adventure,* as a first, physical step, when he left his job in a large company because he wanted to set up on his own. Not only did he venture into the unknown, without a burning idea to drive him on, but he started his business just before the Great Depression.

You can Do it!

Hunting around for something to do, Comino, a first-class graduate in mechanical engineering, set up his printing business in the heart of London through a series of accidents. Because of his Greek roots he had some Greek friends who happened to be in the cigarette business. They needed their paper and packaging to be printed. So he started with two or three machines in a basement in Oxford Circus. Because of his location there he ended up doing jobbing printing for the rag trade.[5]

Comino started from nothing, with virtually nothing, in a depressed economic climate. That combination of circumstances instilled in him the idea that you have to fight for yourself, but if you put in all the hours in the day and use your brains you can do it. At the time he had no business picture. He simply wanted to be independent.

It so happened that the printing trade offered marvellous training opportunities for people, including Comino himself: design, copy-writing, visual aspects of printing, the engineering and chemistry of the printing process. Above all, because the job was so physically as well as mentally demanding, it was useful continually to remind everyone 'You can do it!'. Moreover, in this distinctive environment, both spatially restricted but technically instructive, seeds were being sown for the ultimate conception of slotted angle.

The communal role: the social transaction

Learning involves *a continual interchange between challenge and support.* Those who are brave enough to respond to the call to adventure, more often than not (if they are open to it) find in it their source of social suport. In time such support builds up into the *family feeling* that plays so important a part in any learning organization. For Comino's initial source of support was Fred Riley, and that earthy, warm-hearted influence was subsequently to be nourished by the influx of youngsters from the East End, where poor communities were strongly bonded together.

Riley was one of the first few boys Comino took on as apprentices from the slums of London. While he had enormous innate ability, he had no formal education. Comino gave him (and innumerable others) confidence in himself; in his turn, Riley helped Comino to build up a learning organization. The master had the vision of the learning community but it was the disciple who knew how to turn it into a reality. The resulting 'family feeling' is best exemplified by the response of Krisson conscripts during the war years.

The Krisson Gang

> Dear Gang and all responsible for the parcel I have just received. Quite frankly I do not know how to put my appreciation of what I have just received into words. Apart from monetary value, which I realize is quite considerable, the admirable choice and variety of gifts really makes me think I must have chosen a firm and a gang of workmates in a million . . . a firm which, to my mind, has no equal in the world. This must sound a lot of balderdash to you blokes but to me it's just an inkling of how I feel. Anyway if I ever get a chance to repay the firm for the kindness and consideration it has always shown to me, believe me, I'll take it. *Thanks for everything gang.*[6]

The community feeling has continued to manifest itself not only in a 'Dexion pride', which still exists some fifty years later, but also in the 'classless Dexion society', which stands out in class-ridden Britain. That classless community has provided the context for a family of products and processes that unite 'metal-bashers' turning out a 'grown man's version of Meccano' on the one hand and professional marketing in international arenas on the other.

But such a communal spirit has to be continually renewed if it is to maintain its supportive part in the learning organization. For everything and everyone is relentlessly subject to change.

The intellectual role: learning must be greater than the rate of change

For Comino one of the most important functions of the manager was to stimulate the problem-solving and learning behaviour of others. At Krisson the youngsters were turned into printers, doing staggering things by the standards of the trade. As a result the company found itself in the vanguard of developments in letterpress printing.

Besides on-the-job training there were regular evening classes on problem-solving on the one hand, and on political and economic developments around the world on the other. As Norman Bailey recalled:

> I was a country boy who'd been to grammar school before I joined Krisson·at the age of 17. Comino saw something in me. I went to his home twice a week. We talked till midnight. He pushed Shaw, Wells and Russell at me. He was my university education.[7]

Once again this focus on learning and questioning, rather than teaching and answering, was borne out during wartime.

A Boat Sailing Through the Storm

Thank you for the K.P.L. Bulletin – a typical Krisson masterpiece and something to be proud of. How it brought back personalities and showed in a wonderful way how K.P.L. will be making every effort and sacrifice to keep the boat sailing through the storm.

If I kept count of all the useful things I learnt at Krisson that have assisted me here I am sure I should be amazed. It is only occasionally when I ask myself 'How did I arrive at that?' that I find Krisson's experience is the answer. Take this for example. I was accused of using too much new round belting. I complained that the quality was not as before. I am proving it by running two sets of 16 side by side doing the same work and noting all the breaks, tightenings, etc. I ask you – where did I learn that?[8]

Some thirty years later Demetrius Comino was calling for change and learning to become a way of life among managers.

We must train people how to learn for themselves. Learning must become part of the normal work of every manager. Education must be for change and not for a static world. No solution, no process, no knowledge can be permanent or static in the face of change. What can be basic is a set of Basic Unifying Problem-Solving Concepts. In particular Dexion must be a learning organization with a basis of such concepts.[9]

The commercial role: the emotionally laden transaction

Krisson and then Dexion, particularly in their early days, were companies brimming with ideas. Both companies moved with their times, adapting to a changing environment. But whatever ideas were developed intellectually had to be put to the test in the market-place. That required emotional resilience as well as intellectual ingenuity. It also necessitated a collective ability, within the learning organization, to win friends and influence people.

Krisson, under Comino's influence, unashamedly drew on the Americans for insight into salesmanship. John H. Patterson of National Cash Registers and Dale Carnegie, of public-speaking fame, became gurus to the fledgeling companies. In the 1950s Dexion people were often asked whether their firm was American. 'Our sales literature was direct and simple. It will do this for you. No fluff. We had a direct approach to selling.'[10]

Because neither Comino himself nor his Krisson apprentices had any entrepreneurial or sales background themselves, they felt a need to learn from the most outstanding salesman and sales-oriented culture. They also realized that they needed to undergo a transformation in emotional as well as intellectual attitude. While product and people development was therefore 'invented here', approaches to market development were learned and adapted from American practice. The adaptation proved so successful that Dexion established a reputation as the company for budding salesmen to join because of its professionally based sales training.

Winning Friends and Influencing People

I recently attended a Dale Carnegie class. It was a thoroughly enjoyable evening and our class of 50 were all attending for the first time. Hearty laughter and sometimes sympathy was the order of the day when the almost petrified speakers got up to say their piece for two minutes. The girls of the class made charming pictures as they stood on the platform in front of a grinning, predominantly male audience and tried to free their tongue from its glue-like attachment to the roof of their mouth. Their poor faces registered all colours and they sat down at the end with a sigh of relief.

They were all nationalities and all classes, that is porters and executives. After all had made their speeches the instructor told them their faults and would not let them go until they had corrected them.[11]

As a learning organization Krisson realized that no matter how good its product or service, how friendly its people or how brilliant its ideas for improvements, markets had to be exploited and customers had to be won. To succeed in that respect the company had to outgrow its culturally ingrained limitations, through a combination of training and development. This had to be built into the fabric of the organization.

The organizational role: the coordinating transaction

As the learning organization succeeds in projecting its fledgeling products or services into the market-place, it comes to realize that a further developmental step is required if it is to establish its identity as separate from the owner's. By the later 1930s Comino had already given Krisson an organizational identity of its own, but it was not a substantial enough organization for someone who wanted, increasingly, to change the world. For Comino had no unique product to call his own. So, during the war, he proceeded to devise one, to be produced by a separate division of the existing organization.

Comino had always been strongly influenced by Henry Ford. The challenge of identifying a broadly based need that could be satisfied through mass production greatly appealed to him. He wanted to be able to multiply the impact of his organization's socially, technologically and commercially instigated learning on the world stage.

Through the product concept that Comino was exploring he therefore sought to marry up the need – and willingness to pay – of millions of potential industrial consumers, with an intellectual idea realized in a particular physical form. The marriage between demand and supply is what he was after, an integration of technological capability and commercial need. Moreover, he wanted to implant the social form that his people had so carefully nurtured and developed into a technological innovation. He devoted much more thought to new technology and the social form than to any formal organizational or financial arrangements.

The enabling role: the evolutionary transaction

Comino spent several years pondering on a simple, but versatile solution to his own storage problem. He was also well aware that his problem was similar to one faced by thousands of organizations that had to handle and store materials in confined spaces. While still a small printer, he ransacked the trade journals, spent endless hours at the patent office, and went to the Hanover fair to develop his ideas. Eventually, after some ten years of research and development, and many a false start, he came up with slotted angle. And by the end of the war he had worked out not only the product but also the production process, at least in general terms.

Slotted angle was essentially an *enabling technology*, just as semi-conductors are today: as speedier, more versatile chips are produced every year so the new computers, facilitated by ever more varied computer software, are 'enabled' to perform new functions and satisfy an ever-changing range of customer needs. Similarly the Dexion product turned out to be a universal building material, whose versatility was demonstrated in the 1950s at the time of a series of earthquakes in Greece.

A Universal Building Material

The people of the Greek islands are still clearing up the wreckage of the recent earthquakes and rebuilding their homes. A firm in London is helping in the relief work by sending materials for a number of pre-fabricated houses as a gift to the island. Today a specimen bungalow of this type was handed over to the Greek ambassador.

The firm that made the gift weren't builders before. This is the first house that they have ever put up. What they do is to supply industry with angled lengths of steel with slots in it. These slotted angle lengths make almost anything – storage racks, machinery platforms, gantries, towers, bins and boxes.[12]

Thirty years later the basic slotted angle still sells, but today it is accompanied by an integrated range of allied products, many of which have resulted from subsequent research and development activity.

The creative role: inventing the product

The inherent originality of Comino's invention lay in its combination of simplicity and versatility. Indeed, because of the product's range and scope, Dexion essentially created an industry for materials-storage and (later) handling equipment where virtually none had existed before.

In the 1940s the extent to which Comino would be able to follow in Henry Ford's footsteps by turning his dream of large-scale production into a reality was open to question. Like Ford, Comino was interested in producing an economical product for 'everyman'. Unlike his predecessor, though, his ambition to create a learning organization transcended even his aspiration to beat a path, by means of his new product, to every part of the globe. Ford was quintessentially a car man, an engineer and a manufacturer; Comino was essentially a renaissance man, a humanist and a builder.

Resource Building

Resource building was our objective when we started Krisson Printing in 1927. It still is, and I believe it is largely the basis of our success.

I would go further and say that any individual, any company, any nation that deliberately and continuously has as one of its major objectives the building of its resources will inevitably rise above the others and become a leader.[13]

Innovation: the Return

Learning, or development, for the individual and for the institution, cumulatively involves:

- physical adventurousness and a bias for action;
- social engagement and a family feeling;
- mental ingenuity and a learning capability;
- emotional resilience and sales orientation,
- coordinating ability and integrated controls;
- individual openmindedness and enabling institutions;
- personal creativity and innovative systems.

Innovation, or transformation, for the individual and the organization, turns the potential created into actual performance. The *upward* movement from *physical reality* to *creative imagination* is now reversed into a *downward* movement from *vision* to *action*. The starting point, now, is the vision.

Innovative management: actualizing a vision

Now that the individual and organizational vision, as the culmination of the learning process, has been developed, it has to be communicated. The innovative manager has the task of articulating his or her personal sense of mission, so as to indicate how, in actuality, the vision will serve to solve a universal problem. Moreover, by illustrating how such a vision can transform the world, the innovative manager taps the imagination of all those involved. Finally and quite obviously, this is not a once-and-for-all process but – like each aspect of organizational learning – needs to be reinforced and renewed continually.

Comino's vision was of a self-governing learning community, spread around a world that had become increasingly 'slotted angle conscious'. He saw the company as a constructive element of proven value, offering not a take-it-or-leave-it product, but something that people could fashion for their own ends, something fundamentally simple and progressive.

The vision was at the forefront of the company's activities in the 1960s, once Comino had created the new industry. Dexion's products were being used around the globe to build houses for earthquake victims, to construct grandstands for independence

celebrations, and to equip explorers for expeditions to the poles –
quite aside from its more everyday uses. Towards the end of the
1960s, Comino the innovative manager began to take a backseat role
in the business, devoting his attentions now to the development of
people rather than products or markets. The power of the vision
henceforth, was (potentially if not actually) reduced.

Developmental management: recognizing potential

Recognizing the potential in *people* and *things*, in *products* and *markets*,
is the next important stage in the innovative process. For, whereas the
visionary creates potential, *the enabler recognizes the emerging technological,
social and commercial opportunities.* Developmental management, then,
involves a recognition of the underlying needs within and among
people and communities, products and market-places. Such recognition
leads to organic development of the company and its people.

   In the early stages of its development, Dexion was able to recognize
the 'packets of possibility' in its product–market interface. As a result,
the enabling technology contained within the original 'grown man's
version of Meccano' could be extended into a multiplicity of
applications. Norman Bailey, as managing director in the 1960s, was
able to translate this enabling philosophy into sales management.
'We're not here to tell the sales force what to do, but to enable them
to do what they need to do. Our job is to make it possible. They're
the front line.'[14]

   However, during the 1960s, a series of diversifications took place
that involved a transformation of the business rather than a further
evolution of it. The innovative and entrepreneurial impulses supplanted
the developmental ones. Above all there were shortfalls in executive
capacity.

Analytical management: structuring activity

The analytical manager is engaged in:

- defining policies and procedures;
- establishing strategies and structures;
- articulating the production–market concept;
- allocating roles and responsibilities;
- delineating boundaries between departments and divisions;
- channelling the flow of resources through formalized planning and
  control mechanisms.

Such analytically based activities should represent a channelling of the potential created by the innovator, duly recognized and enriched by the developer.

The executive role played at Dexion by Norman Bailey in the 1960s and 1970s was a somewhat isolated one, preceding as it did the takeover of the company by a new management regime. Bailey recalled that, even in the Krisson days, quarterly reports were issued to parents about all aspects of the apprentices' work. In the 1950s Bailey issued a quarterly report to the sales force; it gave a statistical picture of sales performance, including budgeted versus actual sales, and a commentary on variance.

This kind of analytical role was anathema to Comino from the outset. His meticulous problem-solving processes were applied to production and marketing rather than finance and organization. Moreover, the role of the enabler was never strongly established in the company. Comino himself, aware of the problem if unwilling to confront it head on, maintained in 1965:

> Though we are a successful firm, our success and further progress is hampered by one serious failing. We are not good at routine work, at carrying out procedures according to the rules, promptly and rigorously. The result is that a percentage of our profits are needlessly frittered away.[15]

The reluctance to engage in what we might call *maintenance learning* was to cost the company dear at the time of economic recession in the early 1980s, when cost-cutting became the order of the day. Yet Comino was able to claim, in terms of personal theory if not of Dexion practice, a fundamental belief in the efficacy of systems.

The Well-oiled Machine

> Rules are unintelligent, they make no distinctions, they restrict our freedom and use of intelligence and initiative. Yet if there were no rules the world in general and our business in particular would be chaotic and unworkable. Rules restrict our freedom on details, but they give us freedom on major matters. . . .
>
> It is true that rules tend to make an organization run like a machine, but machines free us from the details and permit us to use our intelligence on more important things. Because we have an engine in a car that looks after the procedures and details of injecting petrol into the cylinders and

igniting the mixture at the right moment, we are free to steer a car. But engines stick to the rules and that is why they operate so smoothly.

It would play havoc with their running if the ignition had initiative and tried alternatives or if the fuel tried to take short cuts. Everything must run to rule and on time; precisely. Rules and procedures are deliberately designed to cut out alternatives in order to make the routine and repeated operations in an organization run like a machine. Just as in a machine it is fatal if people operate one erratically, ignore it or take short cuts.[16]

Yet in practice Comino hated going through the motions – the routine – of running formal meetings. According to Bailey:

I must have run a thousand meetings having the chap with the ultimate authority sitting there, alongside me. Demetrius could not be bothered with following an agenda. That was superficial stuff. He was only interested when it came to some human or industrial policy.[17]

Enterprising management: doing deals

Comino reflected that those of us who drive cars often feel how silly it is to sit waiting for traffic lights to change when there is an obvious opportunity to slip across. This inclination to take a risk, to commit ourselves and to be enterprising is what brings an organization to life. An original invention, serving an underlying need, located within a structured organization, nevertheless remains stillborn. It has yet to be sold.

You can Do it!

In 1949 we granted an American steel company a manufacturing licence to make slotted angle. After two years the company had hardly sold any. There was no market for the product, they claimed. So Comino went over himself. 'Take me round some factories,' he said to the Americans. As he went around he demonstrated how this and that could be made at half the price using Dexion angle. All the applications one could imagine lay under their noses. Demetrius subsequently sent over a team of six salesmen from the UK and demonstrated how the Americans could do it. Cheeky. 'You don't see what's in the product,' he said, 'and I do.'[18]

I started out as a southern region salesman twelve years ago. After a fortnight I'd had enough; that was until I went out on a call with Arnold Dyer. I became transformed. He brought the job alive. We went to see this plant engineer, bringing with us this sample of five foot high speedlock. We plonked it in the reception area. The guy said we were wasting his time. He'd already placed an order with a competitor. Arnold assured him that it was never too late, and persuaded him to take us on a site visit. Through his persuasive powers Arnold turned the guy completely around. It was magical. A challenge. A contest between two opposing forces. With Arnold selling was a way of life. It stayed with me forever.[19]

What are the activities of enterprising management?

- securing a competitive advantage;
- championing a product's cause in the market-place;
- taking a calculated financial risk;
- selling yourself to others;

these are all part of it. In a corporate context this managerial ability is spread throughout the organization to the extent that people's self-centred motives are tapped in the common cause.

One of the American books favoured at Dexion in the 1950s was Frank Bettger's *How I Turned Myself from a Failure into a Success.*[20] Bettger's approach was in sympathy with the 'You can Do it!' philosophy inculcated into the original 'scout troop' at the Krisson Printing works. From the outset Dexion was looking for self-starters in the sales force – people with a will to win. Comino was totally dedicated to the idea of payment for results. From the very start daily records of sales were kept. At the same time people felt themselves to be missionaries for the product. 'I took a cut in salary to join this company in 1972. Dexion enjoyed the reputation for having the best sales set-up in the country. You were expected to give 100%.'[21]

Focusing on Dexion's most important managerial concepts, Comino stressed:

- first, the dominant position of *marketing* in top management, orienting the organization towards its customers;
- second, maximum *delegation*, enabling the organization to move quickly;
- third, a willingness to trust youth with responsibility early;
- fourth, the creation of *stimulation* in the work environment;
- fifth, the establishment of *frank relationships* between bosses and subordinates;
- sixth, the need for *involvement* of all personnel.

One of the younger salesmen in Scotland, Ray Higgins, represents the continuity of this approach today.

My boss Jim started out selling packs of angle. He's never lost the feel. One of the things I love about selling is that you're getting inside the client's problem. We're geared around ideas. We have what I do believe is the best product. But our competitors don't produce a bad one. Anybody can produce a piece of metal. It's the relationships with our clients that count. People in Scotland are consistently successful with Dexion. They know the Dexion people. A lot of the older clients say 'I used to build this out of Dexion Angle.'[22]

The management of change: adapting to the environment

The establishment of any business is not a once-and-for-all operation. Continuing adaptation to change is essential, especially in the fast-moving environment in which business is conducted today. As a result, ongoing programmes of experimentation and adaptation form a critical part of any organizational development. Such uninhibited experimentation is more often the prerogative of youth than of age.

Yet experiment, problem-solving and the generation and selection of alternatives remained as important for Demetrius Comino in his sixties as it had been in his youth. If anything he caused damage to his company in the 1970s by continuing to challenge, to diversify and to probe when Dexion should have been consolidating, focusing and directing its powerfully constituted energies.

PACRA

Progress arises in science, as in evolution, from the increasing weeding out of error. Thus truth, in scientific terms, is not approached as one would seek a goal, by heading straight towards a distant beacon, visible or visualized. The individual scientist may proceed that way, but as for science as a whole, what it regards as truth is but the strip of possibilities left over after all demonstrable truths have been trimmed away. And this will remain a fairly broad band of uncertainty, including the indeterminate, the unknown, and the indeterminable.

In the process of natural selection or evolution, and in the development of science, two clear and distinct processes stand out: throw up, find, collect a wide range or variety of possibilities; eliminate rigorously all those that do not fit a set of criteria. This is the basis of PACRA – purpose, analysis, criteria, resources, alternatives, and of course eliminate and select.[23]

The original slotted angle emerged out of the PACRA process that Comino has described. The learning community established at the Krisson works was replicated, to some extent, by the research, training and development that emerged at Dexion. But it has never assumed the same dominating force. In fact, in the business context in the 1970s, the generation of alternatives overbalanced the rigorous elimination of ill-suited diversifications.

In the 1980s however, a balanced learning community existed in Dexion's Scottish plant:

> We take a philosophical view in Dexion Scotland. The attitude here is that mistakes are to be learnt from. It's a question of getting the basic rules right, and then expressing ourselves as individual sales people. If I'd merely come and gone I'd have seen Dexion as a metal basher. Instead I see ourselves as people who work together to sell solutions to problems. I tend to sell from the perspective of a consultant. Why do you need shelving? What do you want to achieve?[24]

Such processes of action and reflection, trial and error, idea generation and problem-solving have also been built into the high-tech end of Dexion's operations. The Handling and Electronics divisions of the company are in the business of solving complex problems. At the engineering end of the main Storage Division the 25-year-old production controller James Cadman, with youthful enthusiasm, is grasping the experimental nettle.

> If there wasn't excitement. I wouldn't be here. In manufacturing we see changes everywhere. The Japanese will soon be selling techniques, not cars. To bring down cost we have to look towards new manufacturing techniques. I've started putting up notices all over the place. SCM. It stands for 'Short Cycle Management'. We've got people thinking. I'm in the factory solving problems.[25]

People management: establishing a learning community

The 'scout group' of young apprentices that Comino brought into Krisson became not only a family but also a *learning community*. Everyone felt they belonged, there was a sense of community and shared values, productivity was achieved through people, and the whole workforce felt close to the customer. Above all, though, it was a learning community in that everyone learned and developed together, as managers, as businessmen and as human beings.

The challenge that the company has since faced is that of

maintaining and developing a learning community, suitably reformed, within the larger-scale Dexion. Such a community would
need to emerge out of the broadly based vision of the Dexion Group
in the context of Europe 1992, notwithstanding the major disruptions
the company has experienced – it went public in the late 1960s and
was taken over by an American company in the late 1970s.

The takeover followed a period of severe recession, exacerbated by
a prolonged steel strike and a three-day working week. It may also be
seen as a result of the relatively weak managerial and financial control
exercised through Dexion's early life. A change of management
regime and waves of redundancies made sharp inroads into 'family
life'. At the same time Comino's move into the background weakened
the force of the 'learning' side of the Dexion community, for his
learning principles and practices had never been formally codified
within the company. Nevertheless, the family influence, so strong in
the formative years, and the original shared values, continued to exert
an influence in the late 1980s, even if they were less all-pervasive. In
James Cadman's words:

> When I first joined it was a friendly environment. It came out in the
> initial interviews. They were looking for someone who could fit into
> Dexion. Someone who is enterprising, good at communication, and not
> limited to a profession. My initial view of the organization was
> subsequently confirmed. There's an incredible atmosphere. A lot of
> loyalty. Although things don't always go well the company bonds
> together.[26]

The bonding and the learning have become set somewhat apart over
the years. The plight of the company in the late 1970s led the new
management to believe that safety through profit was a higher priority
than learning through trial and error. As the current Chairman of the
Group, Steve Hinchliffe, indicates:

> Dexion had always been seen as a growth company. Sales and personal
> relations in the seventies were good. Problem-solving was of a practical
> rather than of a financial nature. It was also communal in outlook.
> Everyone and his aunt had to be in on a minor problem. Sometimes no
> decision was made at all. I tried to get the appropriate individuals
> responsible.[27]

An appropriate blend of responsibility and reponsiveness, of
communality and of learning, seems to have been arrived at, once
again, by the storage centre at Dexion Scotland and its sales region.

You can't throw a team together and say communicate. We like each other. If somebody feels comfortable with their job they have no need to keep somebody else in their place. Youthful enthusiasm here is combined with experience. The vitality of youth is intermeshed with the wisdom of age. We're doing great things. We're becoming leaders in the new technology. We've a new story to tell. We made the slotted angle years ago. Now we're in the electronics business. We've moved on with our customers. We can give them the whole package. We paint a picture of Dexion as a group.[28]

The family image, then, in terms of people and products, continues to dominate at Dexion.

Action management: making things happen

The image of the Dexion product has both a cerebral and a practical element – the problem-solving and the 'metal-bashing'. For, at the end of the day, any organization has physically to produce something. For all his intellectual sophistication, the physical product was dear to Demetrius Comino's heart. Furthermore, physical productivity is part and parcel of the company's heritage, as Bill Bates, the production manager, explains:

We built our families on the back of Comino. George Thomson, who started out as a sweeper on the factory floor and ended up as our managing director, would come in with Comino's ideas, and between them they'd make it work. During the Skopje earthquake we worked 24 hours a day to get the product out. During the three-day week in 1971 it happened again.[29]

When the company achieved production levels of a million feet of slotted angle a week there were great celebrations. The physical image of the powerful 'metal-bashers' or steel men is also central to the company ethos. Brian Stringer, a youthful but senior buyer in the Storage Division, joined Dexion not only because of its reputation for training and developing its people but also because 'it is a big player in steel, and I love steel.'

Finally, as the umpteenth Dexionite extols the Dexion bedrock that forms the firm foundation of his personal and corporate working life, it is plain that vision and action, invisible dream and visible reality remain connected. To turn such an original vision into continually repeatable action is to complete the productive circle of *learning departure* and *innovative return*. The cycle of *anticipative learning* and *precipitative creativity* revolves as part of the ongoing spiral of business life. And, as in a round of golf, if you fluff a shot or get stuck in a bunker you have to make up the loss later in the game, so in business life any false step or period of standing still means that later you will need to revisit old ground in order to maintain ongoing progress.

It is now time for us to move from vertical to horizontal, from anticipative to participative learning.

Notes

1 J. Botkin, *et al.*, *The Limits to Learning*. Pergamon, 1979, p. 17.
2 D. Comino, 'The Learning Organization'. Unpublished paper, p. 4.
3 Letter from Demetrius Comino to staff, reproduced in the company journal *Dexion Angle*, June 1964.
4 D. Comino, 'Change and What it Implies'. *Dexion Angle*, September 1970, p. 2.
5 N. Bailey, interview with the author, 1989. Norman Bailey was formerly the managing director of Dexion.
6 S. Clift, Letter, *KPL Bulletin*, no. 2, 1940.
7 Bailey, interview, 1989.
8 H. Treasdon, Letter, *KPL Bulletin*, 1940.
9 D. Comino, writing in *Dexion Angle*, July 1966.
10 Comino, in *Dexion Angle*, July 1966.
11 J. Deller, Letter, *KPL Bulletin*, no. 2, 1943.
12 News bulletin, read by Geoffrey Talbot, 'BBC Radio Newsreel', February 1957.
13 D. Comino, writing in *Dexion Angle*. June 1963.
14 Bailey, interview, 1989.
15 D. Comino, 'The Need for Rules'. *Dexion Angle*, June 1965, p. 2.
16 Comino, 'The Need for Rules', p. 3.
17 Bailey, interview, 1989.
18 Bailey, interview, 1989.
19 T. Reynolds, interview with the author, 1989. Tony Reynolds is the sales director of Dexion Storage Division.
20 F. Bettger, *How I Turned Myself from a Failure into a Success*. 1941. The book is discussed in *KPL Bulletin*, no. 3, 1943.
21 Bailey, interview, 1989.
22 R. Higgins, interview with the author, 1989. Ray Higgins is the sales manager of Dexion Scotland.
23 D. Comino, 'Why is Scientific Method so Successful?'. *Dexion Angle*, November 1971, p. 5.
24 Higgins, interview, 1989.
25 J. Cadman, interview with the author, 1989.

26 Cadman, interview, 1989.
27 S. Hinchliffe, interview with the author, 1989.
28 Higgins, interview, 1989.
29 B. Bates, interview with the author, 1989. Bill Bates is production manager of Dexion Storage Division.

10

Participative Learning at Dexion

Introduction

Both individuals and organizations, looking both inward and outward, need to engage in an ongoing dialogue with a large cast of characters – people and institutions – if they are to grow and develop. Like the seven steps of learning and creativity, moving up and down the vertical axis there are seven kinds of individual or parts of the organization, operating on the horizontal axis. These seven, once again, are permutations of action, thought and feeling. They constitute the *participative* mode of the learning organization, if not also the learning society. I shall start with individual characters and move on to organizational forms.

Individuality and Learning

The Seven Dimensions of Participative Learning

We learn with and through other people. The richer the mix of individualities to which we expose ourselves the greater the potential for learning. However, we are able to communicate with the diversity of our fellow human beings only if we are open to that same diversity of qualities within ourselves. These qualities are:

> physical,
> social,
> intellectual,
> emotional,
> conceptual,
> aesthetic,
> imaginative.

And they give rise, in the context of the developing organization, to seven dimensions of participative learning.

Adventuring: the first, physical dimension

> The Greeks, like the British, as a result of geography and tradition, are a seafaring people and inevitably much of their poetry is connected with the sea. One little rhyme goes 'Here ships are lost and you, my little boat, where are you going?' Well, the little Dexion boat did set out. It may well have got lost, but it didn't. It got somewhere. It opened up what has officially been classified as a new industry.[1]

Adventurers and cavaliers have always found themselves a home in the Dexion sales force. As the womanizers and drinkers of yesterday and the action men and women of today they have always kept the company on the move. The figure of Arnold Dyer, who 'brought sales to life' and physically transformed the selling situation from 'no go' to 'go go', is a good case in point.

Adventurers:

- relish moving from place to place, seeking out challenging situations, and they demand instantly effective rewards for their efforts;
- undertake a journey full of incident and charted by physical landmarks (while the analytical manager, for example, may balk at the opportunity of working in Libya or Lebanon, the adventurer will welcome the physical risk involved);
- learn from hard knocks and physical duress, realizing that thought and feeling divorced from action will be meaningless;
- seek out mentors who have demonstrated mastery in getting through scrapes, who have been involved with the rough and the tumble of business and life;
- require coaches who can help them learn how to store up their energy – to relax physically – and who can provide them with a physically and romantically stimulating environment in which to work.

Animating: the second, social dimension

> We have tried in Dexion to think of people, and though I know we could and should have done much more we have developed a spirit and a loyalty

which many people tell us is unusual. We have never had a strike nor anything approaching one. There is little or no formality. Everybody is called by their Christian name and there is no affectation; it was not imposed, it just grew up.[2]

Though Comino was not a gregarious person himself, by recruiting youngsters from the East End of London he imported into his company a warm and sociable group of people who became an animating force.

Animators:

- create a social or communal circle, which grows and develops as the individuals themselves evolve;
- learn through progressively wider association with ever more broadly based communities;
- gain their rewards as each community they form, whether production or sales oriented, comes to represent a social landmark along the way;
- seek out mentors who have already created a community, and who will therefore be closely in touch with the corporate culture as a whole;
- require coaches who create supportive environments within which they can exercise their communicative skills;
- having created a culture with an identifiable and coherent history, mythology and set of social activities, are ready to move on.

Changing: the third, intellectual dimension

One of my crazy ideas from the start had been to take on 14-year-olds from school, including some very bright ones. So I largely left the running of the printing business to these capable young people that I had gathered around me, and set myself the problem of inventing a product that suited my personality and resources.[3]

Comino himself personified that rebellious spirit out of which the urge to change people and institutions is born. This spirit infused the Krisson works, which set out to become an 'alternative' business institution from the outset, determined to 'make a difference' in the world. That tradition of *learning and changing* is carried forward today most particularly by the young graduates in both sales and production, as in the case of James Cadman's mysterious introduction of 'SCM' just to make people think (see p. 214 above).

Change agents:

- naturally seek out a path of learning, undergoing a variety of novel experiences, reading interesting books and going on stimulating courses;
- need to establish, either through external stimuli or their own thought processes, intellectual landmarks in their development;
- love to be constantly on the move, but mentally rather than physically, intellectually or technologically rather than socially or commercially;
- seek out mentors of great intellectual calibre, able to cope with the complexity of an interdependent and changing environment;
- require coaches who will help them to stretch their minds;
- having demonstrated mastery in the design and implementation of a particular project, are ready to move on.

Enterprising: the fourth, commercial dimension

> In 1958 the clouds began to gather. Business became more difficult to get, and success had made us over-confident. I suppose it was crazy, but we did move forward rather than retreat. As a result things at first got worse rather than better. Only on rare occasions was I anxious or afraid.[4]

Comino, like the business genius he so admired, Henry Ford, was not a natural entrepreneur. Both industrial magnates hated the money side of business. But Comino certainly possessed the basic instincts of the Greek trader; moreover, because he was aware of the shortfall in entrepreneurial ability – the capacity to wheel and deal – in both himself and his original scout group, he submitted himself and them to the mentorship of such great American entrepreneurs as John H. Patterson and Dale Carnegie.

Entrepreneurs:

- naturally seek out an emotionally testing path – one that is circuitous rather than direct. They love to take risks that are emotionally thrilling;
- have a workstyle that is full of ups and downs, and of mistakes from which to learn – the best of them treat failures as stepping stones rather than as stumbling blocks;
- view each battle won, each new piece of territory acquired, each acquisition secured, as a landmark in their dramatic journey, for which they seek to be duly and directly rewarded financially;

- seek out mentors who provide an example of calculated risk-taking, wilful assertion and tactical negotiation at its best;
- require coaches who will help them to learn from failure, for they are able to learn only from such emotionally laden experiences;
- having conquered sufficient territory, are ready to move on.

Executing: the fifth, organizational dimension

> We grew to a considerable size with a very simple organization. But as we grew in size and complexity it was not easy to recognize the complications, the overlapping and makeshift solutions that grew with them. Also our costing and accountancy was thoroughly inadequate and did not give us reliable and early information. Whilst we were very small I could see what was happening, make quick imaginative decisions, and I had enough personal control to see them through. Now it was different.[5]

While Comino had the intellectual honesty to recognize his failings as an analytical manager, particularly outside the technical sphere, the old Dexion regime was unable to make up for the shortfall. Only Norman Bailey was properly groomed as an executive and therefore too much responsibility for execution fell on his shoulders. The two realms in which such analytical management is at a premium – marketing and finance – were never apportioned the influence that sales and production, personnel and engineering had. When Dexion was taken over by an American parent company and new management regime in the late 1970s, they immediately addressed the financial and organizational imbalance, though not the marketing or general managerial one.

Executives:

- naturally pursue a linear path of development, rising through the hierarchy in the same way as they accomplish a task, in ordered steps (whereas the orderly task focus was there in Dexion it was not transferred to functional organization);
- learn through a combination of practical experience and formal training, welcoming the opportunity to upgrade their expertise through normally accredited institutions;
- view certified qualifications, like progressively more elevated positions, as landmarks in their development;
- seek out mentors who possess a combination of personal authority and institutional status;

- require coaches who can provide clarity of structure and manageable targets within which to work, so that the budding executive can advance along a planned promotion path;
- having successfully managed a function or a division, are ready to move on.

Enabling: the sixth, evolutionary dimension

> Almost as soon as Ghana was born, the Dexion, on which thousands sat and cheered as the pomp and circumstance went by, began to be absorbed into a national economy – to emerge as houses, schools, farm buildings, work benches, looms, and indeed any structure from a bracket to a building framework which this new country needed.[6]

Dexion in general and slotted angle in particular was a profusely enabling technology. However, when it came to individual people, Comino challenged them intellectually and commercially, but found it difficult to relate to them as whole human beings. Probably as a result, no enduring approach to organizational development emerged within Dexion, despite the profound attention to learning and problem-solving.

Enablers:

- follow a path that is neither linear nor bounded, but is diagonal and associative, picking up threads along the way and weaving them into a technological, commercial or social pattern;
- given the time and space to think and feel deeply, learn through their own insights into people and organizations, products and markets, through intense experience and reflective observation;
- evolve their roles, products and markets organically, viewing significant developments in themselves, their organizations and their cultures as landmarks in their progress;
- seek out mentors who have developed themselves outside the formal hierarchy and have, in the process, significantly enhanced the potential of people and products;
- require coaches who are able to create the sort of physical, social and learning environment that will facilitate development;
- having instigated, over a considerable period of time, an extended product or organization development – one that fulfils a higher business or social purpose – are ready to move on.

Innovating: the seventh, transformational dimension

> A packet of Dexion is a packet of possibilities. It can become virtually anything. There must have been millions of feet of it scattered over the earth's surface, in the deserts, in the jungles, over the North and South poles and even under the oceans.[7]

Slotted angle was indeed a fundamental innovation, perhaps the only one among the family of products that subsequently emerged out of Dexion. Though a strong research and development team was installed in the company during the 1960s and early 1970s, no inventions to match the original all-purpose product arrived on the Dexion scene. That having been said, the original product family was wide ranging enough to create a whole new industry, in materials storage and handling.

Innovators:

- naturally follow the transcending path of a spiral – over time their central idea spirals upwards and outwards, becoming progressively transformed (in the Dexion case from a versatile construction material into something progressive – and ultimately democratic);
- view product–market breakthroughs, intermingled with flashes of Comino-like inspiration, as the landmarks along their innovative journey;
- learn from innovative leaps backwards, whence came their art or science, and forwards into the technical, commercial or social future, even to the extent of creating new industries;
- seek out mentors who have been great innovators in the course of history (as Henry Ford was for Demetrius Comino);
- require more humble and accessible coaches, willing to be dedicated to the innovator's cause;
- having made their technological and commercial breakthroughs, are ready to move on (in Comino's case towards the creation of an enduring learning community).

Summary

Participative learning comes about when the cast of all seven characters engage in dialogue, across their personal divides. In the process a fertile exchange of action, thought and feeling will take place across cultural, social and functional barriers. All too often, if this is to happen, the *image-holder* of the company – usually the managing director or chairman – will need to be able *to absorb and radiate all seven traits* within his own managerial personality.

Comino was undoubtedly an adventurer, an agent of change, an innovator and enough of an entrepreneur and animator to recognize his own limitations. Where he fell short was as an enabler and as an executive. Among the supporting cast of original Dexion characters, Fred Riley and George Thomson stand out as animators, Norman Bailey as an executive, and the collective sales force as entrepreneurs. In the new management regime, as we shall see, there is entrepreneurial continuity, innovative discontinuity and a reinforcement of the executive role, albeit with a financial rather than a marketing or general orientation. Finally, while both animator and change agent maintain an influence from the wings the enabler role is notable for its absence.

The Learning Organization

A learning organization in which all seven kinds of individual are able fully to participate and (prospectively) learn from one another will itself have seven *divisions* or areas within it:

- the *energy field*, often associated with basic manufacturing and sales, with which the *adventurers* are associated in *energy management*;
- the *corporate culture*, including both employee relations and customer services, to which the *animator* contributes in the context of *relations management*;
- the *nerve centre* of the organization, in which the *agents of change* engage in *information management*;
- the *enterprising cells* of activity, including acquisitions and new ventures, where *entrepreneurs* and *intrapreneurs* become involved in *venture management*;
- *resource management*, in which *executives* plan and control the procurement, allocation and dispersal of materials (purchasing, plant and machinery), production, people (personnel) and money (finance);
- the *evolving social and commercial organism*, through which the *enabler* engages systemically in *developmental management*;
- the *creative nucleus*, where the company's originator and subsequent

technological and social innovators become involved, through the *corporate psyche*, in *innovative management*.

The Energy Field

The Salesman's Saga

Dexion Angle is easy to use.
Easily builds whatever you choose.
X is the quantity freely supplied,
Invariably doubles, sir, once you have tried.
One standard angle is all that's involved,
Nuts and bolts tightened – the job is resolved.

Simple to measure it, cut it to length –
Lightning assembly will give ample strength.
Overheads will become things of the past –
Time and labour costs disappear fast.
Take a trial order of five hundred feet!
Extremely versatile, painted and neat,
Dexion Angle you cannot beat!

Anything anywhere – that is the theme,
Nothing impossible, so it would seem.
Get some today and prove it yourself.
Let yourself go – don't be left on the shelf!
Easier production will bring ample wealth.[8]

When I started here in 1964 all we made was slotted angle and speedlock. I began by loading shelves off the plant. At the end of 11 hours I couldn't stand up. I was on my hands and knees.[9]

Our competitive nature drives each of us to do our thing. I've set myself two goals for this year – to beat my sales target and to beat 90 on the golf course.[10]

Manufacturing, construction, distribution, sales

All business activity, but most particularly manufacturing and selling, is fast-moving and physically demanding. In the case of Dexion that physical energy field was traditionally occupied by the steel men on the production side and the sales personnel; in addition one might point to the phenomenal physical dexterity of the contractors who install the equipment on site. The physical transformation of vast quantities of steel into the different parts of the 'grown man's version of Meccano' holds its particular appeal, as does the progressive build-up of mechanical parts into a functional whole.

Not only is the physical construction process often an adventure, especially when you are building grandstands for the Olympic games, but the dispersed nature of Dexion's traditional market has its attractions for the salesman with wanderlust. Nothing represents this better than Comino's description of 'millions of feet of [slotted angle] scattered over deserts, . . . jungles . . . [and] the North and South poles'.[11]

Energy management involves:

- a product line that is physically visible at all times in all places for maximum sensory impact;
- work and training activities that stimulate individuals' physical strength, stamina, dexterity and courage;
- a bias for action, coupled with a sense of urgency, a rapid turnover of materials and product, and just-in-time production;
- management by wandering about – by touch, taste, sight, hearing, smell and physical impact generally;
- an action orientation, typified by trials and tests, speed and immediacy of response, and a 'work hard, play hard' ethos;
- the provision of facilities for exercise and relaxation, both portable and on site.

From physically based energy management we move to socially based *people* or *relations management*, in the context of the *corporate culture*.

The Corporate Culture

Dexion Outing – Eastbourne

Meet	Victoria Station, 8.30 a.m.
Eat	Lunch and Tea at the Cavendish
Play	Fun and games in the briny
Pay	£1 a head. No charge for kids.[12]

To make a profit has always been a company objective but in the old days it was tempered by the idea that we had to satisfy a real need. Dexion was a business which was perceived to be making a contribution to society.[13]

We are all customers at different levels. Our distributors are customers. Those people in the factory – we're their customers. It goes right down to the guy in the plant. The people in the offices. We are proud and protective of product quality. We need to say thank you down the line.[14]

Human relations, customer services

Relations management, within the organization and outside, is geared towards serving the needs of both employees and customers in a practical, down-to-earth manner. In Dexion's case, the original Krisson 'scout group' formed the basis for a community that has lived on for another sixty years. Rare for northern Europe in general, and Britain in particular, a middle-sized company has been created which exudes a basic warmth and friendliness. At Dexion, formalized personnel management has never been allowed to oust human relations, and marketing has never overtaken sales – to both good and ill effect.

Relations management involves:

- ongoing informal exchange of feelings between people within and outside the business – employees and customers, suppliers and distributors;
- a rich tapestry of myth and ritual, ceremony and story line, including tales of creation and resurrection, crisis and resolution;
- a heroic cast of characters who personify the values of the organization;
- demonstrably shared values, exhibited in person and in print, to which people feel they are closely attached;
- a wide range of group activities, of both a working and recreational nature, which make up the organization's family life;
- pride in the product and a primary emphasis on human relations, both in people management and customer services.

Energy and relations management form the grounds of the company, whereas *information management* helps it navigate a path through uneven and unknown terrain. While action pervades energy management and feeling infuses human relations, *information management* is dominated by thinking: it takes place at the organizational *nerve centre*.

The Nerve Centre

The Learning Context

H. G. Wells	*A Short History of the World*
Bertrand Russell	*Freedom and Organization*
A. E. Mander	*Psychology for Everyman*
Susan Stebbing	*Thinking to Some Purpose*
C. M. Beadnell	*A Picture Book of Evolution*
Huxley & Andrade	*Simple Science/More Simple Science*[15]

We had a lot of training. Comino was more comfortable with ideas than with people. For ten years I changed jobs every two. The structures were so fluid.[16]

If you're willing to learn the company will help you. I moved from being an administrator to being a designer on to setting up a French distributorship. When they saw I was keen they were willing to train me.[17]

Technical management, production control, staff training

A learning organization is intimately associated with the processing of information, whether as raw or processed data, techniques or ideas, or fully fledged concepts. Products and markets, people and organizations are interpreted in terms of their information and communication requirements, not only *cognitively* but also *affectively* and *behaviourally*. Moreover, the man–machine interface becomes a critical part of the information management whole.

In Dexion's case the introduction of the all-too-complex information system IMPCON represented a major (and, initially, ill-conceived) exercise in information management. The opportunity now arises, however, to turn a problem into an opportunity and to create a 1990s version of a learning environment. This will necessitate drawing on, but duly upgrading, the original Krisson experience, which was geared towards the management of change. For example, in the 1990s, as opposed to the 1930s, in many instances databases and interactive computer-based programmes will replace reading lists and seminar discussions. However, the basic ethos of individuals' learning interactively at a speed that is greater than the rate of change should remain.

Information management involves:

- the establishment of rolling plans, together with systems for monitoring and upgrading them, over the short and medium term;

- the installation and adaptation of intelligent and interactive machines to process appropriate internal and external information covering people, money and things;
- the recruitment and training of *knowledge workers* to provide wide-ranging information and flexible expertise in marketing and sales, manufacturing and engineering, personnel and finance;
- the establishment of project teams and ad hoc groups that can be quickly formed and re-formed in response to changing circumstances;
- the encouragement of experimentation in individual people and organizational units in all parts of the company, in the context of computerized and social networking;
- the development of a *learning environment* throughout the organization, including the provision of training programmes, interactive learning facilities and group 'think tanks'.

From thought-provoking information management we move on to emotionally stimulating *venture management*.

Enterprising Cells

Confidence

Not only must the manager have confidence in himself but the group must have confidence in him. If he's one to steal ideas and credit that doesn't belong to him then he'll almost certainly fail. And if individuals cannot come to him in the knowledge that they'll be trusted then he again loses. There's nothing people hate more than a betrayed confidence.[18]

People who have been here long enough can remember Dexion's ability to strike opportunities at a profit. There's a huge lump of business in the Middle East. There is vision and opportunity in Interlake, our American parent company.[19]

Myself and Jim put a team together. In six months we tripled our sales. From a dead loss to a winner.[20]

New ventures, business development

Venture management comes naturally to the individual entrepreneur. As a business grows and develops, however, it has to be built into the organizational fabric. No longer can a single individual roam the entrepreneurial field, undaunted and uninhibited. He has to carry the organization behind him. Conversely, if venture management is not consciously built into the business, it will wither away and die in the face of unrelenting bureaucracy.

From the outset Comino sought to build adventurousness into his business, recruiting such self-starters as were likely to carry the American-style entrepreneurial flag, and surrounding them with a supportive learning community. This pattern of recruitment has been maintained ever since, and the development of venture managers has been built into the distribution structure primarily through the owner–manager storage centres. To that extent entrepreneurship is alive and well in Dexion. However, although such adventurous managers are also present in the sales force, they have lost much of the supportive structure that prevailed in the Comino years, including the encouragement they used to have to range freely across interdivisional product lines.

Venture management involves:

- popularizing the inventions that research and development have come up with, duly ensuring that such products or services can be made to appeal to the market-place;
- getting the best people into the sales force in general, or into a particular venture, in order successfully to identify and exploit opportunities;
- putting together a good deal, involving profitable combinations of people from inside and outside the company;
- taking calculated risks in venturing into such unknown business territory as can offer room for manœuvre;
- acquiring, defending and expanding a power base through which venture managers can advance and exploit the autonomy of their venture;
- working under, and in turn offering, direct economic incentives for the venture manager's activities;

In fact, if freewheeling venture managers are to succeed, they must work hand in glove with *analytical managers* who take responsibility for the planning, organization and control of physical, financial and human resources.

Resource Management

GRASP: Getting Results And Solving Problems

The understanding and conscious application of basic GRASP operations can enhance the quality of everything we do – our methods and results, and above all the general quality and effectiveness of our thinking. Specifically GRASP involves:

Purpose We must specify what we want to achieve.

Plan We must work out what actions or operations are needed to bring about our desired result.

Act We must put the plan into action; do whatever is needed to get the result.

Review We must continually review and revise our methods and results.[21]

The degree of natural teamwork leaves room for improvement. We are too compartmentalized. If we had better coordination the finance people may even become human.[22]

Tell me my objectives and then let me deliver.[23]

Operations, marketing, financial and human resource management

The management of resources encompasses the planning, co-ordination and control of physical, financial and human resources. As such, the core activities of production and marketing, finance and personnel – that is the procurement and allocation of goods and customers, money and people – are included here.

Resource management for Dexion, at least in the early days, dealt much more successfully with people and things than with money. As a result the problem-solving approach, which was so important to the company, was more readily applied to technical and social aspects of the business than to commercial and organizational ones. Not surprisingly the new management regime, introduced after the takeover, decided to reverse the balance of emphasis.

Resource management involves:

- the formalization of policies and procedures covering each of the major resources in question;
- the establishment of explicit plans and strategies for all aspects of the business;
- the delineation of formal organizational structures, specifying roles and responsibilities;

- the establishment of specialized departments and divisions, each with clear boundaries and responsibility limits;
- the installation of formal planning and control procedures to monitor and correct deviations between desired and actual performance;
- clarification of lines of communication, both vertically and horizontally, to ensure that resources are procured and allocated efficiently and effectively.

Efficiency and effectiveness are associated with maintenance learning; but they inevitably fall short when innovative learning is required. In other words resource management is more suited to achieving *safety through profit* than to accomplishing *profitable growth*. For that we need to turn to *developmental management*, and the *evolving organism*.

The Evolving Organism

Resource Building

> In Dexion we believe that a company is a living organism; in order to be healthy it must grow and develop. In order to grow, certain tangible and intangible things called 'resources' are needed. Tangible resources are money, buildings, materials, machines, tools, people. Intangible resources are skills, judgment, know-how, prestige, confidence, morale.[24]

> We underrate the talents of people here.[25]

> We have to accept that management is essentially a changing pattern. You can collapse it all into people. People at the top being able to change as the business changes.[26]

Research and development, organization development

Significantly for Dexion, in its formative years, Comino was much more interested in resource building than in resource management. In the 1970s and 1980s there was an inevitable backlash. Now, in facing the 1990s, the company needs to harmonize the *maintenance* and *innovative* forms of management and learning.

Developmental management forms a bridge between the originator's vision and the current exigencies of resource management. As a catalytic, enabling force, its function is to connect the business vision with the emerging technological, commercial and social environment.

Similarly, through its systemic nature, the developmental function recognizes and utilizes the interdependence between itself and the surrounding environment. In the Dexion context it therefore plays a leading part in developing latent product, market and organizational potential across divisional boundaries.

Developmental management involves:

- a recognition of the stage reached by the product, market, people and organization in the course of their evolution, together with an indication of how such evolution can be furthered;
- conscious development of both tangible and intangible resources by catalytic intervention;
- focusing on areas of mutual benefit between individuals, departments, divisions, businesses and countries;
- securing synergy between the significant organizations – including customers and suppliers, divisions and distributors – with which the company is connected;
- identifying and setting up joint ventures locally, nationally and internationally to stimulate product, market and organizational development;
- progressively merging member and group, individual and organization, organization and environment, to the extent that narrow personal, functional or commercial identities are outgrown and new, more significant identities formed.

In Dexion's case, in the 1950s and 1960s, the identity of slotted angle, on the one hand, and of a learning community, on the other, were subsumed under the shared identity of a *progressive democracy*. And the ultimate identity of a company is contained within its nucleus and represented by its vision.

The Creative Nucleus

The Learning Community

The new mind must be built up on broad, stable foundations of solid facts and tested truths, and the structure must be a unity, consistent with itself and its environment. And there must be freedom of movement into all its parts, no sealed chambers, no blocked corridors. And all the doors and windows must be open to let in fresh ideas. It must be built in such a way that it can be altered and added to, so that it will never become fixed and out of date; we've got to become an educational institution obviously of a very original kind. But first we must build up the business.[27]

Social and technical innovation

The nucleus of the organization, which holds the originating idea, transcends a purely commercially based business definition. For the nucleus, all too often lost in the cobwebs of business history, is composed of the most concentrated energy, the violet light of inspiration, the crucible of imagination.

Comino was able to articulate his vision, as far back as the 1940s, while he was developing the Krisson Printing works. The nucleus of the Dexion-to-be, therefore, was the learning community. Slotted angle was a technological and commercial means towards an educational and social end. At the same time the nature of the product was well suited to a classless and technically oriented educational institution.

Creative management involves:

• Uncovering the historic origins and destiny of the organization (in Dexion clearly lodged within Krisson in general and Comino in particular);
• projecting a powerful image to the world, which captures the imaginations of people within and outside;
• imparting fundamental values which are closely in touch with the originator as a person, with the society of his or her heritage and residence, and with the underlying need that the product is serving;
• reaching down to the underlying product or service, in its most profound sense (as happened at Dexion, where slotted angle – the product – provided the basis for the development of democracy);
• the physical transformation of the environment in which the company is set, for the benefit of mankind;
• continuing innovation of both a technical and a social nature.

Conclusion

It is now time to draw all the threads together, representing the full cast of individual and organizational characters within the learning organization. For should any individual or organizational members either misrepresent themselves, or fail altogether to participate, then the learning organization will be limited in some way or another.

It is only though the full integration of the adventurers' energy field – *energy management* – the animators' corporate culture – *relations management* – the change agents' nerve centre – *information management* – the entrepreneurs' enterprising cells – *venture management* – the executives' formal structure – *resources management* – the enablers' evolving organism – *developmental management* – and the innovators' organizational nucleus – *creative management* – that a fully fledged learning organization comes into being.

Notes

1 D. Comino, 'Dexion in Retrospect and Prospect'. Unpublished paper, 1969, p. 1.
2 Comino, 'Dexion in Retrospect and Prospect', p. 2.
3 Comino, 'Dexion in Retrospect and Prospect', p. 2.
4 Comino, 'Dexion in Retrospect and Prospect', p. 3.
5 Comino, 'Dexion in Retrospect and Prospect', p. 4.
6 Comino, 'Dexion in Retrospect and Prospect', p. 5.
7 Comino, 'Dexion in Retrospect and Prospect', p. 5.
8 *Dexion Angle*, September 1958.
9 B. Bates, interview with the author, 1989.
10 T. Reynolds, interview with the author, 1989.
11 Comino, 'Dexion in Retrospect and Prospect', p. 4.
12 News bulletin, read by Geoffrey Talbot, 'BBC Radio Newsreel', February 1957.
13 A. Murton, interview with the author, 1989. Alan Murton was formerly the personnel director of Dexion Storage Division.
14 P. Walsh, interview with the author, 1989. Pat Walsh is the regional sales manager of Dexion Storage Division.
15 Demetrius Comino's recommended list of reading for Dexion staff, published in *Dexion Angle*.
16 G. Murdoch, interview with the author, 1989. Geoff Murdoch is the technical director of Dexion Storage Division.
17 J. Littlewood, interview with the author, 1989. Jenny Littlewood is a designer at Dexion Storage Division.
18 D. Goddard, interview with the author, 1989. David Goddard is managing director of Dexion Storage Division.
19 A. Brooks, interview with the author, 1989. Alan Brooks was formerly the overseas sales director of Dexion Storage Division.
20 G. Abbott, interview with the author, 1989. Geoff Abbott is the Apton sales manager.

21 N. Bailey, 'GRASP: the Comino Trend'. Unpublished paper.
22 J. Sandison, interview with the author, 1989. Jim Sandison was the financial director of Dexion Storage Division.
23 L. Hill, interview with the author, 1989. Len Hill is the distribution manager of Dexion Storage Division.
24 D. Comino, 'Why is Scientific Method so Successful', *Dexion Angle*, November 1971, p. 3.
25 P. Jackman, interview with the author, 1989. Peter Jackman is the production director of Dexion Storage Division.
26 S. Hinchliffe, interview with the author, 1989.
27 D. Comino, writing in *Dexion Angle*, April 1962.

PART III

Developmental Management
in Perspective

11

Towards a Developmental Perspective

Introduction

The Demise of the Old Economic Worldview

As I begin this final chapter I cannot help but remark on the bizarre turn of economic events. The parent company of Dexion is itself, at the time of writing, under threat of takeover. Its fate is shared by the great British American Tobacco company which, despite, or perhaps because of its global reach, is being threatened by a hostile bidder, Sir James Goldsmith. Neither of these two companies is under-performing in any absolute sense. Neither bidder is likely to improve the fortunes of Dexion or BAT in the long term.

So what is actually going on?

In developmental terms we are witnessing the demise of an old paradigm, or economic worldview. The *takeover phenomenon*, as we see it today, is old-style capitalism's last gasp or, should we say, its last grasp. It represents primal manager's final, and ultimately futile attempt to 'keep it simple, stupid.' Indeed it carries with it the KISS of death.

Whereas the onset of *perestroika*, the crumbling of the Berlin Wall and Vaclav Havel's Civic Forum bring Marx under scrutiny, the appearance of the corporate raider and the 'poison pill' in the West ironically signals the demise of Adam Smith. For, at the very time that the Eastern bloc is turning to free enterprise, that same primal force is overreaching itself.

In Zimbabwe, where I spend much of my consultancy time, a young visionary friend of mine travels round the country admonishing his fellow managers and businessmen for their economic myopia. On the one hand it is clearly apparent to him that 'scientific socialism' has had its day; but, on the other hand, the business establishment is failing to come up with a moral imperative to match its economic achievements. As a result socialism is overstaying its welcome, but this is only because it appeals on moral grounds to a people who have been the victims of social and economic abuse for more than a century.

When I turn my mind to Europe, and the prospect of the Single European Market, I am again appalled by the lack of economic and business imagination. How, I asked my fellow management consultants at a European management symposium in Lyons, might we in the late twentieth century compare our managerial originality as Europeans with our creativity in the arts and sciences? Which of our management thinkers today could we compare with Beethoven or Mozart, with Newton or Pasteur, with Michelangelo or Gaudi? How does the quality of our economic evolution compare with our rate of development, say, within the physical sciences?

Economic Transformation

Physics has undergone four major revolutions, spearheaded in turn by Newton, Einstein, the quantum physicists, and now Prigogine and his fellow 'bootstrap' scientists. What comparable changes have taken place in management?

Management, in fact, has been through one major transformation – from a phase of trumped-up entrepreneurship in the late 19th century to one of rational management in the 20th. But while the *practice* of management has indeed been transformed, the *underlying foundations* have remained the same. Adam Smith (purveying the pursuit of self-interest), on the one hand, and Charles Darwin (identifying the survival of the fittest), on the other, have become the guiding spirits for businessmen around the free world. At the same time, in the 'unfree' world, the alternative Marxian foundations have proved a recipe for economic, if not also social and political, disaster.

From our developmental perspective, what is striking is not so much the quantitative economic shifts as the qualitative ones. What we have been witnessing over the last two decades is a global shift in the philosophical underpinning of business and management. As can be seen in Figure 11.1 the developmental approach combines

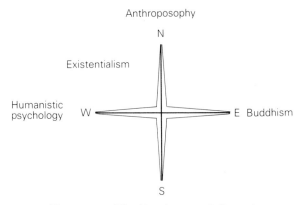

Figure 11.1 The Developmental Ground

Buddhism (*the economics of interdependence*) from the East with Existentialism (*man makes himself*) from western Europe, and central European anthroposophy (*the evolving universe*) with American humanistic psychology (*self-actualization*).

Unlike primal and rational-based management, which are still strongly entrenched in their original European and American contexts, the developmental grounds are widely spread and deeply set.

Developmental Roots

From Chaos to Cosmos

The conceptual roots of developmental management, drawing sustenance from these internationally 'cross-fertilizing' soils, are being laid down not by economists and politicians but by biologists and ecologists, again from all corners of the globe. And, like Agha Hasan Abedi with his 'real management', we are reviewing the laws of nature in order to gain business inspiration.

In the words of Elizabeth Sartouris, the eminent Greek-American ecologist, in her book *From Chaos to Cosmos*:

> Nature teaches us that evolution depends on competition and cooperation, on independence and interdependence. Competition and independence are both important to individual survival, while cooperation and interdependence are both important to group, or social, or species survival.[1]

Our worldwide economic system, she says, as well as our communications technology and information revolution, have bound us into a body of humanity which is now being compelled to evolve from competition to cooperation. No animal, human or business species can in fact evolve by itself. As Ford combines forces with Mazda, British Airways with Sabena Airlines and Siemens with GEC, we are reminded that, increasingly, we all must cooperate by adapting to the movements of others.

> Just as mechanical images inspired the development of industrial and social technology, organic images of self creating networks are beginning to inspire us to reorganize all human society as a more harmonious and humane venture.[2]

Holism and Evolution

Sartouris's developmental perspective is not the sudden and idle fancy of a 'greener than thou' ecologist. Already in the 1920s such an evolutionary perspective was emerging from the most unlikely quarters. General Jan Smuts, the South African military leader, prime minister and world statesman, wrote a book some sixty years ago that has become a classic – among biologists and social philosophers if not among economists and businessmen.

In *Holism and Evolution* Smuts describes the progressive evolution of wholes, rising from the material bodies of inorganic nature through the plant and animal kingdoms to man.

> Holism, in all its endless forms, is the principle which works up the raw material or unorganised energy units of the world, utilises, assimilates and organises them, endows them with specific structure and character and individuality, and creates beauty and truth and value for them.[3]

Evolution, then, traces the grand line of escape from the prison of matter to the full freedom of the spirit. It is just such a trajectory that the developing organization has to travel.

The Developmental Core

The Developing Organization

The developmental core was established by Bernard Lievegoed, drawing on anthroposophical roots and a fertile combination of cultural soils (it is not unimportant that Lievegoed spent his early years in Indonesia). In tracing the evolution of a business from a pioneering to an integrated organism he has remained truer to the underlying nature of a developing organization than most of the practitioners of so-called 'organization development'. As the business undertakes its evolutionary journey so its managers need progressively to change the style and substance of their activities. Moreover, their orientation in time and space should become ever more expansive, as they turn their focus from matter towards spirit (Figure 11.2).

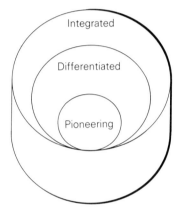

Figure 11.2 The Developmental Core

An Evolutionary Perspective

The intuition of the East

All those executives, most particularly in Britain and the US, who, afflicted with acute 'short-termitis', are caught up with the bottom line, forever anxiously watching their share price rise and fall, are indeed imprisoned in matter. That is not to say that we should ignore the bottom line, but that it needs to be seen in evolutionary perspective.

> We may look upon mechanism as incipient Holism, as a crude early phase. In proportion as Holism realises its inwardness more fully and clearly in the development of any structure; in proportion as its inward unity and synthesis replace the separateness and externality of the parts, Mechanism makes way for Holism in the fuller sense. But its realisation is a matter of degree, and there will probably remain some residuary feature of Mechanism.[4]

Smuts's biological perspective of yesteryear is supported by a modern-day Japanese businessman, the chairman of the mighty Canon group. For Ryuzaburo Kaku there are four stages in the evolution of a corporation:[5]

Stage 1 Capitalism exploits the workers.

Stage 2 Employers realize that the corporation can flourish only with the active participation of its personnel.

Stage 3 The corporation realizes that its progress depends on the health of the surrounding community. It therefore makes common cause with its immediate, local community, but not necessarily with the global community at large.

Stage 4 It is at this final stage that a global consciousness emerges, and the corporation sees itself as contributing to the whole of mankind.

The developmental manager, from Kaku's perspective, will have transcended the first two stages and entered wholeheartedly into the others. All four stages, however, as we shall see, continue to have a part to play in the evolving corporate whole. Even the most highly evolved, interdependent organization, must continue to exploit markets, continually maintaining its primally competitive thrust. However, such primal competitiveness and rational coordination are subject to cooperation of a higher order. As Ken Wilber, the brilliant American developmental psychologist, puts it:

> At each major stage of development there is the emergence of a higher order structure, the identification with that structure, and the dis-identification with the lower structure. Thereafter the higher structure can both operate on and integrate the lower structures.[6]

We fail as a business community today to the extent that we remain so attached to the bottom line, to the short term, or to the business basics, that we are unable to 'dis-identify' ourselves from them. This process of self-release is necessary if we are to rise to a higher organizational and managerial order. It is just such an order towards which Canon's Kaku aspires, even if his vision is limited by the collective nature of Japanese enterprise.

Releasing our selves

As Jan Smuts, reflecting his individualistic European heritage, pointed out:

in the process of evolution we see the advance from material systems to individual organisms. One organism is not merely a duplicate of another, as one molecule of water is a duplicate of another. It is a single individual with a character of its own. And the element of separate individuality increases as the differentiation and variation increase with the advance of evolution. Such individual differences tend to increase, and at the same time their blending in the individual tends to become ever more unique.[7]

This notion of variety and unity, advancing together in potential unison, is as relevant to the individual and the organization as it is to the European Community. Greater wholeness leads not only to more intensive individuality, in the self, but also to more perfect order, in the environment.

The implication of all this, for individual managers and for whole corporations, is that they have to let go of their superficially individual personality to realize their true individuality. This, in fact, is the unique task of mid-life, to discard your narrowly based identity – as a marketing manager, or as IBM – and develop a more broadly based and interdependent being, as a blend of your personal and corporate selves. In that context, the current financial infrastructure, which dictates that the shares of independent, though 'public', corporations are held by the stock market, is hopelessly obsolete. No wonder the mightiest executives in the US and Europe are shivering in their boots: their boots are ill fitted for modern-day walking!

So where does the more developmentally conscious manager or businessman go from here?

Towards the Learning Organization

From analysis to perception

The incomparable Peter Drucker, in his book *The New Realities*, gives us, if not the complete answer, at least a very good clue.

For Drucker, as for Smuts, the new realities mark a shift from a mechanical worldview, in which the analysis of the component parts was all-important, to a *biological approach to management*, in which it is the perception of the whole that is critical. Moreover, whereas matter is the basic mechanistic building block, *information is the basic biological element*. Since information knows no boundaries, Drucker says, it will also serve to form the basis for newly interactive communities of people.

From Analysis to Perception

The computer is in one way the ultimate expression of the analytical, the conceptual view of a mechanical universe that arose in the late seventeenth century. It rests in the last analysis on the discovery of the philosopher–mathematician Gottfried Leibniz, that all numbers can be expressed 'digitally' that is by 1 and 0. It became possible because of the extension of this analysis beyond numbers to logic in Bertrand Russell and Alfred Whitehead's *Principia Mathematica*, which showed that any concept can be expressed by 1 and 0 if made unambiguous and into 'data'.

But while it is the triumph of the analytical and conceptual model that goes back to Descartes, the computer also forces us to transcend that mode. 'Information' itself is indeed analytical and conceptual. But information is the organizing principle of every biological process. Life, modern biology teaches, is embodied in a 'genetic code' that is programmed information. And biological process is not analytical. Biological phenomena are wholes. They are different from the sum of their parts. Information is indeed conceptual. But meaning is not; it is perception.[8]

Drucker suggests that our new, information-based and biologically inspired economies are crying out for a new philosophical synthesis. He himself, probably because of his overly rational orientation, has not quite found it. In maintaining that 'knowledge has become the real capital of the developed economy',[9] Drucker pays little attention to non-rational qualities based purely on feeling. However, his 'new realities' certainly bring the *learning organization* onto centre stage.

The heart of productive activity

In the learning organization:

- working harder is displaced by *working smarter*
- rationally based marketing evolves out of primally based buying and selling
- system and information are substituted for guesswork, brawn and toil.

As Charles Handy states in *The Age of Unreason*, 'learning becomes a central part of coping'.[10] Similarly, Bill Abernathy and his colleagues at Harvard Business School claim:

What is needed is a view of production as an enterprise of unlimited potential, an enterprise in which current arrangements are but the starting point for continuous organizational learning.[11]

Finally, in her intriguing analysis of the post-industrial revolution, the Harvard industrial psychologist Shoshana Zuboff states:

> Learning is the heart of the productive activity; learning is the new form of labour.[12]

There is no doubt, then, that the *learning organization* is a more highly evolved institution than its entrepreneurially or hierarchically oriented counterparts. But it still falls short of the kind of synthesis for which Drucker is calling. In fact, as I have indicated in my own management textbook,[13] the information-based organization and economy will not necessarily lead us on to the next step in our managerial evolution. First, managers in Europe and the US must release themselves from their rational straitjackets.

Developmental Dynamics

The developmental polarity

The developing organization, like the developing manager, evolves through a series of stages. The first two such stages we have termed *primal* and *rational*. Each stage has both *hard* and *soft* attributes. Thus the primal enterprise may be entrepreneurially oriented (tough) or communally oriented (tender), while the rational organization may be dominated by hierarchical (tight) or networked (loose) structures.

The developing organization, as it increases in scale and complexity, has to transcend its primal or rational order, but without losing those attributes that depend on the material body (primal) and the informational brain (rational). The evolving manager therefore has to be able to utilize, interdependently, enterprise and community, hierarchy and network, without being restricted only to these independent or dependent elements.

In the course of evolving in this way, the individual or organization is progressively transformed by a series of processes involving disassembly and reassembly. It is an inevitably painful process, but a necessary one if wholesome learning is to take place. The *developmental perspective*, once it is adopted consciously – by individuals and the institution, in relation to the product and the market-place – gives rise to associations in both time and space.

Developmental time and space

In the same way that you, as an individual manager, forge a genuine link between your past and your future, the institution to which you belong forges a genuine vision for itself, born out of its unique history and reaching towards its unique destination. In the same way that you connect the different selves you have uncovered in mid-life, so the self-renewing organization transforms 'arm's-length' relationships with customers, suppliers, unions or governments, into intimate and interdependent associations. The image of the consciously evolving, or self-renewing manager or organization is therefore a *molecular* one as Figure 11.3 shows.

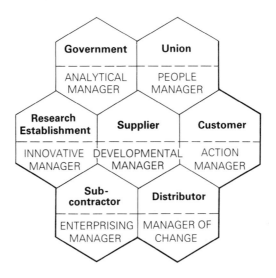

Figure 11.3 The Molecular Organization

The interdependent 'molecules' thus created link together different individualities – people or institutions, products or markets, social communities or physical environments – over space and time. Over *time* you become transformed, as an evolving entity, one developmental stage linking with the next; across *space* you grow and develop, as an evolving entity, one form of individuality linking with another. In the process the learning organization, evolving over time, and the co-partnership, evolving across space, become the norm rather than the exception.

Developmental Branches

In reviewing the branches of developmental management, we locate two leading elements:

- manager self-development and organizational self-renewal in time: the 'hard thrust';
- individual and organizational synergy in space: the 'soft touch'.

Individuation

Manager self-development and organizational self-renewal

The hard thrust of the developmental is neither that of economic man exploiting scarcity, in his Darwinian struggle for survival, nor of organizational man allocating resources effectively, in his Weberian pursuit of bureaucracy. Rather it is the thrust of the whole man, actualizing himself (to use Maslow's terminology)[14] in his drive to become himself. This process of *self-actualization*, or *individuation*, involves more *psychological and social risk-taking* than commercial and technological risk-taking.

Smuts pointed out that there was more to Darwin's theories than normally meets the evolutionary eye:

> Darwinism, in fact, implies two factors: an internal factor, operating mysteriously in the inmost nature and constitution of living organisms, and an external factor working along independent lines on the results achieved by the internal factor. The inner factor, *Variation*, is positive and creative, producing all the raw material for progress. The external factor, *Natural Selection*, is essentially negative and destructive, eliminating the harmful or less fit variations.[15]

Whereas primal management is built upon the premise of natural selection – the external factor – *developmental management* is built upon the foundations of *variation* – the *internal factor*. While both factors are present within the Darwinian universe, Darwin emphasized the first at the expense of the second. Today that part of the business world that focuses on images of the predator and the prey is clinging to the destructive end of the Darwinian continuum, hoping against hope, while those concerned with developing a learning organization are working at the creative end, with every reason for optimism.

In fact both the death force and the life force are a necessary part of individuation, for the person and organization. The developmental psychologist Ken Wilber points out that at each stage of our personal or corporate development both deep and surface structures are at work. The deep structures – called *transformations* – determine all the potentials and limitations of a particular stage. The surface structures – called *translations* – are constrained by the forms of the deep structures, but are free to order themselves variously within that constraint.[16]

Most of the new business techniques being advocated today are translations – 'discounted cash flow' or 'management by objectives', for example – rather than transformations – such as the invention of the joint-stock company. Once a particular stage of development comes into being, according to Wilber, it maintains itself through a series of more or less continual translations.

Having emerged from their primal and entrepreneurial state, analytical managers are easily able to translate their rational management principles from finance into marketing or from dis-counted cash flow into managing by objectives. What remains difficult, and is the essence of the hard developmental thrust, is individuation, self-actualization or the process of transformation.

> Whenever Eros (life force) exceeds Thanatos (death force), at a particular level, translation proceeds and stabilization occurs. . . . When Thanatos exceeds Eros, however, the particular translation involved winds down, is eventually surrendered, and translation to a different mode ensues . . . by accepting the death of the lower level, whereby consciousness transcends it.[17]

Unfortunately, and no matter how often managers in Europe and the US talk of managing change, they remain stuck in either the primal or the rational groove. They have been generally unwilling to let the known world go, to surrender their primal individuality and independence or their rational order and dependence. They stop growing at thirty-five! Separation anxiety at any level, Wilber tells us, is the inability to accept the death of that level, and if that inability persists development stops at that stage. Hence, at the institutional level there are never-ending reorganizations, and at the business level the rash of hostile takeovers and mergers multiply interminably.

To sum up. The process of individuation – for person or product, organization or society – provides the developmental cut and thrust that overrides separation anxiety. Thus a preoccupation with the generalized notion of *intrapreneurship* at the primal level, or *management competence* at the rational level, is bound to limit our developmental scope. Our primary concern should be with *managerial, functional* and *organizational individuation* (of the kind outlined in Chapter 5). Unfortunately most approaches to manager self-development are translations rather than transformations, because their scope – in historical time and geographical space – remains so limited. The introduction of new technology, firmly linked as it is with the transformation of production processes, offers greater hope for personal and organizational, as well as product, individuation.

Synergy

Joint personality and organizational interdependence

So much for the hard edge of developmental management. In fact the soft edge is much further advanced and this is principally because of Japan's dramatic entry onto the economic stage during the last twenty years.

As an organization evolves, and becomes progressively transformed, both its hard and soft attributes change their basic form:

> *Hard* ruthless entrepreneurship⌐
> toughminded administration⌐
> whole-hearted individuation
>
> *Soft* communal group⌐
> interactive network⌐
> interorganizational harmony

It is plain that the Japanese have evolved, more comprehensively than their Western counterparts, through the soft ends of the developmental polarity. The phenomena of *joint personality*, as opposed to individual personality, and *organizational interdependence*, as opposed to institutional autonomy, are all-pervading within Japanese business.

However, economic and technological forces, if not cultural ones, are now catching up with European and American business. The advent of new business practices and relationships –

> co-partnerships
> piggy-backing
> risk-sharing

joint production
intensified supplier–customer interaction
fully-fledged consortia
genuine joint ventures

has had a marked effect.

Rosabeth Moss Kanter is perhaps the best-known of recent management analysts to comment on these forced changes. In her book *When Giants Learn to Dance* she refers not only to 'the desperate search [of companies] for synergies', but also to their desire to become 'PALs' with one another.

> Lean, agile, post-entrepreneurial companies can stretch in three ways. They can *pool* resources with others, *ally* to exploit an opportunity, or *link* systems in a partnership. In short they can become better PALs with other organizations – from venture collaborators to suppliers, service contractors, customers and even unions.[18]

Understandably, Kanter's Americanized, developmental stance is closely linked to that of the lean and agile primal manager.

Yoneji Masuda, on the other hand, is a Japanese futurologist, whose economic and sociological analysis is developmentally and synergistically much more far-reaching. For Masuda, in the *information society* we are entering, information will expand through 'synergistic production and shared utilization', so that the economy at large will be transformed from an exchange economy into a synergistic one. The spirit of the information society, he says, will be globalism, 'a symbiosis in which man and nature will live in harmony'.[19]

Developmental Fruits

We now turn finally to the fruits of developmental management.

The fruits of primal management, as we have already noted, are economic and political in substance, and personal or communal in their appeal. Rational management is socio-technical in substance, and appeals to a professional or institutional appetite. The fruits of *developmental management*, finally, are *psychological* and *ecological* in nature, appealing to the *whole person* with a *global awareness*.

The whole person is made up of actions, thoughts and feelings, which, in business terms, are converted not only into management and organization but also – since business is nothing more than an extension of the human being – into products and markets. It is the developmental manager who, for the first time, becomes consciously and purposefully aware of this. This awareness is carried into the *learning organization* both horizontally and vertically.

Horizontal Participation

Developmental managers recognize and enhance the individuality of a cast of diverse human characters, stimulating and promoting their interdependence – or joint personality – within the organization. By this horizontal process each of these individuals progresses towards self-actualization or wholeness.

But the process does not stop there. For such managers are also engaged in fostering interdependence between institutions, enabling them in turn to progress towards wholeness. Action-oriented businesses are linked with organizations founded on thinking – universities and research establishments – or more strongly on feeling – social and voluntary services. Similarly business cultures that are more behaviourally oriented, typified by the US, intermingle with more affectively oriented organizational cultures, such as Japan, and more cognitively oriented ones, as in Europe.

Vertical Learning and Innovation

Interrelating actions, thoughts and feelings through interpersonal and inter-institutional participation – the horizontal dimension of learning – constitute only part of the developmental fruit. The other part involves the complementary processes of *learning* and *innovation* – the vertical dimension. These two processes, from a developmental perspective, are common to individuals and organizations and equally to products and markets.

We may see learning as the *internalized* or *introvert* process, grounded in reflection, and innovation as the *externalized* or *extrovert* process, giving rise to action. Each process may be represented in seven stages – learning as the seven Is and innovation as the seven Es (Table 11.1). It is only by following the upward journey of evolution through learning and the downward journey of self-actualization through innovation that individuals and organizations engage with their own wholeness.

Table 11.1 Learning and Innovation

Learning	Innovation	Attribute
Imagining	Envisioning	Creation
Intuiting	Enabling	Development
Interpreting	Executing	Analysis
Involving	Energizing	Emotion
Interacting	Experimenting	Intellect
Infusing	Enthusing	Sociability
Immersing	Enacting	Energy

Conclusion

The 'bottom line' for the developing organization is not the company's net profit, but the growth of the individuals and communities with whom it is involved. Any company that aims to succeed today knows that it can only hold on to young and talented professionals if it provides them with scope for continuing growth and development.

As any living organism grows and develops it reaches ever more confidently towards wholeness. Since they do not allow the fulfilment of this urge, the parochially independent and nationally dependent kinds of organization have had their day. Each is bound to remain an unfulfilled part of an ever more integrated whole – the global economy, which is powerfully symbolized by our planetary ecology. The notorious hole in the ozone layer may be seen as a potent metaphor for the gap in our commercial, organizational and managerial awareness.

At a micro-level both the youthful entrepreneur and the 'adult' rational manager need to be put in their place at a relatively early stage of organizational evolution. At a macro-level the independent enterprise and the public corporation need to be seen as interim structures along the way to organizational self-renewal.

The only large-scale company today that is truly immune from takeover is the one that is more highly evolved than its so-called 'predators'. If it is developmentally managed, such a company's identity will be interfused with the corporate identities of hundreds, if not thousands of other organizations around the world. Similarly the individuals and organizations within the company will be continually renewing themselves, thereby actualizing their interdependent potential. The core structure underpinning such an institution will be molecular, so that individuals, departments, organizations and societies bound up with it can *co-evolve*. Continual and continuing processes of *pioneering, differentiating* and *integrating* will ensue. Entities large and small, public and private will both *individuate* and *interfuse* on an ongoing basis.

The managers responsible for the organization will draw continuing *behavioural, intellectual* and *emotional* nourishment from their developmental roots in *ecology, biology* and *humanistic psychology*. Moreover, the philosophical grounds upon which their operations are based will

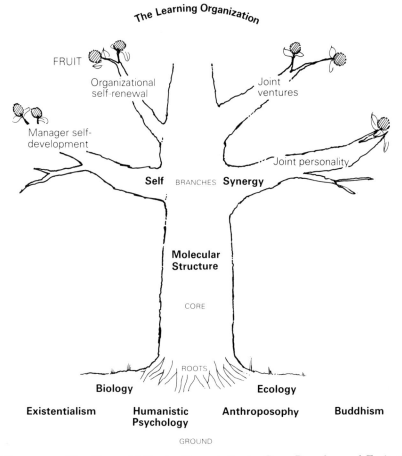

Figure 11.4 The Tree of Life: the Ground, Roots, Core, Branches and Fruit of Developmental Management

reach across the globe, from ancient *Buddhism* to modern *existentialism*, from *anthroposophy* to *humanistic psychology* (Figure 11.4).

As a direct result not only will individuals grow, psychologically and managerially, at the mid-point in their lives, but the prevailing economic ideologies of capitalism and communism will evolve appropriately. For a new creative tension needs to be established between individualism and collectivism, a tension that is reciprocally humanizing rather than mutually constraining. While *primal* and *rational* management can and should continue to play their part, it is *developmental management* that is now required to take the lead, whether in the Deutschebank, the city of New York or Soviet Russia.

Notes

1 E. Sartouris, *From Chaos to Cosmos*. Pocket Books, 1987, p. 214.
2 Sartouris, *From Chaos to Cosmos*, p. 192.
3 J. C. Smuts, *Holism and Evolution*. N.I.P. Press, 1987, p. 107.
4 Smuts, *Holism and Evolution*, p. 153.
5 H. Dixon, 'Giving the World a New Philosophy', *Financial Times*, 13 February 1989.
6 K. Wilber, *The Atman Project*. Quest Publications, 1980, p. 35.
7 Smuts, *Holism and Evolution*, p. 232.
8 P. Drucker, *The New Realities*. Heinemann, 1989, p. 213.
9 Drucker, *The New Realities*, p. 74.
10 C. Handy, *The Age of Unreason*. Century Hutchinson, 1989.
11 W. Abernathy, *et al.*, *The Renaissance of American Manufacturing*. Basic Books, 1983, p. 35.
12 S. Zuboff, *In the Age of the Smart Machine*. Heinemann, 1988. p. 71.
13 R. Lessem, *Global Management Principles*. Prentice Hall, 1989.
14 A. Maslow, *Motivation and Personality*. Harper & Row, 1964.
15 Smuts, *Holism and Evolution*, p. 183.
16 Wilber, *The Atman Project*, p. 126.
17 Wilber, *The Atman Project*, p. 41.
18 R. M. Kanter, *When Giants Learn to Dance*. Simon & Schuster, 1989, p. 118.
19 Y. Masuda, *The Information Society as Post-industrial Society*. Institute for the Information Society, 1980, p. 37; new edn, Basil Blackwell, 1990.

Index

Page references in *italics* indicate tables and figures.

Index by Meg Davies